P9-CRM-201

THE PURITAN EXPERIENCE

THE PURITAN EXPERIENCE

Studies in Spiritual Autobiography

Owen C. Watkins

Schocken Books · New York

*Published in USA in 1972
by Schocken Books Inc.
67 Park Avenue
New York
NY 10016*

© *Owen Watkins 1972*

Library of Congress Catalog Card No. 70–150987

Printed in Great Britain

Contents

v

Preface

This book is an attempt to fill a gap in Puritan studies which has been apparent since works by Tindall and Haller drew our attention over thirty years ago to the significance of the spiritual autobiography as an expression of popular Puritanism. Well over two hundred narratives of this kind are known to have been written before 1725, and I hope that the survey which follows will be useful to those wishing to know more about the scope and variety of these writings, as well as the literary and religious tradition which fostered the major works in the genre, by Bunyan, Baxter, and Fox.

Some material from chapter 10 appeared in an article in *The Friends' Historical Society Journal* in 1953, and parts of chapters 1 and 7 have been published in a lecture given at the invitation of the Fellowship of Evangelical Churchmen to commemorate the tercentenary of the publication of *Grace Abounding* in 1966.

It is a pleasure to thank those who have helped me at different times and in different ways: Mr Laurence Lerner for advice and encouragement in the early stages of the work, Mr Michael Mason for some brief but valuable criticisms of my style, Mrs W. M. T. Nowottny who supervised my first studies in this field, and Dr J. I. Packer and Professor Roger Sharrock who have read and commented on some of the chapters. I owe an especial debt to Dr Geoffrey Nuttall, whose sustained interest and patient criticism have encouraged me throughout the inordinately long period when the book was being written; and without the constant support of my wife, Barbara, the task amid other pressing claims would have been prolonged even more.

I also wish to record my appreciation of the facilities of the

British Museum, and the co-operation of librarians of the Friends' House Library, Dr Williams's Library, the National Library of Scotland, and the University of Edinburgh.

I am indebted to the University of Leicester Research Board for a grant towards the cost of preparing the manuscript for publication.

OWEN C. WATKINS

Chapter 1

Personal Religion

Puritan autobiographies were the product of a Puritan conviction that the highest art a man could practise was the art of living, that the only masterpiece worthy of the name was to be achieved in the most complex and difficult of all forms of creative endeavour: a human life.

This is one reason why, in the voluminous writings of seventeenth-century Puritans, there is not much that we should call literature, if by literature we mean that which gives the receptive reader a unique experience which he values for its own sake. When they produced literature in this sense they did so in the same way as the British were said to have acquired the Empire – in a fit of absent-mindedness. For they valued literature not for its own sake, but just in so far as it promoted right attitudes and right conduct. Their creative energy was mostly taken up with interpreting the concepts and values they considered crucial to human destiny, and so their chief publications were sermons, treatises, and handbooks – doctrinal, devotional, practical, and controversial. But they also believed, with many ancient authorities, that 'examples are more powerful than precepts',[1] and thus the esteem given to expository works was shared by history and biography, especially the latter. So Richard Baxter recommended the reading of such books because

> the true History of exemplary Lives, is a pleasant and profitable recreation to young persons; and may secretly work them to a liking of Godliness and value of good men, which is the beginning of saving Grace: O how much better work is it, than Cards, Dice, Revels, Stage-Plays, Romances or idle Chat.[2]

1

Spiritual autobiographies, with few exceptions, were not written because the writers thought their lives were 'exemplary' ones in this sense, but because, as Thomas Goodwin pointed out, 'That God pardon'd such a Man in such a Condition, is often brought home unto another Man in the same Condition.'[3] They hoped through the record of their own experience to offer experimental proof of some of the eternal truths of Christianity. God was consistent in his dealings with men throughout history, but since He called everyone individually, each saw some aspect of His glory that was hidden from others. Working within an agreed framework of doctrine it was therefore possible to have as many variations as there were believers, and so the conditions were present for the emergence of an accepted literary form. By a spiritual autobiography I mean a narrative dealing primarily with the writer's religious experience, covering the whole of his life or a substantial part of it, and written sufficiently long after the events for a coherent view to have been possible. However, a few writings which do not entirely conform to this definition will be discussed because they add to our understanding of works of this kind.

It was a genre that became popular with Puritan readers in the second half of the seventeenth century, and was the outcome of conditions that were distinctively English, notably the contribution made to reformed theology by the English Puritan divines in their doctrine of divine grace. They took up the work of the continental reformers on justification (what God had done for sinners at Calvary) and completed it with detailed studies of sanctification (what God did within the soul and body of the believer). Their achievements in this field were recognized by the Protestant churches of Europe, who highly valued the works of 'the affectionate practical English writers'.[4] For well over a hundred years Puritan pastors from Greenham to Baxter laboured incessantly through preaching, writing, and counselling to help people of all ages and conditions to find the way of salvation and work out the application of the gospel to every part of their lives. One of the results was that men and women with no special literary skill developed an ability to analyse and communicate their religious experience; the Puritan culture provided a body of theory, a technique, and a language with which to do so – and there were many dedicated pupils.

From what I have said so far it will be clear that I shall normally

2

be using the word 'Puritan' to denote that aspect of sixteenth- and seventeenth-century religious life in Britain which was centred on pastoral and personal issues rather than political or ecclesiastical ones. We shall be concerned less with 'turbulent and factious spirits . . . adverse to the government of the church'[5] than with 'doctrinal Puritans'. In the early days these were Calvinist divines within the Church of England, many of whom were in some respects non-conformist, and their common bond was an urgent pastoral concern which came to be shared by the growing numbers of separatist preachers. After about 1640 the heirs of these men were, in fact, found mainly in the separatist churches, and most of the spiritual autobiographies were written by Presbyterians, Independents, or Baptists. These men I shall sometimes refer to as 'orthodox Puritans', when it is necessary to distinguish them from the individualist prophets and the Quakers, who were also part of the whole Puritan movement, though representing distinct developments from the main tradition.

Before turning to the autobiographies themselves, I shall survey briefly the most important factors within Puritanism that fostered their development: notably the range and purpose of Puritan preaching, the teaching on conversion and the Christian life which it embodied, and the kind of personal response which it demanded. These matters have been the subjects of many thorough studies in Britain and America during the past thirty years or so, and I am unlikely to throw any new light on them in this introduction, which is intended to supply the minimum context needed for the discussion which follows.[6] Readers who are already familiar with the field may prefer to turn directly to chapter two which, while it also consists of introductory matter, deals directly with autobiographical records.

Faith and knowledge

The severity of Calvin's theology, said C. S. Lewis, 'sprang from his refusal to allow the Roman distinction between the life of "religion" and the life of the world. . . . Calvin demanded that every man should be made to live the fully Christian life. In academic jargon, he lowered the honours standard and abolished the pass degree.'[7] The analogy is an apt one for the English Puritans, because in working out the implications of their Calvinism

3

they committed themselves to a massive exercise in popular education. Faced though they mostly were with 'an ignorant, rude and revelling People', they did not hesitate to require as full an understanding as possible of the whole Christian religion. The first 'direction to a sound conversion' that Baxter urged upon the inquirer was: 'labour after a right understanding of the true nature of Christianity, and the meaning of the gospel.'[8] Since faith was a response to the acts of God, it had to be based on accurate knowledge of what these acts were. So even a bare appeal to repentance would involve more than a few central themes like guilt, atonement, and forgiveness. The message had to be understood in the full context of Christian doctrine: in effect, some grasp of everything mentioned in the Apostles' Creed, with particular attention also to the decree of election, justification by faith, and the work of the Holy Spirit in conversion and sanctification.

This was an immense demand to make, and there were many who pleaded their ignorance and incapacity. Baxter's reply to such objections summarized the *raison d'être* of a hundred years of Puritan evangelical concern:

> (1) Every man that has a reasonable soul should know God that made him; and know the end for which he should live; and know the way to his eternal happiness, as well as the learned; have you not souls to save or lose as well as the learned have? (2) God hath made plain His will to you in His word; He hath given you teachers and many other helps; so that you have no excuse if you are ignorant; you must know how to be christians if you are no scholars. You may hit the way to heaven in English, though you have no skill in Hebrew or Greek; but in the darkness of ignorance you can never hit it. (3) . . . If you think, therefore, that you may be excused from knowledge, you may as well think that you may be excused from love and from all obedience; for there can be none of this without knowledge. . . . you account seven years little enough to learn your trade, and will not bestow one day in seven in diligent learning the matters of your salvation.[9]

Of course, though knowledge was the essential foundation for every part of the Christian life, it was not enough in itself. Repentance, faith, perseverance, and growth in grace all involved a full

4

emotional commitment and the practice of good works. William Perkins defined theology as 'the science of living blessedly for ever'[10] and Puritan teaching in general emphasized the necessity of a total response. 'For the Puritans,' says Dr J. I. Packer, 'true Christianity consisted in knowing, feeling and obeying the truth; and knowledge without obedience, feeling without acting, or feeling and acting without knowledge were all condemned as false religion and ruinous to men's souls.'[11] The problems involved in integrating these three elements of personal religion lie behind much of the heart-searching and reflection recorded in spiritual autobiographies.

Puritan teaching on conversion and the Christian life was based on the Epistle to the Romans and the doctrine of justification by faith derived from it. The plight of man was his complete self-centredness; he had inherited from Adam a warped organism which, while causing him to act always and only from self interest, so distorted his perception that he could not see where his self-interest lay, nor could he recognize that this condition must inexorably lead to self-destruction. He was 'dead in sin' because utterly unresponsive to God, and every faculty was infected by rebelliousness, though each retained some remnant of the image of God. He could therefore be rescued only through divine initiative, an act of pure grace – which had in fact been carried through in the atoning work of Christ. To benefit from this, to achieve new life, the sole agency was faith: this alone enabled a man to come to Christ in true repentance and appropriate all the benefits of His sacrifice. But faith, like everything else, was the gift of God, as the texts in *Romans* demonstrated: 'So then, it is not of him that willeth, nor of him that runneth, but of God that sheweth mercy,' and 'Therefore hath he mercy on whom he will have mercy, and whom he will he hardeneth.'[12] The only thing a man contributed to his salvation was the sin from which he was redeemed; but since the process was one of eternal life and death, it was inevitable that once aroused he would not be content with a passive part, and there were certain features of Puritan preaching which helped to determine the nature of his activity.

Preaching for conversion

The Puritans inherited without question and almost unchanged

5

the scholastic model of human nature. In relating this to their concept of regeneration they were concerned mainly with the relations between the faculties of the rational soul: the reason, the will, and the affections. They had also to consider the imagination, which could sway the entire being by the way it presented desirable and repulsive things to the reason, will and affection. Reason, as the king of the faculties, should be in control, acting with the will to rule the affections; but in fallen man both the will and the affections are in revolt, while reason itself is imperfect. Thus the affections act independently to forestall reason, which itself is misled by the corrupted imagination; and the dominant activity of the will is to command the reason to provide excuses for self-justification and continued rebellion against God. Thus, to quote Perry Miller's summing up of the situation, 'Sinful man tries all his life to see things as they are, to apprehend truth and to act by it, but at every endeavor his senses blur, his imagination deceives, his reason fails, his will rebels, his passions run riot.'[13] A harmonious combination of the faculties could be achieved only by a simultaneous seizure of them all by divine grace, accompanied by a rational apprehension of the truth. Conversion therefore consisted of both physical and spiritual renewal, so that grace had to invade the soul through a sense impression of some kind. The spoken word was the one agency by which, on the plane of nature, the innermost faculties could be reached, and this was why the sermon was regarded as the most effective channel of grace. Here the reason could first be persuaded by proofs, demonstrations, and the silencing of objections; then, since the aim was not only to persuade men but to work upon their hearts, the will and the passions could be moved by eloquence. Eloquence itself was to be used only to make logic persuasive, and not for its own sake, for obvious reasons.

Preaching, then, was the most important of the means appointed by God to bring men out of their bondage to sin and call together those who were to be His people. And because He was no respecter of persons, but chose the foolish things of the world to confound the wise, the Puritans were constrained to present the gospel in a way that anyone could understand, however simple and ignorant. In principle they gave a plain exposition of the Scriptures, with no parade of their own learning and no embellishments of style. Their method of analysing a text was derived from the logic of

Ramus, but this need not concern us here; it is enough to say that plainness and perspicuity were considered essential if the vital message were to be understood by all: '*Humane wisdome* must be concealed, whether it be in the matter of the sermon, or in the setting forth of the words: because the preaching of the word is the *Testimonie of God, and the profession of the knowledge of Christ*, and not of humane skill.'[14] So wrote Perkins, one of the earliest of the spiritual brotherhood. He warned the preacher that he must not 'tickle the itching eares of his auditorie with the fine ringing sentences of the Fathers', but must 'observe an admirable plain-nesse and an admirable powerfullnesse'[15] so that the unlearned man might be able to grasp the eternal issues in which he was involved. But Perkins made it clear that this did not mean that the preacher himself was to be unlearned:

> If any man thinke that by this meanes barbarism should be brought into pulpits; he must vnderstand that the Minister may, yea & must priuately vse at his libertie the artes, philosophy, and varietie of reading, whilest he is in framing his sermon: but he ought in publike to conceale all these from the people, and not to make the least ostentation. *Artis etiam est celare artem: it is also a point of Art to conceale Art*.[16]

Biographies of Puritan preachers indicate the high esteem in which plain and powerful exposition was held. In all the sermons of Samuel Crook, which were many thousands, 'his expressions were choice, grave, solid, weighty, savory, and seasonable; his applications home, and pertinent, strongly set on from divine authority by a sweet and moving elocution, a masculine eloquence, fervent zeal, and strength of love to the souls of his hearers.'[17] And the ministry of John Dod 'was so spiritual, and yet so plain, that poor simple people that never knew what Religion meant, when they had gone to hear him, could not choose but talk of his Sermon.'[18]

The procedure was first to enlighten the unregenerate man about the nature of sin, then to lead him to a conviction of his own guilt before God. Only when thoroughly roused and humbled by the deadly pollution of sin and his congenital inability to love God and neighbour was he encouraged to find comfort in the promises of the gospel. The roles of law and gospel apparent in the opening chapters of Romans provided the conceptual framework for this strategy. If the promises were taken up before the law had done its work, the sinner might be sorrowful for something other than his offence against God: the fear of punishment, for instance, or the wish to be free from one particular sin which happened to offend his conscience. Richard Sibbes said that often the cause for a relapse after conversion was 'because men never smarted for sinne at the first, they were not long enough under the lash of the law'.[19] For a man in an ill course of life to snatch at comforts before the appropriate time was

> as if some ignorant man should come into an Apothecaries shop stored with varietie of medicines of all sorts, & shold take what comes next to hand, poyson perhaps in stead of Physicke. There is no word of comfort in the whole booke of God intended for such *as regard iniquity in their hearts,* though they doe not act it in their lives.[20]

Sibbes's comparison here is a reminder that none of the spiritual brotherhood believed in the right of every man to interpret Scripture for himself. The Reformation had not abolished the need for spiritual directors. Once the sinner was thoroughly penitent the preacher must apply the gospel with all the skill at his command:

> When their Soules once begin to feele all sins, even their best beloved One, heauy and burdensome; to prize *Iesus Christ* far before all the world, . . . to resolue to take him as their husband, and to obey Him as their Lord for ever, &c; and all this in truth: I say then, and in this case, wee may haue comfort to minister comfort. Then, upon good ground, wee . . . may tell them, with what a compassionate Pang, and deare compellation, God Himselfe labours to refresh them.[21]

The judicious pastor was then to use all his powers to heal the afflicted conscience with the balm of the gospel, for 'God knowes that as wee are prone to sinne, so when the conscience is throughly awaked, wee are as prone to despaire for sinne.'[22]

Preachers had to be equally proficient in applying the law and the gospel. So as well as their reputation for plain preaching they were noted for their power in both conviction and consolation. When Thomas Wilson opened the curses of the law to his auditors, they 'heard not so much Words as Thunderclaps', but he was a

Barnabas in consolation also.[23] And we are told of Robert Bolton that,

> though in his manner of preaching he was a *Sonne of thunder*, yet unto bruised reeds and those that mourned in spirit, hee was as sweet a sonne of Consolation as ever I heard, and with a very tender and pitifull heart powred the oyle of mercy into their bleeding wounds.[24]

As we should expect, we find that many converts recorded long periods of dejection, doubt, and even despair. Yet this was not in itself an essential stage in true conversion. 'There is a gospel sorrow and humiliation after believing that is a duty,' wrote John Owen, ' . . . but this legal sorrow is an effect of the curse of the law, and not of its command.' God in His sovereignty 'deals with the souls of men in unspeakable variety. . . . Some walk or wander long in darkness; in the souls of others Christ is formed in the first gracious visitation.'[25]

The two essential elements, then, were conviction of sin, followed sometimes sooner, sometimes later, by an experience of forgiveness. Spiritual autobiographies nearly all emphasize this twofold progress, and many of those who 'wander long in darkness' confirm a conclusion of Sibbes's that 'Nothing is so certaine as that which is certaine after doubts.'[26]

Self-examination

When a repentant sinner sued for grace he would know that if he were one of the elect a power would be bestowed on him which would keep him faithful to the end. If, on the other hand, he were not fore-ordained to salvation, his conversion was a false one, and although he might for a while be able to subdue the effects of sin, it would not be destroyed at the root and he would never achieve complete victory. In that case he was doomed to be one of the reprobates who would glorify God by demonstrating that human nature, even at its highest, could not renew itself or obtain salvation on its own initiative. Thus the convert kept watch on his moral and spiritual life for the fruits of the Spirit, which were the outward signs of saving grace in the heart. To be certain that these marks were genuine it was necessary to make a rigorous distinction between the effects of grace and behaviour that was the result of natural causes. Thomas Shepard, in a series of sermons on hypocrisy, warned his hearers of some of the principles of conduct that might lull them into false security: the hope that godliness would bring outward blessings, the praise of other religious people, pressure from a sensitive conscience, trusting in a good example, or trusting in 'the gilded rottenness of some moral performances, wherein a man saith that he does what he can'.[27] All these were sandy foundations, and it was the task of the good pastor to transpose abstract doctrine into a rule of practice so that by diligent self-examination the perplexed believer could accurately dissect his soul. The warrant for this was found in Paul's injunction to the Corinthians: 'Examine yourselves, whether ye be in the faith.'[28]

> Oh that I might prevail with Christians, to take pains with themselves in this great work of examination. Their salvation depends on it. It is the note of an Harlot; she is seldom at home, *Prov.* 7. 11,12. *Her feet abide not in her house: now she is without, now in the streets.* It is the sign of an Harlot-Professor, to be altogether abroad, spying the faults of others; but is never at home with his own heart . . . let these few things be seriously weighed.
> 1. Without self-examination we can never know how it is with us. If we should die presently, we cannot tell to what Coast we should sail; whether to Hell or Heaven. . . .
> 2. If we will not try our selves, God will try us. He will examine us as the chief Captain did *Paul, by scourging, Acts* 22. 24. He will ask that question as Christ, *Whose image and superscription is this?* And if we cannot shew him his own image, he will reject us.
> 3. There is a secret corruption within, which will never be found out but by searching. . . . Little doth a man know what Atheism, Pride, Uncleanness is in his heart, till he searcheth.
> 4. . . . the benefit is great which way soever things turn. If upon examination we find that we have not grace in truth, then the mistake is discovered, and the danger prevented. If we find that we have grace, we may take the comfort of it.[29]

So there appeared many handbooks which showed the ordinary man how to relate his inner experience to some ascertainable outer experience. Of the countless anatomies of the soul that went through edition after edition in the seventeenth century the best known to the modern student, because of its influence on Bunyan, is Arthur Dent's *The Plaine Mans Pathway to Heaven. Wherein every man may clearly see whether hee shall be saved or damned.* Almost every Puritan preacher of note produced a similar work. Baxter gave a list of the signs of saving grace in at least four of his books,[30] and in such writings as Mrs Anne Skelton's *Infallible Signs of Saving Grace* ordinary church members offered to the public the results of their experience. There was some variation in the marks of grace identified by different writers, but in addition to well regulated outward conduct, delight in religious observances, and a love to fellow Christians, there was general agreement that the true believer needed to be sure that his whole life was directed to the glory of God, hating sin essentially because it was loathsome in His sight. Every faculty should show some indication of renewal, and since there was no principle known to man which sinful nature could not misuse or Satan contrive into a snare, every response needed to be checked with the word of God, and every disguise of nature unmasked by meticulous self-examination. Submission to Scripture was the acid test:

> The Rule by which a Christian must try himself, is the Word of God. Phancy and opinion are false Rules to go by. We must judge of our spiritual condition by the Canon of Scripture. This *David* calls a *Lamp unto his feet, Psalm* 119. 105. Let the Word be Umpire to decide the controversie whether we have grace or no. We judge of colours by the Sun. So we must judge of the estate of our souls by the light of Scripture.[31]

As well as being a weapon in the fight with evil, self-examination had a very positive end in the quest for assurance, which could not be gained without much self discipline. Assurance was by no means necessary for salvation and was, indeed, a rare blessing of a mature faith, experienced after many conflicts, doubts, and temptations. For the only completely reliable confirmation of election came through the inward witness of the Spirit, when it reinforced the witness of the believer's own spirit. Thomas Goodwin identified two ways in which this might happen: 'discoursively' or 'intuitively'. Of the first he said that the Spirit 'writes first all graces in

11

us, and then teaches our consciences to read his handwriting'.[32] The second way was well described by Sibbes: 'The Spirit doth not always witness . . . by force of argument from sanctification, but sometimes immediately by way of presence; as the sight of a friend comforts without help of discourse.'[33] In both cases the experience involved something above and beyond heartfelt trust in God, and the application of the promises, and the appearance of gifts and graces in the heart: it was a direct and certain testimony that could not be mistaken, any more than the light of the sun can be mistaken for the light of a glow-worm. It was to be striven for and wrestled for as the crown and summit of earthly bliss; and the practice of self-examination, though fallible in itself, was a precondition for receiving such a gift. Orthodox Puritans were therefore highly suspicious of the vulgar prophets and Quakers who claimed to have gained this blessing on incredibly easy terms.

Spiritual warfare

It was through self-examination also that the warfare of the spirit became fully revealed to the Christian. An unregenerate man might struggle with his conscience in a way which resembled and foreshadowed the holy war between flesh and spirit; but this involved a straightforward conflict between the faculties, and so was natural, and as it were all on the same plane. With conversion the inward struggle became vastly more complex:

> . . . under this work God is pleased secretly to communicate a *principle of grace* or spiritual life unto the will. . . . so the Spirit begins now to 'lust against the flesh', as Gal. v.17, aiming at and intending a complete victory or conquest. There was, upon bare conviction, a contest before in the soul, but it was merely between the mind and conscience on the one hand, and the will on the other. . . . but the conflict begins now to be in the will itself.[34]

This was the warfare described in treatises on the Christian life, and in all manner of popular literature:

> I sing my SELF; my *Ciuil-Warrs* within;
> The *Victories* I howrely lose and win;
> The dayly *Duel*, the continuall Strife,
> The *Warr* that ends not, till I end my life.

And yet, not Mine alone, not onely Mine,
But every-One's that under th'honor'd Signe
Of Christ his Standard, shal his Name enroule,
With holy Vowes of Body and of Soule.[35]

Richard Kilby described how his sins were

. . . like vnto a company of desperate rebels besieged in a
castle, yeeld they will not, vntill they be famished out.
They have succour from the remembrance, and from the
corrupted imagination, from the outward sences, specially
the eies, and the eares: and who can say how full of
temptations the world is, temptations fitted to worke vpon
the sight, and the hearing.[36]

The pollution of sin in every faculty, then, was not entirely
removed until death, but remained by guilt and imputation of
Adam's disobedience. The justified man was, however, enabled to
co-operate with the Holy Spirit by faith in putting to death, or
mortifying, the remnants of inward corruption. Books like Lewis
Bayly's *The Practise of Piety* and Robert Bolton's *The Saints
Selfe-enriching Examination* taught him how day by day to withstand the devil, who by temptation from within and without tried
ceaselessly to deprive God of His glory and man of his soul. No
faculty was immune from temptation, and perseverance and courage were needed in the long and weary analysis by which secret
sins were brought to light and laid before the God of 'consuming
fire' for mortification. Self-examination for the Puritan was thus
something much more than introspection as practised by the
'melancholy' man, who watched himself but did not dissociate
himself from his sin in spite of his remorse, and refused to take
the steps of mortification. 'The end of self-examination', said
Richard Lucas, 'is not only to know your faults, but to mend
them.'[37]

So in this battle the believer learned to fear the terrible power
of indwelling sin and to maintain absolute resistance to the devil.
He had to guard against his peculiar weaknesses at all times,
especially at periods of great joy, sorrow, or fatigue. He had to
beware of what John Cotton called 'man's perverse subtilty in
inventing wayes of backsliding'.[38] It was essential for him to
experience the full guilt of his sin in the light of God's love, to
meditate on the power and love of Christ, and to implore the aid

13

of the Spirit for all his infirmities. His sins had to be searched out and dealt with one by one, for although the whole process of salvation was a unity it could only be experienced piecemeal on this side of eternity. Once alerted to the forces involved and their dispositions, the Puritan watched with awed and fascinated attention the mysterious battles taking place within his own soul:

> . . . I would have beleeved but could not; I would have put away thoughts of temptation but could not: the temptation grew stronger and stronger, my heart was broken by reason of sorrow; yet for a time, marvellously kept up to strive; I saw I could not hold out, and was ready to yeeld, and give over the combat. But, I found the Lord coming in for my helpe, in a needful time, when I was without strength. I apprehended the power of Christ very sensibly set against the power of the Devill, and he began to give ground. I had sustained many hundred charges concerning the odious nature of my sinne, and the sad curse denounced against the same. After a little retreate of the enemy, I began to take a little boldnes, but never with more trembling, and despairing in my selfe, or more cleaving to Christ as a Conquerour: I could then truely say, *my rejoicing is in another, and I have no confidence in the flesh.*[39]

The Puritan way

Many people responded to all this as a new and exciting pattern for a significant and adventurous life. It is difficult for us to recapture this excitement, even from the literature of the time, because so much in Puritanism has become the common heritage of the nation; we have become over-familiar with many of its less attractive manifestations. This particular pathway to the New Jerusalem has been flattened out and trodden down by so many generations of pilgrims, and so many have left a detailed account of their journey, that the way has for a long time been regarded as the safest, drabbest, and most respectable of all. We no longer embark on a hazardous expedition, but join a conducted tour through the litter left by thousands of picnic parties.

But it all looked very different three hundred years ago. The risks to be taken were new ones, and the challenges were fresh and invigorating. Men had welcomed the Reformation or reacted against it with a violence that sprang at least in part from an uncertainty of their own powers, and as Mr Christopher Hill has reminded us, 'Right down to 1640 men could not be sure that Protestantism had come to stay in England.'[40] The Puritan intellectuals who formed the spiritual brotherhood were at once more sensitive to the Reformation ideals and more eloquent in giving expression to them than most of their contemporaries were. One they emphasized most forcefully was that individual men and women could achieve a personal relationship with God, and that this relationship could permeate all daily life with the light of eternity. To do this they used Scripture and their own experience to throw light on each other. Robert Harris said 'that a Preacher had three Books to study, 1. The Bible. 2. Himself. 3. The People'.[41] And Robert Bolton's 'singular dexterity in comforting afflicted and wounded spirits' was said to have been due to the 'grievous pangs' of his own new birth.[42] There is no evidence that a preacher habitually recounted his own spiritual travails in the pulpit, but ideally he 'never taught any godly point, but he first wrought it on his own heart'.[43]

And this, essentially, was what the Puritans meant by 'experience'. Vavasor Powell referred to it as 'the inward sense and feeling of what is outwardly read and heard; and the spirituall and powerfull enjoyment of What is beleeved'.[44] Mrs Jane Turner, who published an autobiography in 1654, described it as 'truth brought home to the heart with life and power',[45] and Samuel Petto called it 'entercourse and communion' between Christ and His people.[46] It was always something personal, and the existence of the records which we are to examine is evidence of the effectiveness with which a particular way of life was communicated to many humble and poorly educated people. This caused them to extend their range of self-awareness, as the doctrines which they learned became almost simultaneously embodied in personal experience and afterwards articulated through narrative and testimony. 'Now to a poor soule', said John Rogers, 'all such things as are in the soule, are made known by *experiences*; *experience*, we say, *proves principles*.'[47]

So as their pastors, in plain and persuasive language week by week, explored the relation between doctrine and experience, men found they were being given a lens with which to bring their inward lives into focus, a process that became more systematic and meaningful as they named and discussed what they found there.

NOTES

1 E.g. Seneca, Augustine, and Gregory Nazianzen.
2 Samuel Clarke, *Lives of Sundry Eminent Persons*, 1683. Epistle 'To the Reader', sig. a3v.
3 Thomas Goodwin, *Works*, 1704, Vol. V, p. xii.
4 Richard Baxter, *Christian Directory*, 1673, sig. A3. Cf. G. Waterhouse, *The Literary Relations between England and Germany in the Seventeenth Century*, Cambridge, 1914, pp. 101–11.
5 Francis Bacon, *Works*, ed. Spedding, Ellis, and Heath, 1872–4, Vol. XIV, p. 449. Quoted in Christopher Hill, *Society and Puritanism in Pre-Revolutionary England*, 1964, p. 21. Cf. ch. 1 for a survey of the definition of a Puritan.
6 See, in particular, William Haller, *The Rise of Puritanism*, New York, 1938; Perry Miller, *The New England Mind; The Seventeenth Century*, Cambridge, Mass., 1954; Geoffrey F. Nuttall, *The Holy Spirit in Puritan Faith and Experience*, Oxford, 1946; Gordon Stevens Wakefield, *Puritan Devotion*, London, 1957.
7 C. S. Lewis, *English Literature in the Sixteenth Century*, Oxford, 1954, p. 42.
8 Richard Baxter, *Practical Works*, reprint of 1838, Vol. II, p. 589. I owe this reference, and a number of others in this chapter, to Dr J. I. Packer.
9 Baxter, *Works*, II. 481f.
10 William Perkins, *Works*, Cambridge, 1608, Vol. I, p. 11.
11 J. I. Packer, *The Practical Writings of the English Puritans*, Annual Lecture of the Evangelical Library, 1951, p. 23.
12 Romans ix. 16, 18, referring back to Exodus xxxiii. 19.
13 Perry Miller, *op. cit.*, p. 284.
14 William Perkins, *The Art of Prophecying*, in *Works*, Cambridge, 1609, II.759.
15 Perkins, *Works*, 1617, II. 381; *Works*, 1609, III. 430.
16 Perkins, *Works*, 1609, II. 759.
17 W.G. [William Garret], *Anthologia. The Life and Death of Mr. Samuel Crook*, 1651, pp. 21f.
18 Samuel Clarke, *The Lives of Thirty-Two English Divines*, 3rd ed., 1677, p. 177.
19 Richard Sibbes, *The Bruised Reede and Smoaking Flax*, 1630, p. 15. For the procedure described here by Sibbes cf. Robert Bolton, *Instructions for a Right Comforting Afflicted Consciences*, 1631.

20 Richard Sibbes, *op. cit.*, sig. a9.
21 Bolton, *op. cit.*, p. 163.
22 Sibbes, *op. cit.*, sig. a6.
23 Clarke, *Lives of Sundry Eminent Persons*, p. 20.
24 Edward Bagshaw, *The Life and Death of Mr. Bolton*, prefaced to *Mr. Bolton's Last and Learned Worke of the Foure Last Things*, 1635, p. 20.
25 John Owen, *A Discourse Concerning the Holy Spirit*, in *Works*, ed. William H. Goold, reprint of 1966, Vol. III, pp. 360f.
26 Sibbes, *op. cit.*, p. 68 (second paging).
27 Thomas Shepard, *The Parable of the Ten Virgins*, Aberdeen and London, 1855, pp. 271ff.
28 2 Corinthians xiii.5.
29 Thomas Watson, *Heaven taken by Storm*, 1669, pp. 60ff.
30 Cf. *Treatise of Conversion, Right Method for a Settled Peace of Conscience, The Saints Everlasting Rest, Sermon of Judgment.*
31 Thomas Watson, *op. cit.*, pp. 56f.
32 Thomas Goodwin, *Works*, 1863 reprint, Vol. VI, p. 27.
33 Richard Sibbes, *A Fountain Sealed*, in *Works*, 1862, Vol. V, p. 440.
34 John Owen, *op. cit.*, Vol. III, p. 356.
35 George Goodwin, *Auto-Machia*, translated from the Latin by Josuah Sylvester, in *Tobacco Battered*, n.d., p. 147.
36 Richard Kilby, *Hallelu-iah*, Cambridge, 1618, p. 123.
37 Richard Lucas, *The Plain Man's Guide to Heaven*, cited by G. A. Starr, *Defoe and Spiritual Autobiography*, 1965, p. 32.
38 John Cotton, *A Brief Exposition . . . upon . . . Ecclesiastes*, 1654, p. 160.
39 'Experiences of J.M.' in Samuel Petto, *Roses from Sharon*, 1654, p. 24.
40 Hill, *op. cit.*, p. 49.
41 Samuel Clarke, *Lives of Thirty-two English Divines*, p. 332.
42 Edward Bagshaw, *op. cit.*, p. 16.
43 Nicolas Estwick, *A Learned and Godly Sermon Preached . . . at the Funerall of Mr. Robert Bolton*, 1633, p. 66.
44 *Spirituall Experiences of Sundry Beleevers*, 1652, Epistle.
45 Jane Turner, *Choice Experiences*, 1653, p. 202.
46 Samuel Petto, *op. cit.*, sig. O4.
47 John Rogers, *Ohel or Beth-shemesh. A Tabernacle for the Sun*, 1653, p. 355.

Chapter 2

Recorded Experience

The kind of self-examination I have been describing largely replaced oral confession to a priest, which was of course abolished at the Reformation. It quite soon became a recognized practice, however, for confession to be made in writing, usually in the form of a diary. Here a man would write of his progress and setbacks in the lifelong struggle with the enemy. In such a book the practice of mortification could be systematized and he could record the outcome of his meditation. Moreover – and this came to receive particular emphasis – by remembering mercies received day by day at the hand of God he might prevent lapses into ingratitude and unfaithfulness. Jane Turner's spiritual autobiography grew out of notes of this kind, she 'finding from sad experience, that . . . I am prone to forget the particulars, the remembrance of which I find to be much for the glory of God, and my own comfort and profit'.[1]

Confessional diaries

We can see precisely what was involved here by looking at the confessional diary of Richard Rogers, selections from which have been published in recent years. Rogers became Vicar of Wethersfield, Essex, in 1574 and was an influential member of the early Puritan spiritual brotherhood. His diary embodies the essential features of the Puritan tradition of self-examination, which were to remain basically unchanged until well into the eighteenth century. His primary consideration was the need for self-knowledge:

It is an other thing that I desire, to know mine owne hart better, where I know that much is to be gotten in understaunding of it, and to be acquainted with the diverse corners of it and what sin I am most in daunger of and what dilig[ence] and meanes I use against any sin and how I goe under any afflic[tion].[2]

But while searching out secret and persistent corruptions he was aware that his ultimate purpose must avoid self-centredness, must in fact enable him to view his whole life in a more balanced perspective. Thus he hoped 'that I may so observe mine hart that I may see my life in frame from time to time, . . . I should then be oftner with more certaintie be doeinge of good to my selfe and to others' (p. 72). He did not pursue this activity in isolation, but had regular conference with fellow pastors and derived support and stimulus from them:

No smalle helpe hereto was our whetting on one the other who beinge 4 daies togither communicated many thinges togither: . . . We spake of . . . how hardly we enter into watchful[ness] over ourselves against any inward or outward evil, and how soone we waxe weary of that course (p. 64).

Some weeks after this particular meeting he had to lament his failure to maintain the vigilance there resolved upon: 'we haveinge some weekes before purposed great watchfullnes over our hartes, me thought I had veary slightly regarded or looked to finde out any, ether olde or new corruptions in my self' (p. 70). The key to his whole strategy may be found in his use of the word 'watchfulness', which occurs again and again, and if his systematic self-scrutiny most commonly produced occasions for self-reproach, it did sometimes lead to an identifiable victory. Having complained of 'wandringes and more unsetling of my minde then I have felt these many dayes' he could add, 'if I had not in time espied, and found it out, and cut of the course of it, much unsetlednes with answerable frute had undoubtedly folowed' (p. 75).

His record is of a delicate balance between success and failure in reaching his appointed standards, of growth in grace and lapses from it. The struggle was continuous and attention could never be relaxed; if it were, failure of some sort was sure to follow: 'I, somewhat pleased and satisfied my selfe in my dayes woorck, and pitied of others, as one wearyed through labour, did the lesse geve my selfe to grow upp by the direction of the doctrine delivered that day' (p. 75). If Rogers's diary leaves us with the impression

19

that he was a morbid and overscrupulous introvert, it is as well to remember that we do not get a full picture of a man from notes of this kind any more than we can judge a garden by looking through the contents of the incinerator. As Professor Haller has pointed out in his discussion of Rogers,

> The Puritan preacher was no Rousseau. He was a professional intellectual more or less consciously preparing himself and his generation for a revolution. When he fell weary of the coil of business, discouraged by external difficulty, by the sense of his own failure, and by the futility of his own effort, he retired to his study and poured his heart out in his diary. At such moments the healthiest mind seems morbid.[3]

And as I have already indicated, Rogers's ultimate aims were positive ones: 'I doe not so much complaine of the great evil that I doe as of the litle good,' he wrote, and 'I love and wish allways to be free and at liberty to delight in that wherin I may boldly delight without repent[ance].'[4]

The habit of diary keeping received frequent mention in the biographical accounts of Puritan saints which were published throughout the next century. Samuel Fairclough, we are told, kept such a record from the age of twenty.[5] John Carter 'kept a constant Diary, or day-book, . . . He cast up his accounts with God every day'.[6] Samuel Bolton, when he died, 'left a *writing* behind him wherein he hath recorded al the *outgoings of God* towards him, and all the *experiences* of Gods shining with the *light* of his *countenance* upon him, and also of his *withdrawings* and *hiding* his face from him.[7] Perhaps the most articulate expression of what the journal meant in the daily life of a Puritan is given by James Janeway in his life of his brother John:

> he did write down every evening what the frame of his spirit had been all the day long, especially in every duty. He took notice what incomes and profit he received; in his spiritual traffique; what returns from that far-country; what answers of prayer, what deadness and flatness, and what observable providences did present themselves, and the substance of what he had been doing; and any wandrings of thoughts, inordinancy in any passion; which, though the world could not discern he could. . . . This, made him to retain a grateful remembrance of mercy, and to live in a

constant admiring and adoring of divine goodness; this,
brought him to a very intimate acquaintance with his own
heart; this, kept his spirit low and fitted him for freer
communications from God; this, made him more lively and
active; this, helped him to walk humbly with God, this
made him speak more affectionately and experimentally to
others of the things of God: and, in a word, this left a sweet
calm upon his spirits, because he every night made even his
accounts; and if his sheets should prove his winding-sheet,
it had been all one: for, he could say his work was done;
so that death could not surprize him.[8]

Many writers compared this kind of diary with an account book,
and the definition of the debit and credit sides may have been
sharpened by its relevance to the doctrine of justification by faith:
a man could bring to God nothing but the debt of his sin, while
on the other hand God offered him nothing but grace, and at the
end of a month both spiritual and financial balances might be
undertaken together:

> 31 day spent in seeking to cast up my accounts with god &
> to see all ye debt discharged by ye full satisfaction allready
> made by my . . . blessed Saviour Jesu Xt.
>   I have Considered my Concerns ys moneth and find yt my
> Recepts have been 10L.3s.6: and have disburst and payd
> 9L.4s.6: Blessed be ye God of my mercys that sends me
> Recepts answerable to my charges and disbursms Amen.[9]

Thomas Watson made a similar connection when pinpointing the
difficulty of self-examination and the reluctance of many Christians
to undertake it:

> Many Christians are like trades-men that are sinking; they
> are loth to look over their Books, or cast up their accounts,
> lest they should find their estates low: So they are loth to
> look into their guilty hearts, lest they should find something
> there which should affright them.[10]

Those who overcame their reluctance did so because they were
convinced that disagreeable realities could not be overcome unless
they were known and faced up to, and in any case it was only by
undertaking such a work that evidence of saving grace in the heart

could ever be found. ' 'Tis my desire', wrote Oliver Heywood, 'to search & see what obedience & grounds of hope I have . . . that I may give diligence to make my calling, and election sure, not in itselfe, but to my selfe.'[11] Reflection was an essential part of this process, and so writers constantly referred back to earlier entries, as Rogers did, and made cumulative use of the knowledge so gained. Hannah Allen said that in periods of acute temptation she would read over earlier experiences that she had written down,[12] and Robert Blair the Covenanter, with a systematic diligence characteristic of the Scottish divines, said that 'every Lord's-day the notes of the preceeding week were considered and laid to heart, and at the end of every month the notes thereof were perused, and at the end of the year a view was taken of the whole'.[13]

Many references imply that notes were made daily, but this was by no means the invariable practice and some surviving records show quite long intervals between entries. Their length and nature also vary considerably. Some, like those of Rogers's contemporary Samuel Ward, are little more than brief reminders of matters to be confessed: 'My anger att Mr. Newhouse att supper for saying he had eaten all the bread', and 'My proud thoughtes in that I had prayed in some good sort'.[14] Others are written in shorthand or code. Some consist of prolonged meditations, almost like private sermons.

It is difficult to be sure just how widely that practice was followed in the early seventeenth century. An anonymous *Note Booke for the Year 1693*, now in Dr Williams's Library, indicates that well over a century after Rogers, exactly the same concerns as his were being confided to the diary of another country pastor: 'Thursday spent mostly in a free & friendly converse wh some sober psons – my heart in a good frame' and 'frid: This Morning lost in Sloth and Sleep I find worldly thoughts and things great obstructions to ye things of heaven . . .'[15] Published references to the diaries of deceased preachers come in the forties and fifties, many of which were probably begun after the writer heard almost by accident of what someone else was doing. Robert Blair commenced his journal after being licensed as a preacher in 1616, 'having heard of the practice of some diligent Christians, who daily took brief notes of the condition of their souls,'[16] while

Henry Newcome started his record while at Cambridge in the 1640s, where sooner or later every facet of Puritan tradition must have caught his attention.[17] He continued it intermittently.

In contemporary works of practical divinity there are fewer references than we might expect, and it was not until 1656 that a specific treatise on the confessional diary appeared. In *The Journal or Diary of a Thankful Christian* John Beadle described the duty that all believers had of keeping a record of God's mercies, arguing that the beginning of *Genesis* was God's own diary of the creation of the world, and that Moses kept a journal of the Israelites' wanderings in the wilderness: 'and was not their voyage a type of our pilgrimage? their journey from *Ægypt* to *Caanan*, a signe of our passage from bondage to liberty, from darknesse to light, from a vale of tears to the joyes of heaven?'[18] He went on to recommend items that the Christian should record: not only the means and persons used by God to convert him, all deliverances from danger, and all answers to prayer, but also the ordinary experiences of daily life: 'What Times we have lived in, what Ministers we have lived under, what Callings we were of, what Wealth was bestowed on us, what places of Authority and Command were committed to us' (p. 60). The God who numbered the hairs of a man's head could not fail to be concerned with every detail of his existence.

This advice was not acceptable to everyone. Baxter, writing in 1660, agreed that 'To those Christians that have full leisure, this course is good; but', he added warningly, 'I urge it not upon all. Those that . . . cannot spare so much [time] . . . must . . . record only the extraordinary, observable, and more remarkable and memorable passages of their lives, lest they lose time from works of greater moment'.[19] It is interesting to find these points being taken up and developed in a later age. The early nineteenth-century editor of Ebenezer Erskine's diary thought the practice could be dangerous because it might supply fuel for spiritual pride, because of the possible injudicious use of the work by surviving relatives, and because the writer was certain to be tempted to write with an eye on posterity. Perhaps his fears reflect an attitude that developed after a long history of the publication of private memoirs, although Erskine himself stopped making regular entries after about fifteen years, having apparently come to regard it as a prop to be discarded with developing spiritual maturity: 'I think',

C

23

he wrote in this connection, 'the Lord has for some time been teaching me to *live rather by faith than by sense*'.[20]

And we cannot tell to what extent, if at all, a confessional diary was read by people other than the writer. Apart from a reference by Vavasor Powell to an occasion when he could not consult his earlier record 'having lent it to a Christian Friend that was far distant',[21] we do not hear of any being circulated. To judge from the number of times we are told that a diary or other auto-biographical record was discovered among a man's papers after his death it would seem that they were mostly kept private during his lifetime.

Biographies

However, records of this kind certainly contributed important material to the biographies of famous Puritan preachers, which were often appended to their funeral sermons, preached by a friend or colleague. Here, when it came to be printed, everyone could read of the deceased man's conversion and spiritual conflicts, and in so doing they could find help for themselves. So through these and other biographies the study of the workings of God in the actual lives of men became a means of edification as highly regarded as the more formal instruction of sermon and treatise. Printing the lives of worthy men was like 'engravings with the point of a diamond, raising up for them an everlasting monument', wrote one enthusiastic biographer.[22] It is 'a super-Ægyptian embalming', asserted another, when their memory is preserved 'with the Spices and sweet Odors of their Excellencies'.[23] In a less lyrical vein, and of more immediate concern, was the thought that 'The common people are more apt to enquire what Ministers do, then what they saie'.[24] These life histories were thus the answer to the Papist challenge, Where are your saints to testify to the truth of your religion? And they refuted the impudent lies which the devil and slanderous tongues circulated of the best men the moment they were dead, and often before.

The demand for works of this kind was met in a number of ways. A few lives appeared in the 1630s and 40s by way of preface to preachers' collected writings, but the biographical appendix to the funeral sermon was far more common, and continued to grow in popularity until the late 1650s. Not many appeared as separate works, perhaps because they were reckoned too slight to warrant individual publication. Examples that did appear – such as John Ley's life of Mrs Jane Ratcliffe (1640), or William Hinde's life of John Bruen (1641) – contained in addition to the narrative much improving commentary and exhortation to the reader. More sensational examples of biographical enterprise concerned the deathbed struggle of a despairing soul in *The Last Visitation; Conflicts and Death of Mr. Thomas Peacock*, and the repentance of the condemned criminal John Atherton, described in Nicholas Barnard's *Penitent Death of a Woefull Sinner*. The substance of many of these narratives, augmented with information obtained privately, was assembled by Samuel Clarke in a whole series of collections which appeared between 1650 and 1683, and these popular compilations must have helped to reinforce in the minds of the Puritan public the concept of an ideal Christian life – one corresponding with the doctrinal pattern already delineated.

In view of the example of men like Richard Rogers in the sixteenth century and subsequent widespread commendation of the benefits of self-examination and diary-keeping, it is a little surprising to find that very few spiritual autobiographies were published until the second half of the seventeenth century. An explanation that immediately springs to mind is that with the establishment of the Puritan regime there was a relaxation of the political and ecclesiastical pressures which had inhibited the publication of such material under the old order. But it cannot have been entirely the lack of opportunity, for of the works that appeared in the latter part of the century, and the many others printed only within the last hundred years or so, only a handful were even begun before 1650. All this would suggest that while the established Puritan teaching on conversion and sanctification laid out the essential framework for a narrative of spiritual experience, the emergence of the spiritual autobiography as a recognizable literary form was the result of additional stimulus from other sources.

Early autobiographies

Before we consider these, however, it will be convenient to survey briefly the autobiographical writings that were published earlier.

First, there was the life of William Cowper, Bishop of Galloway, which was printed in 1619 from a short account he wrote at the beginning of his last illness three years earlier. The Preface commends it to posterity 'that they may know how to walke in a good Conscience before God', but it is mainly an account of his education, calling, and career; and although he refers to many infirmities and temptations he gives no details of them, saying merely, 'it were tedious here to set them downe all, as they were done and fought'.[25] A similar reticence is noticeable in other autobiographical narratives, such as the beginning of John Bastwick's *Confession of the Faithfull Witnesse of Christ*, published in 1641 to justify his anti-episcopal activities. John Lilburne the Leveller often refers to his religious experiences in his early pamphlets, but nowhere gives us a connected narrative until he wrote a brief note on his acceptance of Quakerism in 1656.

Three writers at this time did publish books which more nearly foreshadow the technique and conventions of later spiritual autobiographies. The first of these was Richard Kilby, who in 1608 published *The Burthen of a Loaden Conscience*, and ten years later, *Hallelu-iah: Praise Yee the Lord, for the Unburthening of a Loaden Conscience*. In the former he gives a brief account of his youth, and in a meditation on the Ten Commandments confesses how he has repeatedly broken them all. The later book, which was written in 1616, is more explicitly autobiographical. After giving fuller details of his youth, Kilby devotes most of his space to the narrative of his struggle against sin and temptation during a period of great suffering from the stone. This seems to have been the outcome of his occasional meditation and reflection, for most of his story is an almost day-to-day record after 19 April 1616. It recounts his broken vows and repentances, his pain, his relaxation with friends, and the great difficulty he had in preaching. He conveys with considerable power the torture of his disease and the fervency of his prayers, and gives enough of the physical details of his suffering to keep it painfully in the reader's consciousness. He writes a plain prose with carefully balanced sentence structure and is free from the stylized jargon that characterize the testimonies of a later period. It is, in fact, a straightforward and often very moving account of a man's struggle with a tender conscience and his search for God in time of affliction. The forcefulness with which he conveys this is not surpassed until Bunyan's time.

In 1642 a converted Jesuit missionary, Richard Carpenter, published his *Experience, Historie, and Divinitie,* in which he told how he had travelled 'in his raw, greene, and ignorant yeares, beyond the seas' to France, Spain, and Rome.[26] A fragment of his experience is given in each chapter, which leads in to a lengthy meditation, an exhortation to the reader, and appeals to papists to renounce their errors. The book derives much of its pattern from the confessional diary, and indeed he urges the reader to 'make a weekely Bill of Gods benefits, and thy sinnes' (p. 120). The narrative is largely unlocalized and forms the slenderest possible thread linking his various points, though in one place we get an intriguing glimpse of his father confessor at the Jesuit College in Rome, 'who said freely amongst his companions, that hee had laboured in digging under the Parliament house, till every shred of his shirt was wet.' 'This man', adds Carpenter, 'was not a fit Ghostly Father for young Schollers, looking towards *England*' (pp. 133–4).

Finally, *A Narration of the Life of Mr. Henry Burton,* published in 1643, is a narrative of the sufferings he endured for his pamphlets and preaching against the bishops. It is a lively record of trials and imprisonments in Lancaster Gaol and Guernsey, with details of the visions, dreams, and consolations which alleviated his captivity until his return to London in triumph as a popular hero. Burton gives us only a little insight into his inner life, and is best in the reporting of his journeys and imprisonments; he plays up to his admirers in the self-portrait that he gives (it was written 'partly to satisfie the importunity of many godly friends')[27] and shows the heartiness and bluff honesty that the English have always admired in their public heroes.

All these works obviously owe something to the Puritan tradition of self-examination. Burton's story, with its emphasis on his persecution, belongs however less to any tradition of spiritual autobiography than to the narratives of sufferings, of which there are innumerable examples from the early days of the Reformation to the time of the persecution of the Quakers under Charles II. Kilby's work, on the other hand, has obvious affinities with both the confessional diary and contemporary handbooks of practical divinity. His aim was mainly didactic: 'to glorifie God, and to shew unto all people the horrible bondage of sinne; that they might plainly see it, truly feare it, and timely prevent it'.[28] He used his experience as experimental evidence of the truth of his teaching, as later writers such as Bunyan were to do, but doctrine rather than narrative was the shaping factor for Kilby, as it was even more for Carpenter. In fact, it was left to the radical Puritans of the Commonwealth period to establish the spiritual auto-biography as a popular literary form.

Contemporary influences

We are now in a position to take note of some of the specific factors which at this time combined to encourage the publication of detailed spiritual autobiographies. One which has already been touched on was the growing interest in biographies which em-phasized the spiritual life of the subject. The 1640s saw an increase in the number of those appended to funeral sermons and prefaced to collected writings. As we have seen, the first Puritan biographies to be published separately also appeared at this time; and in 1650 the massive collections of Samuel Clarke began to appear.

Secondly, there was a widely noticed upsurge of innovation and experiment in religion – the outcome of seventy years of expert preaching which encouraged individual religious experience and expression. There was expectation in the air, the most famous expression of which is Milton's analysis of the situation as he saw it in 1643: 'Now once again by all concurrence of signs, . . . God is decreeing to begin some new and great period in his Church' and he portrayed his fellow countrymen,

> sitting by their studious lamps, musing, searching, revolving new notions and idea's wherwith to present, as with their homage, and their fealty the approaching Reformation: others as fast reading, trying all things, assenting to the force of reason and convincement. . . . For now the time seems come, wherein *Moses* the great Prophet may sit in heav'n rejoycing to see that memorable and glorious wish of his fulfill'd, when not only our seventy Elders, but all the Lord's people are become Prophets.[29]

The sense of living in a period of unusual activity by the Holy Spirit was shared by all Puritan preachers, even the most con-servative, and if they did not all view the emergence of 'sects and schisms' with Milton's optimism, perhaps they were justified by the outcome of events – at least insofar as many who were busiest in 'revolving new notions' and 'trying all things' were not so adept at 'assenting to the force of reason and convincement'.

The collections of spiritual experiences which were published in the early days of the Commonwealth were all related by their editors to this feature of the time: Vavasor Powell said that many recorded their experiences because 'The special and unspeakable love, and care of our good Lord, . . . hath so manifestly appeared to his people (especially of late yeares)',[30] Samuel Petto declared, 'It seemeth to be one work of this Generation to declare Gods works. Many opportunities and advantages are afforded, for the drawing out experiences, which for many years have been denyed.'[31] And John Rogers, introducing a third collection, said, 'I believe that they are some of the *flowers* of the *Spring* in these dayes.'[32]

Thirdly, there was the part played by personal testimony in the reception of new members by the gathered churches, i.e. those that restricted their membership to professed believers (in contrast to those formed on the parochial principle) who believed that 'A Union of hearts rather than a vicinity of Houses, is to make up a Congregation'.[33] The three collections just mentioned contained between them over a hundred narratives of spiritual experience, mostly written because the gathered churches required some evidence of effectual calling from those who wished to enter into communion with them. Applicants usually met this requirement by publicly relating the manner of their conversion or by handing in a written account of it. 'Every one to be *admitted*', explained John Rogers, 'gives out some *experimental* Evidences of the work of *grace* upon his *soul* (for the *Church* to judge of) whereby he (or she) is *convinced* that he is *regenerate* and *received* of God.'[34] If the church meeting was then satisfied that the applicant was sincere in his profession and sober in his life they accepted him into fellowship. It was emphasized that only God could really know the truth about a man's regeneration; the task of the church meeting was simply to assess 'its evidences and fruits in their external demonstration, as unto a participation of *the outward privileges* of a regenerate state, and no farther'. So wrote John Owen;[35] and Rogers explained what this meant in practice: 'when *poore soules* powre out their experiences, and tell the *means*, and shew the *effects* of their *Call*; we cannot but (in the *judgment* of

29

charity) beleeve the *cause* of this their *Call*, their *faith*, their *holinesse*, is the *Decree of Election*.'[36]

A Presbyterian, Mrs Elizabeth Wilkinson, wrote her account before being admitted to the Lord's Supper, and some years later the young Baptist Thomas Mowsley was moved to describe his conversion following some talks with his minister. But it was the Independents like Rogers and Owen who made most frequent use of the personal testimony in this way, so much so that Baxter accused them of extirpating godliness 'by taking a very few that can talk more than the rest, and making them the Church'.[37] At all events, people were encouraged to be articulate about their experiences, and some of the early Quakers who had previously been Independents spoke of having attended weekly meetings where they related to one another 'how our Hearts had been kept towards the Lord all the Week; with an Account of most Days Passages between God and our own Souls'.[38] The exchanges of experience which Richard Rogers and his fellow clergy enjoyed some sixty years earlier were now firmly established among ordinary church members, who thus formed a receptive public for anything of this kind that was published.

A fourth and final factor contributing to the development of the spiritual autobiography, then, was the cumulative effect of having other people's experiences available. In 1653 Jane Turner expressed some apprehension at publishing her narrative, because she might have seemed 'to walk in an untrodden path, having never seen any thing written before in this manner and method'.[39] In fact, a second edition of *Spirituall Experiences* (the testimonies recommended by Powell) had appeared in January 1652–3, 'enlarged with the Experiences of forty two Beleevers', and in it he referred to earlier books, saying, 'What hath been printed of this nature, hath both been acceptable and profitable to many precious Christians.'[40] John Rogers evidently came across this book as he was preparing his own collection, for he said, 'I am this very week prevented by a little piece, tituled, *Spiritual experiences of sundry Beleevers*, recommended by Mr. *Powel*.' He particularly hoped that the reading of these confessions would encourage others to make theirs public also: 'Oh how *beautifull* they would be abroad! . . . And indeed it is a *burning shame* they should lye *buried* alive, and not be brought into the *light*, which are *given* in to all the *Churches* in this *age*.'[41]

30

Rogers was here thinking of the testimonies collected by other ministers under similar circumstances, and in this respect his appeal seems to have met with no response. Nevertheless, many more spiritual autobiographies were published individually after this. What impresses us about them as a whole is not so much the host of reasons which the writers offer for publicizing such intimate details of their lives, as the evidence we get of the close relationship they enjoyed with their readers. They knew who they were writing for: their friends and fellow-worshippers, all those who took a serious interest in personal religion, and all those on the fringe of church life who had not yet committed themselves. They read one another's stories with intense interest and concern, they discussed the problems of the spiritual life and the implications which public debate on such matters had for the reputation of the Church in the world at large. They replied to criticisms and attempted to clear away misunderstandings. Above all they hoped to build one another up in the faith through the painstaking analysis and discussion of personal experience. A cohesive social life and a common culture are implied in all this activity, with free interplay between writers and readers, the published material being only a fraction of the ongoing dialogue. Anyone could join in. Misgivings like Jane Turner's soon ceased to be appropriate and it was implied that anyone who was truly converted could and should give an account of the process.[42]

The ultimate aim was to promote the glory of God: no glimmer of the light He had given was to be kept under a bushel,[43] and every testimony added further evidence for the infinite variety of His dispensations: 'all these variety of notes *concur* to make up the *tune* of the *song* of the *Lamb*.'[44] The benefits were more precisely delineated, however, by reference to the effects on all kinds of readers: unbelievers might be led to want spiritual blessings, slothful Christians might be shamed into action, and those in distress might be encouraged when they read how God had brought others out of similar ordeals. Bunyan, we remember, wrote 'for the support of the weak and tempted People of God', while certain other writers hoped to convey a more specific message by their experience: Richard Kilby on 'the horrible bondage of sinne', Hannah Allen on the folly of 'making inward comfort an idol' and Henry Hills 'to own his own shame, and caution others' on the dangers of apostasy. Jane Turner wanted 'to provoke self-examination and spiritual quickening'.[45]

Some of the first narratives to be published show writers more on the defensive than was evidently thought necessary later. They justified themselves at considerable length against objections such as the possibility that evilly disposed men might make a bad use of these personal disclosures. They found their authority in numerous texts which urged the proclamation of God's dealings with men, and especially in the example of Paul in Acts 22 and David in the Psalms, 'And indeed', said Samuel Petto, 'the book of Psalmes is presented to the eys of men both good and bad, and doth consist for the most part of Experiences.' Therefore, he added, 'Be as ready to impute thy non-acquaintance with such works, unto thy defect, as unto their mistake.'[46]

Self-defence was also an important motive for some, particularly the vulgar prophets, who hoped an appeal to experience would be harder to refute than one based on argument. And Francis Bampfield, the Sabbatarian Baptist, claimed that he had several loud divine calls to record his life story as the only way to repudiate those who were persistently defaming his ministry. Richard Baxter, in contrast, though not unconcerned for his reputation, wrote partly to forestall the biographical labours of 'some *overvaluing* Brethren, who I know intended it' (my italics).[47]

Chronology and classification of works

When we consider these works as a whole, the most obvious way of classifying them is according to the writer's denomination. By 1650 the main tradition of Puritan church life was to be found in the Presbyterian, Independent, and Baptist churches, the last two being the more radical in doctrine and church order. The process of political and ecclesiastical events had steadily reduced the numbers of men like Perkins, Sibbes, and Preston, who in an earlier generation upheld the Puritan position from within the established church. After 1662 the identification of Puritanism with dissent was complete. Whether or not it would be misleading to speak of any of the Puritans of the Commonwealth period as 'Anglicans' – and it might be argued that the term itself was anachronistic – we certainly find that the spiritual autobiographies came either from Presbyterians, Independents, and Baptists, or from men and women of more radical convictions. There was of course a lot of difference between, say, a Covenanter like James Fraser and the Baptist prophetess Anna Trapnel, but they both subscribed to the fundamental assumptions of Puritan doctrine which lay behind the habits of self-examination and diary-keeping; it will therefore be convenient to discuss all these 'orthodox Puritans' together. We are then left with two other clearly defined groups of testimonies: those of the vulgar prophets and individualists of the Commonwealth, most of whom were antinomian and expounded a vague mystical pantheism; and the confessions and journals of the Quakers, who found salvation only in acceptance of an 'inner Light' and who were highly critical of Puritan faith and practice in many ways that affected their conversion stories. Logically and historically all three groups of confessions originated in Puritan tradition, though the writers' immediate frames of reference varied considerably according to where their denomination or sect or private theology stood in relation to the general development of Protestant thought. The Quakers and the Ranters, for instance, might be regarded as embodying in very different ways the principles of the Reformation carried to a logical conclusion (as they themselves would have said) or distorted by the disastrous over-emphasis of some considerations at the expense of others (as their opponents would have claimed). We shall, indeed, be considering writers from every point on the theological spectrum from Calvinism at its most meticulously intellectual to the uncontrolled subjectivity of the Ranters. Hence within all groupings many differing stand-points are represented, and these are reflected in the pattern and tone of the narratives; however, the three broad categories I have indicated – orthodox Puritans, vulgar prophets, and Quakers – provide the best framework for our survey and the works themselves will therefore be discussed under these headings.

Apart from a change of emphasis by some of the Quakers towards the end of the century, there was little development in the form of spiritual autobiographies once they began to be published in any numbers. What we find are three closely related types of confessional writing which appeared almost simultaneously about the middle of the century. The first ones to make an impact on the public were probably those of the individualist prophets, who published their experiences in order to support their claims to

33

have received extraordinary illumination. Their flamboyant behaviour attracted a good deal of notice, some of it from Parliament itself, and their dozen or so autobiographical books and pamphlets, all of which appeared during the interregnum, achieved a reputation far beyond their readership. Quaker narratives were beginning to come out at the same time, and new ones appeared so frequently that they soon outnumbered all other works of the kind put together; the flood continued well into the eighteenth century.

The publication of the more orthodox Puritans' experiences followed a somewhat curious sequence which it is difficult to explain fully. In view of the popularity of biographies of well-known preachers and their known custom of recording their spiritual life, it might have been expected that a large proportion of Puritan autobiographies would have consisted of the posthumously published narratives of leading ministers. But the fact is that following the brief autobiography of William Cowper, published in 1619, we have to wait over half a century for another work of a similar kind to appear: then in 1671 we get the life stories of Henry Jessey (died 1663) and Vavasor Powell (died 1670); there is nothing further until 1692, which gave us the narrative of Hanserd Knollys, while in the following decade or so there came the memoirs of Edmund Trench (1693), Richard Baxter (1696), and Thomas Goodwin (1704). All the other seventeenth-century publications were by laymen with the exception of three preachers – John Rogers, John Bunyan, and Francis Bampfield – who published their experiences in their own lifetime. Most spiritual autobiographies by Puritan ministers were not published until the nineteenth century, when they appeared mainly under the sponsorship of various learned societies.

Another way of classifying the Puritan autobiographies would be according to whether they were published in the writer's lifetime or not, and we would then notice two clearly defined periods. Up to 1666, with the first edition of *Grace Abounding*, very nearly all the confessions were by living writers; the only exceptions were Cowper's life already mentioned and the experiences of two Presbyterian women, Mary Simpson and Elizabeth Wilkinson, printed with their funeral sermons in 1649 and 1659 respectively. After this, starting with the memoirs of Jessey and Powell in 1671, we get practically nothing but posthumous narratives, again with very few exceptions indeed, notably the memoirs of Francis

Bampfield and the experiences of a Mrs Hannah Allen, published in 1683, which dealt with some happenings of twenty years earlier. The Quakers do not fit into this pattern exactly, but the same tendency becomes apparent at a somewhat later date when in the 1690s conversion stories by living writers began to be replaced by complete journals of the first generation of itinerant evangelists.

If any significance can be attached to this development, it might be as evidence for a decline in the belief that current events were the outcome of exceptional initiative on the part of the Holy Spirit; hence there was no longer the same urgency to publicize the experience of individuals. If that were the case, it would also help to explain why the Quakers continued to publish narrative confessions by living writers long after others had ceased to do so, for their whole concept of conversion relied more heavily on individual witness to the dynamic operation of the Spirit.

NOTES

1 Turner, p. 2. (Where no book title is given, the reference is to the spiritual autobiography listed under the author's name in the Bibliography on pp. 241–60.)
2 'The Diary of Richard Rogers', in M. M. Knappen (ed.), *Two Elizabethan Diaries*, 1933, p. 62.
3 Haller, *The Rise of Puritanism*, pp. 38f.
4 Knappen, *op. cit.*, pp. 89, 54.
5 Clark, *Lives of Sundry Eminent Persons*, 1683, p. 162.
6 J. Carter [Jnr.], *The Tomb-stone*, 1653, p. 28.
7 Edmund Calamy, *The Saints Transfiguration*, 1655, p. 25.
8 James Janeway, *Invisibles, Realities*, 1673, pp. 58–9.
9 'A Note Book for the Year 1693', MS. in Dr Williams's Library, London, entry for 31 March.
10 Watson, *Heaven Taken by Storm*, p. 58.
11 Heywood, p. 134.
12 Allen, p. 8.
13 Blair, pp. 32–3.
14 'The Diary of Samuel Ward', Knappen, *op. cit.*, pp. 114, 116.
15 'A Note Book for the Year 1693', entries for 6 and 7 January.
16 Blair, p. 31.
17 Cf. Newcome, p. 14.
18 John Beadle, *The Journal or Diary of a Thankful Christian*, 1656, p. 11.
19 Baxter, *Works*, XVII. 601f.

35

20 Donald Fraser (ed.), *The Life and Diary of the Reverend Ebenezer Erskine A.M. of Stirling*, 1831, p. 176.
21 Powell, p. 12.
22 Henry Scudder, 'The Life and Death of Mr. William Whateley', in William Whateley, *Prototypes*, 1640, sig. a.
23 John Norton, *Abel being Dead yet Speaketh*, 1658, p. 4.
24 John Wall and Simeon Ashe, in Samuel Clark, *Marrow of Ecclesiastical Historie*, 1650, Epistle 'To the Christian Reader'.
25 Cowper, sig. B2v.
26 Carpenter, title page.
27 Burton, Preface.
28 Kilby, *Burthen*, Dedication.
29 Milton, 'Areopagitica', in *Complete Poetry and Selected Prose of John Milton*, Modern Library ed., New York, Random House, n.d., pp. 714, 715–16.
30 *Spirituall Experiences*, Epistle.
31 Petto, sig. O4.
32 John Rogers, p. 355.
33 John Cook, *What the Independents Would Have*, 1647, p. 7, cited by G. F. Nuttall, *Visible Saints*, 1951, p. 108.
34 John Rogers, p. 354.
35 John Owen, *The True Nature of a Gospel Church*, ed. Huxtable, 1947, p. 26.
36 John Rogers, p. 361.
37 Baxter, *Reliquiae Baxterianae*, 1696, III. 67.
38 J. Crook, p. 19.
39 Turner, sig. B8.
40 *Spirituall Experiences*, Epistle.
41 John Rogers, pp. 355, 449.
42 Cf. Janeway, *op. cit.*, p. 80.
43 Cf. Fraser, sig. A4.
44 John Rogers, p. 417.
45 Bunyan, title page; Kilby, *Burthen of a Loaden Conscience*, Epistle; Allen, Epistle; Hills, sig. A2v.; Turner, sig. B6v.
46 Petto, sigg. O4v, O5v.
47 Baxter, *Reliquiae*, I. 136.

Chapter 3

Theme and Variations

The normal pattern of a Puritan conversion followed the sequence: peace, disturbance, and then peace again. Bunyan said of *Grace Abounding*, 'It is a Relation of the work of God upon my own Soul, even from the very first, till now; wherein you may perceive my castings down, and raisings up; for he woundeth and his hands make whole' (pp. 1f). The casting down and raising up, the wounding and making whole, referred to the two landmarks already mentioned – conviction of sin and coming to Christ.

Law and grace

Some clear examples can be seen in the testimonies assembled by John Rogers when he was pastor of an Independent congregation meeting in Christ Church Cathedral, Dublin, in 1653. He explained in an introduction that the believer had a twofold call, which he defined as first a 'legal' call, and second an 'evangelical' one. What this amounted to was that conviction of sin usually led a man to diligent attendance on the means of grace (sermons, prayer, Bible reading, meditation) which he afterwards recognized as a period of 'legal work', since it was an attempt to satisfy God's justice through the performance of duties. The statement of Jeremy Heyward, which happens to be the shortest in the collection, can be quoted in full to show the steps to conversion, which are highlighted in the editor's marginal notes.

> THE Lord hath opened my *eyes* to see *sin*,
> and showne me my *self*, and I lay under
> his *wrath* half a year, and so long as I   Under sense of
> sought to make out my own *righteousnesse*,   sin.

37

I lay thus; and yet this while, I followed the meanes, heard the *Word*, and I saw at length nothing but *Christ* would serve me, and till then I could have no *comfort*, wherefore one *first day* of the *week*, I fell to *prayer*, I prayed *thrice*, and at the third time I heard him say, *Loe! my grace is sufficient for thee*, whereby I was much satisfied ere since rowling my *self* on Christ, and *living* in him alone; and I finde so *great a change*, that I can say, *whereas I was blinde, now I am sure I see.*[1]

By prayer and the voice of God.

Confirmed in Christ.
Effects.

Puritan conversion stories as a whole form an extended commentary on the universality of these two stages of experience. In the Dublin collection all the writers interpreted their awakening after a common pattern, though outward influences were varied enough: the example of parents, friends or husbands who had been converted; afflictions such as bereavement, poverty, or illness; offences like disobeying parents, breaking the sabbath, or habitual drunkenness. The inadequacy of the first stage alone is elaborately documented in testimonies of all kinds. The Covenanter James Fraser said that his first conviction of sin led him to try to satisfy his own conscience rather than love God, and he 'mourned for Sin, not because it offended God, but because of the Consequents of it'.[2] A reformation of outward behaviour was one of the earliest signs of an awakened conscience, as it was with Bunyan:

> Wherefore I fell to some outward Reformation, both in my words and life, and did set the Commandments before me for my way to Heaven: which Commandments I did also strive to keep; and, as I thought, did keep them pretty well sometimes, and then I should have comfort; . . . for then I thought I pleased God as well as any man in *England* (para. 30).

Bunyan's tone subtly conveys his complacency here, and Thomas Halyburton likewise found that he obtained temporary peace of heart at this stage. 'Amendment I thought sufficient atonement,' he wrote, and the evidence of his improved behaviour misled him theologically: 'Common Gifts increasing as the Light grew, I took them for special Grace, and thus have taken up, with the foolish Virgins, *the Lamp* of a Profession *without oil*.'[3] The 'legal' relationship with God, dominated by the letter of the law rather than its spirit, is strikingly illustrated in George Trosse's attitude when he found an ingenious way of escaping from a vow he had made to give up drinking in taverns: 'I either put my *Head* out of the *Window*,' he said, 'or *went* out into a *Gutter* to *drink*.'[4] And Thomas Mowsley indulged in a like equivocation after he had vowed to leave off gaming for a year:

> . . . this was about *November*, or *December*, which for a little while I kept; and now observe the great subtilty of the Devil in this particular, for no sooner was it the first day of *January*, but presently I was told that my vow was out of date, and . . . I was willing to make my conscience submit.[5]

Looking back on this kind of behaviour, many writers would have agreed with Vavasor Powell that 'the spirit of fear and bondage . . . did bind me like a Prisoner, to answer every breach of the Law'.[6]

Release came when the gospel was experienced in the heart as well as with the understanding, and this was the high-water mark of the conversion process. Halyburton spoke of the relief that came to him in January 1698 with 'a Discovery of the LORD, as manifested in the Word'; he felt the gospel invitation as a personal one and drew a distinction between 'the Discoveries now made, and the Notions I formerly entertained of the same Truths'.[7] Jane Turner found that 'the abounding love of Christ did compell and constrain me to cast my self upon him for life and salvation, in a way of believing, and not in a way of working'.[8] Anna Trapnel, like many others, spoke in terms of the covenant of grace superseding the covenant of works: 'I must declare I was passed from Mount *Sinai*, into the Regions of Mount *Sion*.'[9] The unity of the entire process was effectively summed up by Adam Martindale; it was, he said, 'like a sharp needle, drawing after it a silken thread of comfort in due season'.[10]

Although doctrine and experience interacted to throw these two key events into prominence, many were still anxious not to over-simplify the record. God had had powerful dealings with them before conviction, and their experience after conversion included many notable landmarks. And if some could not identify the time

D   39

of their first spiritual experience or the actual moment of rebirth, there was an influential body of opinion holding that this was in any case impossible without an exceptional revelation by the Holy Spirit. Giles Firmin called it 'a meer Vanity and Devils Delusion' to worry about it as long as the change had taken place; and Henry Hickman said that those 'stained with enormous Crimes' would know when their reclamation began, but ordinary Christians were unlikely to be aware of 'the Nick of Time in which they ceased to be Natural, and began to be Spiritual'. These two writers were quoted by the Nottingham businessman Joseph Barret to forestall readers' criticisms that his own account was not precise enough about such matters.[11]

Even James Fraser, who divided his spiritual autobiography into twelve chapters, each with numerous sub-sections, had to admit that in some important respects 'the Lord . . . almost perfected his Work ere I thought he had well begun'. It may have been the very persistence of his efforts to capture the ebb and flow of his spiritual life that led him to say that 'A Man's whole Life is but a Conversion'.[12]

Collections of testimonies

The problem was to find a pattern without oversimplifying, although many of the writers were content just to find the pattern. To the extent that they lacked the skill to capture the flux of their inward life in individually discovered language, they relied more heavily on the framework of doctrine or some other externally supplied scheme. We have seen how John Rogers encouraged his congregation to take their bearings with reference to a 'legal' and an 'evangelical' call. And he had more to say about the form a testimony should take, notably that it should consist of two parts: preparation (the circumstances of conversion) and qualification (its effects on the convert's life and attitudes).[13] And so his testimonies nearly all conclude with the writers' resolve to resist sin and obey the voice of God, and with a note of how the working of the Spirit was known to them; this could be either 'ordinarily', by the transforming effects of grace on the judgment, will, and affections, or 'extraordinarily', by dreams, voices, or visions. These two modes correspond approximately with the 'discoursive' and 'intuitive' modes of assurance spoken of by Thomas Goodwin, though Goodwin would no doubt have questioned the validity of much of the evidence here.[14]

Of the thirty-eight narratives in Rogers's collection, most appear to have been taken down at the time of delivery, but at least two were written out beforehand. Rogers claimed to have 'dealt *faithfully* with all, as I finde them in my *Notes*, as near as I can to a *tittle*, taken out of their *owne mouths*, without *respect of persons*; excepting some of the most *ordinary sort*, which I have taken *summarily*'.[15] Jeremy Heyward's account, quoted above, was probably one of those summarized, and we cannot doubt that Rogers's editorial method reinforced the tendency for the accounts to display a standard scheme of interpretation; his frequent marginal comments certainly do so.

A slightly different emphasis is apparent in the sixty-one testimonies in the enlarged version of *Spirituall Experiences*. Many of them refer to the preaching of Henry Walker, who was the minister of the church at Martins Vintry, London, at about this time, and this was probably the church which the contributors belonged to. The original testimonies were said to have been 'Held forth by them at severall solemne meetings, and Conferences to that end'.[16] They all embody three features: a brief account of the circumstances of conversion, the quotation of some texts that helped to bring peace to the troubled soul, and an enumeration of signs by which the believer was assured of his state of grace. References to contrasting phases of experience under the law and under grace are much less pointed than in the Dublin collection. Individual differences again are mainly in outward circumstances, the bond of a common outlook revealing itself in the passages of Scripture and marks of regeneration quoted. The range of texts – often given in the Geneva translation – is surprisingly small, and the same ones constantly recur: Matthew xi.28, John vi.37, and Isaiah lv.1 are by far the most popular, the first being quoted twenty-four times.[17] The signs of regeneration, listed by numbers at the end of each account, resemble one another even more, and correspond to those given in contemporary treatises. They are, however, used less as proofs of a redeemed condition than as a public avowal of sincerity and faith.

These narratives tend to be longer than those published by Rogers, allowing a little more room for specific details of early life. There is an emphasis on an outwardly pious childhood and youth involving a bondage to some kind of fear – fear of hell, fear of the devil, fear of loving the world overmuch, fear of bringing dishonour on the gospel. After conviction a substantial period of what one writer calls 'griefe . . . interlaced with comforts' is a part of everyone's story, and release when it comes is normally the result of long meditation on the Scriptures rather than visions, interior voices, dreams or intuitions such as figure prominently in the Dublin collection. It is clear from Rogers's own autobiography, which will be discussed in a later chapter,[18] that he was susceptible to these kinds of paranormal experience and so encouraged his congregation to speak about them; for the contributors to *Spirituall Experiences* pastoral influence obviously was very different.

Nevertheless, temptations to suicide are recorded quite frequently, and one narrative in particular features an incident which, in various settings, occurs in many of the biographies of Puritan saints. This is where the believer does not merely despair of salvation, but is so completely overwhelmed by his fears as to be in a pathological condition. The memory of some sin convinces him that he is a reprobate, and he refuses to listen to any word of comfort. We usually read of him being visited by a local pastor, who reasons with him for many days in a vain attempt to alleviate his despair. So it was with the young man E.R., who said,

> . . . my parents did send for Mr. *Newstubs* a Minister in *Edmundsbury*, and one Mr. *Rogers* another Minister of *Deddam*, who tooke a great deale of paines with me, and asked mee whom I did beleeve in; and I told them that I did beleeve in God that hee would damne me; and they asked me, if God would damn me because I did beleeve in him; I answered no, but it was for that sin committed against God, and my innocent sister; and they asked mee, whether I was not sorry for that act, and I told them yes, for I had cause enough to be sorry, for I must be damned for that sin. . . .[19]

Later, when told that Christ would pardon a repentant sinner, 'I told them no, that he would never open my heart but with terror, for I was borne to be damned, and that Christ never dyed for such a sinner as I was' (p. 362). The preachers' formidable experience and Biblical knowledge are of no use: the victim has already searched every verse for himself. Prayer, ingenuity, and earnest persuasion are likewise without effect, for they are matched by answers even more ingenious. No matter what black sins have been forgiven others he knows only that he himself was born to be damned. Time and again the Puritan preachers, practised physicians of the soul though they were, had to admit defeat in the face of this wilful obstinacy. The victim completely abandons himself to all his morbid fears and takes a perverse delight in resisting all attempts to save him and in his uniqueness as the one soul whom not even God Himself can save. E.R. eventually recovered – after the ministers had left – but his answers exactly reproduce the arguments of others in a similar state of depression.

The experiences of M.K.

One account in *Spirituall Experiences* stands out from the rest because of its greater length and more pretentious style. And its position as the last contribution to Part One of the book (which constituted the first edition) suggests that the compiler recognized it as the weightiest item. Indeed, if we wanted to select one testimony which should be representative of the Puritan spiritual autobiography as popular literature it would be hard to find a better example.

The story is that of a woman, M.K., and her life story falls into a number of phases, each initiated by a personal crisis, but which together present a familiar pattern. Her mother's death led to spiritual indifference in adolescence, but the sudden death of her father reawakened her concern to the point of despair because she felt it had been a punishment for her sins. After marriage her turmoil increased as her husband lived beyond his means, and she barely withstood the temptation to murder the man she held responsible. Meditation and prayer resulted only in further self-condemnation: 'I saw there was no remedy, but the more I strove, the faster I stucke.'[20] At this point a religious experience convinced her of the reality of God and ushered in the hope of forgiveness, though it was only after eleven years of striving that, with guidance from sermons and the Scriptures, she finally abandoned the attempt to merit divine acceptance by self-purification and good works.

At every stage in the narrative M.K. relates her experiences to her social environment, and at every stage they bear witness to a thriving Puritan tradition. Her mother was 'a godly vertuous and religious Gentlewoman' who instructed her daily from the Scriptures and the commentaries of Erasmus; she had 'serious thoughts' about God in childhood, often awoke in the night to pray, and derived her pattern of Christian faithfulness from stories of the Marian martyrs. Childish piety was followed by a falling-away in youth, and the reaction when it came characteristically brought 'excessive sorrow' in which she 'refused all comfort' from her friends. In desperation they helped her in the most effective way they could think of, which was to persuade her to go to London because 'the word of God was more plentifully preached there'. If this was the only reason for her making the move – and no other is suggested – it eventually proved to be justified because of the influence of a funeral sermon by the redoubtable John Dod. Dod's preaching was reputed so to have struck home to sinners' hearts that he was accused of having spies and informers at work for him,[21] and M.K. herself testifies that 'this Minister did not onely preach to the people, but shewed me as it were in a looking-glasse mine own condition'.[22] Consequently she would go to hear up to five sermons by Dod every week, had private consultations with him, and learned from him to compare her own condition with those of people in the Bible. Self-examination and private prayer were thus carried on with constant reference to norms derived from Scripture and pastoral tradition. Long periods of reflection and moral effort were accepted as normal and necessary, and pastors tried patiently to help their charges through them; the cumulative effect on the convert of meditation, study, and experience was to create the conditions for the next glimmer of understanding that came, and no single experience was felt to be conclusive. It was a continuous learning process. M.K. attributes such occasions of conscious progress in her own life to revelations by God of the fact and nature of His love for her, and in generally acknowledging the divine initiative harmonizes her experience within the framework of Calvinist teaching about the sovereignty of God.

It is clear that M.K. had some pretensions both to gentility and to a wider background of reading than most of her contemporaries in this collection. This may account for the slightly strained and self-conscious tone of her narrative, but in one place at least she manages to convey the power and immediacy of the kind of experience that must have lain behind many less articulate records.

It comes as the climax to months of depression, despair, and fantasies of damnation. One evening her pet dog startled her by jumping on the bed, and her immediate reaction was that the devil had at last come in person to take her away:

> I screamed forth aloud, but when I perceived it was the dog, and not the Devill, I began to thinke, That *surely there was a God that had preserved me all this while.*
>
> In a most grievous agony I spent that night weeping, and although it was Winter, yet I sweat that the water ranne from off every part of my body. Being in this sad condition, I thought it was not right, but surely some meanes might bee used to get out of it. I rising the more early in the morning, went up into the highest roome that was in the house, and looked forth at the window to see if I could see God, there I beheld the Trees to grow, the Birds to flie, the Heavens how they hanged, and all things that were before me, then I thought *they could not make themselves, no more then I could make my selfe, and that we must needs have a Maker, and this Maker must be strong and powerfull*; then I fell downe upon my knees crying out on this manner, *O God, if there be a God, shew thy selfe to me a poore miserable wretch,* that am at the point to perish; *Then I thought I saw the Lord but with a frowning countenance,* hee looked upon me as if he had said, *Thou hast displeased me, and I will not heare thee,* and turning his back went from me, which sight was as a dart thrust through my soul for the space of halfe an houre, divers thoughts entred into my heart, but before I rose from off my knees, I resolved to become an earnest suiter to him, and not to do any thing more that should displease him, hoping that he would be intreated for that which was past.[23]

Here as nowhere else in the whole of the book we are given some glimpse of the authentic spirit of Puritan devotion. In the empty room, in the stillness and cold light of dawn, the lonely soul cries out to God and becomes aware for a moment of a stirring beyond its own consciousness; something alive pierces through from the outside and presses downwards like a living weight, and there is a dim sense of vast reserves of energy there which can only be experienced as a denial or a barrier because restlessness and perversity have destroyed the capacity for any other kind of perception. Enough is suggested here to convince us that this is an account of a genuine religious experience, and a link with what men in all ages have felt when thrust into the presence of a holy God.

Conformity and variety in structure

There were many pressures predisposing these writers to conformity. As well as the clearly defined doctrinal tradition they were brought up in there was the cohesive nature of the gathered church community and the aim of mutual edification which called forth the original narratives. The fear of being unique or eccentric was therefore a potent factor, and it helped to shape experience itself as well as the way it was recorded. A complaint was indeed made that feeble Christians were not to be satisfied until they had the same experience as others. Joseph Barret had 'sad thoughts' when he realized that he had 'not met with those strong Convictions as poor Sinners ordinarily do', though he was reassured after reading that this was usual with those converted like him at an early age.[24] One reason why William Kiffin commended the record of Hanserd Knollys's ninety-three years was because it would help to convince readers 'that God deals no otherwise with them than he doth to those that formerly have feared him'.[25] Unusual features might need special explanation, as when Anna Trapnel feared the validity of her experience might be questioned because it did not conform to some people's presuppositions: 'And if I vary concerning some experiences in this, in respect of doubting, and questioning union after sealing, it is my own experience, I must not second anothers experience; it may be some may scruple at it, and therefore I thought fit to mention it.'[26]

The Puritan pastors, with wider knowledge of what was happening to different people, emphasized the variety of dealings with God that they might have. So the writer of the Preface to Halyburton's *Memoirs*, published in 1715, listed what was essential in an individual's experience of 'preparatory Law-works' but went on to say that 'there is a great Variety among the Lord's People as to the Time of their awakening, the Duration of it, the Means by which, &c., Measure of Terrour, or Down-casting, the Distinctness about their Exercise, and the like'.[27] To the modern reader the variations probably appear less significant than they did to the writers' contemporaries, who were less aware of the assumptions they derived from their Puritan culture.

The confessions that were independently written conformed less closely to a common structural pattern than those produced for a church meeting. Professor G. A. Starr, in a perceptive discussion, has said, however,

> It can be stated almost as a law of spiritual autobiographies that the greater the attention paid to events before conversion, the less emphasis given to what happens afterwards, and vice versa. A work that traces in detail the progress of sin, with conversion finally snatching the author from the very jaws of hell, will rarely have much to say about subsequent relapses. But where the author's fortunate environment or precocious piety has preserved him from great wickedness before conversion, the trials to which he is later exposed furnish the required exemplary matter.[28]

Certainly, examples can be found to illustrate this. Of the writers who give most of their space to what happened after conversion, Bunyan is a notable example; his work and that of Mrs Mary Simpson were published, as their title pages indicate, specifically to help readers understand the trials of a converted and committed Christian. And James Fraser of Brea has six or seven times more material after conversion than before, though as his story is longer than most he is still able to give us fifty pages of detailed analysis on his unregenerate experience. But Fraser is hardly as typical as Professor Starr suggests, for all the other writers who reach their conversion early in the narrative go on to devote most of the subsequent pages to their participation in affairs of church and state: see, for instance, the works of Blair, Brysson, Kiffin, Livingstone, and Shaw. The only clear case of a writer whose conversion comes at the end, snatching him from the jaws of hell, is George Trosse. Because he was unrepentant for so long, he could be compared in his preface to other 'Returning Sinners' such as Augustine and Perkins who had been 'reclaim'd from a wicked Course'.[29] In fact, when these works are considered as a whole, the 'law' which Professor Starr formulates becomes either less tenable or less meaningful. If it means that conversion hardly ever comes exactly half way through an autobiography, then it could be supported: it does so only in three or four instances,

47

notably Halyburton, Rogers, and Trapnel. But this is in itself neither surprising nor significant. More important is the fact that where a decisive conversion experience is related it normally comes somewhere in the middle third of the story, leaving at least one-third of the total space for each of the periods before and after. About half the works under discussion in this section have no such clearly defined conversion experience. Some say their conversion was so gradual that they cannot tell when it was (e.g. Barret, Cowper, Heywood, Jaffray, Newcome). Others simply do not identify such a point in time (Powell, Trench, Disney, Mowsley, Wilkinson). Others again do not order their experience chronologically (Bampfield, Jaffray, Pringle).

The material, then, can be shaped in many different ways. So far I have mainly been concerned with those writers who use the accepted stages of development already discussed. Jane Turner's chapter headings indicate a pattern that would immediately have been recognized as the norm, even though some of her responses might have been challenged:

> 1. The first Note of Experience of the good Providence of God towards mee in a state of Ignorance and Darkness before Conversion [pp. 10–21].
> 2. ... How I was brought to see my self in a miserable state by Nature, ... and so converted to duty, ... [pp. 22–48]
> 3. ... How I was brought to apprehend and believe the free Grace of God in the Gospell, ... [pp. 49–79]
> 4. ... how I was convinced and brought to submit to Baptism and Church-fellowship commanded by Christ [pp. 80–108].
> 5. ... concerning Notions, and Pretended Spiritualities, in which Satan transforms himself into an Angel of Light; and how far I was deceived by it, and how the Lord was pleased to recover me out of it [pp. 109–79].
> 6. ... Qualifications, the habits of Grace or fruits of the Spirit, how and by what means I have and do daily find an increase and decrease in those things [pp. 180–208].[30]

Fraser and Halyburton are more elaborate and detailed, but show the same sequence, and all three writers follow up every portion of narrative with extensive reflections.

A different emphasis in the writer's purpose brings about

48

different ways of shaping his material. John Livingstone and Robert Blair, being largely concerned with their part in public affairs, divide up their life-span with reference to the time spent in the ministry at different places. Walter Pringle recorded his memoirs for his children in forty-five dated sections, written at intervals over four years. They are not in strict chronological sequence, but bring in particular topics that were on his mind at the time of writing, making each entry a kind of meditation. Hence his children were advised 'to read no more than one day's writing at one time'.[31] Francis Bampfield's concern to vindicate his office as minister caused him to compare his experience as closely as possible to that of the apostle Paul, under the headings, Name, Outward Privileges, Conversion, Call to Office, Baptism, Sufferings, Evidences and Assurances, each of which provides evidence of exhaustive parallels between the two of them ('tho the Preheminence is given unto Paul').[32]

Few writers employ any consistent formal device. The young apothecary Thomas Mowsley begins his story as a dialogue between a minister and himself, but the account soon lapses into simple narrative. A more sophisticated formal treatment is found in Henry Hills's account of his apostasy, in which he applies the parable of the Prodigal Son phrase by phrase to his own experience; though commended to the reader as 'a new experimental exposition of the Scriptures', the applications are strained and unconvincing.

A devotional framework is sometimes used, not for the whole work but for an important section within it. George Trosse organizes some five years of his experience in relation to his sins against the Ten Commandments.[33] Oliver Heywood introduces his narrative with a list of findings based on aspirations and self-analysis.[34] The narrative line is never felt to be important for its own sake: comment and reflection are essential to give meaning and coherence to a sequence of happenings. Without this, it is felt, the story will satisfy only the reader's curiosity and will be treating him as less than a rational creature made in God's image with the duty and potential to understand as much of the Creator's world as possible.

Prose fiction and the 'Private Gentleman'

The full influence of narratives of spiritual experience on the development of prose fiction is outside the scope of this study, but mention must be made of an anonymous work which appeared in 1708. This is entitled, *An Account of some Remarkable Passages in the life of a Private Gentleman; With reflections thereon. . . . Relating to Trouble of Mind, some violent Temptations, and a Recovery; . . .* It was evidently fairly popular, for an enlarged edition appeared in 1711, and this was reprinted several times. It was at one time thought to be from the hand of Defoe, but no evidence for this attribution has been put forward. Professor Starr, in his study of Defoe, draws attention to inconsistencies in the work which suggest that it is not a genuine autobiography, and he assigns to it an important place in the development of prose fiction from the spiritual autobiography, arguing that it shows 'a major shift of emphasis' in the conventional structure, and that it embodies 'newer features typical of the fiction to come'.[35] In particular, there are certain important analogies with Robinson Crusoe.

If I take issue again with Professor Starr, it is not because I would quarrel with his main thesis that much in the theme and structure of *Robinson Crusoe* derives from seventeenth-century spiritual autobiographies. With extensive reference to the language and traditions of Puritan devotional writings he argues convincingly that Crusoe, in his rebellion, waywardness, and isolation, acts out in his life the spiritual progress of a typical Puritan, and that Defoe uses this pattern of experience as a basic element in his plot, his main achievement being the skilful way he unites instruction with narration. But I am not convinced that the Private Gentleman's *Account* plays any significant part in this development. It appears to bear far less relation to prose fiction than many earlier autobiographies, and indeed to be remarkable only for the inclusion of much moralizing comment that is less coherently organized than in most other works of this kind. Closer analogies with *Crusoe* can be found elsewhere.

The 'major shift of emphasis' that Professor Starr refers to is the amount of attention that the Private Gentleman gives to his troubles immediately preceding conversion. Other writers, he says, concentrate either on the sins of their natural state or on the temptations suffered after conversion. But, as we have seen, the Private Gentleman is by no means unique in his detailed treatment of the horrors of an inflamed conscience just before peace and forgiveness are achieved: John Rogers, Anna Trapnel, Jane

Turner, and Thomas Halyburton all devote between a quarter and a half of their records to their trials during this period. And as early as 1608 Richard Kilby in *The Burthen of a Loaden Conscience* treated his experiences at length in a manner almost identical to the Private Gentleman's a century later. In any case, it is hard to see how this particular emphasis in the *Account* contributes to the development of prose fiction.

Of the specific features in spiritual autobiographies which were taken up in *Robinson Crusoe* the Private Gentleman seems even less representative. Professor Starr finds that both men flout parental authority, express spiritual disaffection through the language of physical distance, are insensitive to providential warnings, and later learn to see God's hand in their troubles. 'There is a river in Macedon, and there is also moreover a river at Monmouth, . . . and there is salmons in both': it needs all Professor Starr's ingenuity to identify the parallels, and these are features that the account shares with most other spiritual autobiographies of the time, as is the sense of isolation during trouble of mind. But most important is the fact that the *Account* has a far weaker narrative line than most, with less circumstantial detail and more generalized exhortation to the reader. His whole account has an abstract and bookish tone that is reinforced by his frequent recommendations of standard Puritan treatises, and which contrasts forcibly with Defoe's notorious attention to detail, and almost as much with many particular memories embodied in the more evocative confessional writings. Richard Norwood, Thomas Ellwood, George Trosse, and even the Bunyan of *Grace Abounding* spring to mind as writers whose stories seem to embody much more potently the aspects of eighteenth-century prose fiction that developed from spiritual autobiography. But I doubt whether we need to look for a transitional document.

NOTES

1 Rogers, p. 415.
2 Fraser, p. 28.
3 Halyburton, p. 36.
4 Trosse, p. 10.
5 Mowsley, p. 89.
6 Powell, p. 6.
7 Halyburton, p. 70.

8 Turner, p. 58.
9 Trapnel, *A Legacy for Saints*, 1654, p. 14.
10 Martindale, p. 36.
11 Barret, p. 32f.
12 Fraser, pp. 72, 91.
13 Rogers, pp. 448–50.
14 See p. 11 above.
15 Rogers, p. 417.
16 *Spirituall Experiences*, title page.
17 'Come unto me, all ye that labour and are heavy laden, and I will give you rest.' Matt. xi.28. '. . . him that cometh to me I will in no wise cast out.' John vi.37. 'Ho, every one that thirsteth, come ye to the waters, . . .' Isa. lv.1.
18 See Ch. 6, pp. 93–5 below.
19 *Spirituall Experiences*, p. 359f. The John Rogers mentioned here is not the Independent and Fifth Monarchy Man, but John Rogers, Vicar of Dedham from 1605 to 1636; he was said to have been one of the most awakening preachers of his time. See D.N.B. and cf. pp. 58–9 below on Thomas Goodwin's youthful reaction to his reputation.
20 *Ibid.*, p. 174.
21 For Dod's career, see Haller, *The Rise of Puritanism*, pp. 56–62.
22 *Spirituall Experiences*, pp. 178f. For a discussion of M.K.'s language see pp. 211–12 below.
23 *Ibid.*, pp. 175–7.
24 Barret, pp. 52–3.
25 Knollys, sig. A2v.
26 Trapnel, *A Legacy for Saints*, p. 12.
27 Halyburton, 'To the Reader', sig. ¶4.
28 G. A. Starr, *Defoe and Spiritual Autobiography*, pp. 46–7.
29 Trosse, 'Preface', sig. A4.
30 Turner, pp. 10, 22, 49, 81, 109, 180.
31 Pringle, p. 429.
32 Bampfield, title page.
33 Trosse, pp. 27–44.
34 Heywood, pp. 136–50.
35 Starr, *op. cit.*, pp. 62, 52.

Chapter 4

The Puritan Environment

It is not always easy to tell how much in the common pattern of Puritan experience came directly from the Puritan way of life and how much from seventeenth-century conditions in general. Many attitudes and responses which the modern reader might confidently label as characteristically Puritan belong to the age as a whole, and this is true even in the strain of piety which we find in the spiritual autobiographies. Many people who were not Puritans were 'of a strict and holy conversation' and tried to live a sober and godly life, though even in their own day they were liable to be confused with Puritans in the public mind. But there were certain values which, without being exclusively Puritan, were given special emphasis in the writings now under consideration.

These factors were important in the development of a man's life and outlook, and a few of them will be illustrated here to indicate the more significant ways in which both the content and the presentation of spiritual experience were shaped by Puritan culture.

Childhood

'I am forced to judge', wrote Baxter, 'that most of the children of the godly that are ever renewed, are renewed in their childhood.'[1] Puritan parents took seriously the Biblical promise, 'those that seek me early shall find me',[2] and many confessional writers relate childhood episodes which show how rapidly they had internalized the fundamental concepts they had been taught from a very early age. Hanserd Knollys describes how he fell out with his brother on the way to school and was at once convicted of sin:

And I said, Brother, we have sinned, come let us be Friends, and pray God to pardon this, and other our Sins; whereupon we both kneeled down upon the plowed Land, and I prayed, wept and made Supplication to God, as well as I could, and found so great Assistance from God at that time, that I never used any set Form of Prayer afterwards; which done, we both kissed each other, and went to School.[3]

Whether or not Knollys's objections to set prayers can be explained quite so simply as this, it is clear that they go back almost as far as he can remember. Thomas Halyburton had his conscience awakened when he was eleven, Thomas Mowsley when twelve. Of the writers in *Spirituall Experiences*, M.K. would awaken in the night and 'rise out of . . . bed to prayer' many times before she was twelve; while E.R.'s fearful crisis over reprobation occurred when he was eleven.[4] Bunyan at nine or ten was plagued with nightmares of hell fire, though this experience is mentioned by others less often than might be supposed.

The few who do mention being troubled by bad dreams mostly write from an orthodox Puritan position which discounts the mystical element in religion. More individualist writers are inclined to speak of dreams as conveying some kind of vision or revelation. Thus, Thomas Tryon, an Anabaptist vegetarian with an addiction to astrology, says that in dreams he had before he was eight God showed him 'the Kingdom of Love, and the Kingdom of Darkness'.[5] And when Arise Evans, the Welsh prophet, was fourteen he prayed for wisdom and fell down on his knees at 'seeing the Sun at its rising, skip, play, dance, and turn about like a wheel'.[6] One is tempted to conjecture that differing responses were divergent interpretations of the same kind of phenomena, were it not that perception is essentially subjective, and so it is meaningless to talk about the 'same' phenomena in this context. There is, nevertheless, this striking contrast between those with a conservative theology and the more radical brethren in their attitude to dreams and paranormal phenomena: in both cases their adult convictions coloured the selection of incidents from childhood and the significance they attached to them.

The experiences of Puritan children must often have been engendered by the expectations and reactions of family, neighbours, or schoolmasters. Arise Evans was greatly impressed by the women of his household, who insisted 'that they thought upon God at every breath they drew': an observation that may have helped to bring about the irrational intensity of his later behaviour.[7] When Joseph Barret found his heart 'powerfully wrought upon' while learning his primer, he ran to his mother in the next room and begged her to teach him to pray and sing psalms.[8] Her gratified response may be contrasted with the way Richard Norwood's parents reacted when he tried to convey his sudden admiration for Paul's passages on the resurrection in 1 Corinthians xv, 'thinking they had scarce taken notice of them before. But they made little answer (so far as I remember) but seemed rather to smile at my childishness.' This and other signs of indifference in ostensibly pious adults caused him to wonder whether they did not in fact know religious beliefs to be false, but 'were willing that we children should be so persuaded of them, that we might follow our books the better and be kept in from play'.[9]

Norwood's scepticism was to lead him in his teens into a kind of seventeenth-century version of the beatnik experience. Like other, more commonly mentioned, sins of childhood it was a reaction to the scheme of values which the Puritan world presented. If all the writers we are concerned with order their life stories within a conceptual framework derived from this scheme of values, and if in doing so they frequently impose a standardized pattern on their experiences, this may be part of the price to be paid for having so many narratives written at all. For some pattern there must be, some consistent criteria for selecting from the infinite number of happenings that make up a lifetime. An Augustine or a Rousseau can work out their own from the wider context of their culture as a whole, but the skills needed are immensely complex, and it is only the existence of a fairly clearly defined model – or a recognizable range of models – that will enable the ordinary literate man to get writing at all on anything that will make sense as autobiography. The constituent elements of the seventeenth-century Puritan model, and its variations, should be becoming apparent as we proceed. The point I want to emphasize at the moment is that this framework did more than impose a pattern: it gave a man something to define his individuality against. With a map in his hands that identified the main landmarks, he could plot his own travels in relation to them in terms that were understandable to himself and to others, and the unique sequence of twists

E   55

and turns showed that his route was an individual one. The Puritan life-pattern provided him with a stick to measure his growth against, so that the form, proportions, and outline of his spiritual life could be the more clearly discerned.

One such model concerned the effects of original sin in childhood. John Owen traced these through a succession of stages which he derived from an examination of Augustine's *Confessions*, and for which Augustine provided the normative examples. Childhood incidents such as the ones I have cited can be plotted on this sequence. Owen postulates five stages. First, sin is apparent in the self-centred appetites of infants, and 'the indignation and little self-revenges wherewith they are accompanied in their disappointments when all about them do not subject themselves unto their inclinations'. Secondly, in the process of growth and development, the principle of sin operates with increasing frequency and success in focusing the mind on 'vain actings, . . . perverse and froward appetites', and 'corrupt inclinations in every kind'. Thirdly, general irregularities are succeeded by actual sins against the conscience, notably lying and stealing. Fourthly, Sin gains ground as 'the objects of lust, by the occasions of life, are now multiplied', though at this stage the conscience is sometimes awakened by God. Finally, 'Custom of sinning takes away the *sense* of it; the course of the world takes away the *shame* of it; and love to it makes men greedy in the pursuit of it.' So a man comes 'unto the utmost of a recoverable alienation from God'.[10] That all men are not equally corrupt in outward behaviour is due to the restraining, or common, grace of God operating through instruments of social control such as the family, education, and the codes of conduct upheld by society at large.

Owen quotes Augustine to illustrate each of these stages, and although they are not enumerated in spiritual autobiographies as they are in Owen's treatise, the more analytical writers, such as the Covenanters, clearly use a similar framework to interpret their early spiritual experience. Thomas Halyburton, like Augustine, can assess his conduct in infancy not from memory but because he assumes that he behaved in the same way as everyone else, and he measures his sins against established doctrinal standards. Having enjoyed all the advantages that godly and protective parents could supply, he concludes that his constant aggression and self-centred pride were 'not to be imputed . . . meerly to contracted Custom, or occasional Temptations: But it really was the genuine Fruit and Result of that lamentable Byas Man since the Fall is born with. Sure the Spring must be within, when not withstanding all the Care to keep me from them, I impetuously went on in sinful Courses'.[11] Particular sins included 'lying to avoid Punishment, Sabbath-breaking, Revenge, Hatred of my Reprovers'.[12] When his conscience was awakened during a storm while sailing to Holland at the age of eleven, he attributed the cause to a mixture of natural fear and the desire for self-preservation. His frequent convictions after this 'were only like the Starts of a sleeping Man, occasion'd by some sudden Noise' – an image which was itself borrowed from Augustine.[13]

Even more analytical was James Fraser, who in relating God's dealings with him 'under some common Work of the Spirit', lists eight reasons why he gave up saying morning and evening prayers soon after he was nine, identifies seventeen steps in his later backsliding, and quotes eleven reasons why he was a Pharisee in early adolescence.[14]

The 'restraining grace' that Owen speaks of is widely recognized in the records of Puritan childhood. Oliver Heywood's parental discipline prevented evil practices from being 'habituated . . . through custome'.[15] Adam Martindale, 'a little fat short legged lad', records deliverances from death in early childhood: when his head was cut open, when rescued by his sister from drowning in a marl pit, and when he nearly fell in a disused coal pit.[16] Puritan teachers insisted that God's providential care was to be found essentially in the happenings of everyday life; and so in looking back on his childhood and youth the believer was continually discovering more occasions when he had been the unwitting object of divine nurture. Augustine found his memory reviving as he wrote,[17] and some of the incidents that Bunyan added to later editions of *Grace Abounding* suggest that isolated and forgotten incidents were recalled as he found that they could be related to his dominant theme.

Sermons

Two channels of special influence on young Puritans were sermons and books. Sermons affected everyone, and since the preaching was invariably expository in method, confessional writers most

57

frequently record their impact by quoting the text that made such an impression upon them. Hanserd Knollys suffered a double blow when he heard two sermons in one day at Cambridge which effectively convicted him of sin.[18] Gervase Disney devotes six pages of his autobiography to 'good sayings' from sermons he heard.[19] Individual preachers receive frequent and honourable mention, but the extracts and summary accounts that we are given usually convey little of the precise quality of a preacher's manner and style: in consistent Puritan fashion, the man is lost in his message, though in the reporting of John Rogers we get a vivid glimpse of the mighty Fenner in action at a time when Rogers was about ten years old:

> yet then hearing Mr. *William Fenner* full of *zeal*, stirring about and *thundring* and beating the *Pulpit*; I was *amazed*, and *thought* he was *mad*; I *wondred* what he meant, and whilest I was *gazing* upon him, I was *struck*, and saw that it was we that were *mad* which made him so; O sayes he! you *knotty! rugged! proud piece of flesh!* you *stony, rocky, flinty hard heart!* what *wilt thou doe when thou art roaring in Hell amongst the damned! &c.*[20]

Such was the esteem in which preaching was held that we come across very few admissions of sermons being despised or thought tedious, even in a writer's unregenerate days. The progress of Captain John Spilman was probably, however, quite a common one:

> once in a *carnall condition* as I was, I did slight the *Ministers of Christ*, especially your long *Preachers*, and could not abide that any should *preach long*; but at last I was *catched* by one, and hee was on *Heb.*8.8.10. the *new Covenant* made in Christ, which was applied to *me* very *home*, and touched me to the *heart.*[21]

For Thomas Goodwin, different preaching styles came to exemplify the conflict between the spirit and the flesh, for prior to his conversion he had 'resolved to follow the World, and the Glory, Applause, Preferment and Honour of it' by learning 'to preach after the Mode' in the 'witty' style of Richard Senhouse whom he much admired at Cambridge. He despised the 'plain' style: 'and I often thought thus with my self, they talk of their *Puritan* powerful

Preaching, and of Mr. *Rogers* of *Dedham,* and such others, but I would gladly see the Man that could trouble my Conscience'. But later, as he responded to the sermons of men like Sibbs and Preston, this 'Master-Lust was mortified'.[22]

It was not only the hearers of sermons who were affected by their important part in the Puritan way of life, for Henry Newcome noted that 'The meditation and preparing of the sermons did much awaken me to a sense of the weightiness of my charge as a minister, much otherwise than ever before I had thought of'.[23]

Books

Newcome also supplies evidence of the debt that a typical pastor owed to the practical writings of the great Puritan divines. He made notes on all the books he read, but tended to neglect his own because he borrowed so many from friends and had to read those first.[24] Samuel Bolton, who had no money to buy books, also borrowed them 'and abridged them all in his note-bookes'.[25] Particular books are mentioned almost as often as sermons. Bunyan's debt to Dent, Bayly and Luther is well known; Bayly's *Practise of Piety* seems to have been very influential indeed, to judge by the number of times it is referred to by different writers.

The impact of a book could be quite dramatic. 'I read Shepherds Sincere Convert in one of my calm fits', wrote James Fraser, '. . . but I had not read four Leaves of him when I was thrown on my Back.'[26] Augustine's *Confessions* had a similar effect on Robert Blair at the age of twenty-three, and it is perhaps not surprising to find Augustine's experiences referred to more often than those of any other man except the apostle Paul.

One indication of his influence is in the way that the events of his life are found to supply parallels to the writer's own spiritual progress. Halyburton comments that he shared with Augustine the habit of postponing the serious consideration of particular sins;[27] John Shaw went to hear Thomas Weld preach at Cambridge 'as sometime Austin to hear Ambrose, more for company and novelty than conscience'.[28] The number of robbed orchards which figure in Puritan confessional writings probably reflects the normal activities of boyhood rather than the special example of Augustine, though his celebrated reflections on robbing the pear tree may have helped his successors to remember and emphasize

59

similar escapades of their own. When William Hinde wrote the life of John Bruen 'as a Path and President of Piety' for the inhabitants of Cheshire in 1641, he compared him with Augustine in outward affairs as well as in spiritual matters: at sixteen Bruen was sent to Oxford as Augustine had been sent to Carthage; both men were converted when thirty-two, and both had fathers of a similar temperament. With considerable ingenuity Hinde was able to shape almost the whole of his biography around the correspondence between the two men.[29]

We have already seen from John Owen's use of the *Confessions* that Augustine's experience could be taken as a norm, and following the five stages of development in sin already listed Owen speaks of the typical way that the work of grace progresses. Some sparks of celestial fire remain under the ashes of our fallen nature, and God begins to work upon men through various outward means 'to cause them to take some real and *steady consideration of him*' and of 'their own distance from him'.[30] This he may do through afflictions, deliverances, the observation of others, preaching, or reading. Augustine illustrates them all:

> Now, there is scarce any of these instances of the care and watchfulness of God over the souls of men whom he designs either to convince or convert, for the ends of his own glory, but the holy person whom we have proposed as an example gives an account of them in and towards himself.[31]

And Owen goes on to draw from the *Confessions* examples of how when awakening has begun God overrules a man's outward affairs, how sin is incited and provoked until the soul sees its own disability, how its first attempts at reformed behaviour tend to be half-hearted and convictions stifled. Continued aggravation brings a renewed conviction, with the soul 'torn and divided between the power of corruption and the terror of conviction'.[32] But, with the 'secret insinuation' of grace, the spirit now begins to lust against the flesh aiming at a complete conquest, so that the believer pursues holiness and rejects sin with the same urgent intensity with which he formerly craved after sin and shunned holiness. And as with Augustine, this change of attitude comes with the receiving of the word.

Blair, Fraser, Halyburton, and other Scottish divines narrate an experience which closely conforms to this sequence, though their immediate model would have been the Calvinist doctrine of regeneration rather than Augustine's life. The doctrine could not be deduced from the *Confessions* alone, and even Owen uses the work merely for corroborative details after his main argument has been deployed.

In fact, the man whose autobiography shows the most pervasive influence of Augustine appears to have been quite unaware that this doctrinal pattern could be found in the earlier work. Richard Norwood, writing in Bermuda in 1639, had been directly influenced by at least four of Augustine's major works, which he had taken up because of the 'honourable mention of him' in sermons and almost every author.[33] He quotes a passage from the *Tractate upon John* as the immediate means by which his heart was opened to receive the Word, the effect being comparable to that of Romans xiii.13 on Augustine himself. Although Norwood's manuscript was first published in 1945 as his *Journal*, it is a straightforward autobiography, and he himself headed it 'Confessions'. Both the tone of his narrative and the balance between internal and external experience reflect similar features in Augustine, as do utterances addressed to God near the beginning and at the very end. Norwood's themes and his handling of them will be discussed more fully in the next chapter; for the moment it is enough to observe that the progress of his quest, the false trails he followed, and his discovery of God's predestinating grace are markedly Augustinian rather than Calvinistic in tone.

Calling to the ministry

After conversion, an event of major importance for many men was a calling to public ministry, though not all who experienced this write about it at any length. This is somewhat surprising in view of the insistence of the Puritans that everyone who undertook the work had to be certain of an individual vocation to it. It is the vulgar prophets and the Quakers who emphasize the matter most forcibly in their narratives, because lacking both educational background and identification with an established denomination they could invoke only the authority of personal experience. The more radical Puritan preachers found themselves in a similar position, and the most elaborate account of a calling to the ministry is given by Francis Bampfield. He was indeed an Oxford graduate ordained in the Church of England, but he later ministered to a congregation of Seventh Day Baptists, and wrote his autobiography to defend himself against many detractors by testifying to the special gifts of the Spirit he had received. He therefore compares himself to the apostle Paul, both in relation to what was 'outward, common, and ordinary referring unto Men', and to the 'inward, special, and more than ordinary, relating unto God'.[34] Seven folio pages are needed for the details, and 'if he have been a Fool in glorying', Bampfield concludes, 'they are others who have necessitated him thereunto'.[35] Bunyan's account of his ministerial calling, also described at length, lacks any of this stridency. He is hardly at all on the defensive, and while some of his points can be paralleled in the records of other mechanick preachers, his tone reminds us much more of the kind of reflective analysis seen in Baxter's self-review. Bunyan shows how his situation as a man set apart for the preaching of the Word was reached through a process of escalation through ten or a dozen phases: it began with the invitation 'to speak a word of Exhortation' at a private assembly, and developed as the practice of utterance, encouragement from the Scriptures, prayer and fasting, concern for men's souls, and a 'secret pricking forward' in his mind interacted at every stage with a growing response from his hearers. His narrative shows how these factors dovetailed into each other until people 'came in to hear the Word by hundreds, and that from all parts, though upon sundry and diverse accounts'.[36]

Fraser devotes an entire chapter to his call, including ten pages of self-analysis about it. Inadequate reflection in the first place caused both Richard Kilby and Hanserd Knollys to enter the ministry even before being fully converted. This at least was their later judgment. Kilby concludes that he became a minister through vanity and was not converted until eighteen years afterwards.[37] Knollys became uneasy when his preaching appeared to be causing only moral reformation in his hearers, and a senior colleague's counselling led him to discover that he was still building up his own soul on a covenant of works, 'having bin only under legal Convictions, and a Spirit of Bondage'.[38]

John Livingstone at first rejected his father's plans for him to become a minister, but yielded after spending a day in a secret cave with 'much confusion and fear, anent the state of my soul'.[39] On the other hand, Joseph Barret, a Nottingham businessman, was strongly attracted to the ministry, and summarizes in his auto-biography the long process of heartsearching he needed to undergo before deciding against it. 'I am afraid there was too much of wretched Self at the bottom,' he concludes, 'tho' it lay very much undiscovered.'[40]

External and internal experience

Apart from the impact of sermons and books, and the implications of a real or imagined call to the ministry, spiritual autobiographies vary immensely in the amount of attention given to external matters. It is possible to identify five levels of association between outward events and a subject's inner life.

The first, and simplest, situation is when there is hardly any connection at all, and a writer describes something which for some reason he thought memorable enough to record but with no obvious significance for his inward development. This is usually mentioned almost in passing as a piece of information which helps to set the scene of the subject's spiritual life. Thus, Gervase Disney tells us that he was not apprenticed to a bookseller as he wanted to be, because his father had been told that it was 'a declining Trade'.[41] And sometimes there are short passages of eye-witness reporting, like Knollys's account of his voyage to New England: 'By the way my little Child dyed with Convulsion fits, our Beer and Water stank, our Bisket was green, yellow and blew, moulded and rotten, and our Cheese also, so that we suffered much hard-ship, being 12 weeks in our passage.'[42] But it is rare to find detail of this kind unimproved by commentary or reflection: the con-fessional diary, in which narrative was only the means to another end, was evidently still an influence even if not consciously felt.

A second reason for the environment being mentioned may be when a place or a circumstance is connected with a spiritual experience by simple association. Walter Pringle of Greenknow, writing for his children, told them of the exact places at which certain things happened to him, perhaps in the hope that these landmarks would later remind them of what he had written; his first experience of prayer came 'at the north-east end of Stitchel Hall, before there were any new building or a garden there', and many years later he committed his newly born son to God 'at the plum-tree, on the north side of the garden door'.[43] The private associations which places acquired in this way must have been fairly freely spoken of among the members of some church communities, for Bunyan appealed to the emotional response which they engendered when he asked his own people, in the Preface to *Grace Abounding*, 'Have you never a Hill *Mizar* to remember? Have you forgot the Close, the Milk-house, the Stable, the Barn, and the like, where *God* did visit your Soul?'[44] And he himself described later in the book how encouragement came to him on two separate occasions at a particular place on the road.[45] Deep experience impressed Robert Blair at the age of seven with the circumstances of an English preacher's sermon: 'and though it be now sixty-three years since that time, the countenance, carriage, and voice of the speaker remain fresh upon my memory.'[46]

A third kind of connection between the outer and inner worlds is found when a man's spiritual condition is directly produced by outward circumstances. In his diary entry for 30 July 1588, Richard Rogers observes: 'The weather, being heavy, troubled me againe, as before, and that unsetled me at study for the good part of the day, and that for thincking that thinges would be deare.'[47] Autobiographers inevitably preserve fewer minute details of this kind, but they are at no loss for examples of temptations which made their mark because of constantly recurring pressures from a wordly environment: 'flippant company', 'dissolute lads', 'Poetical Books, Romances and the like', and 'the persuit of the pleasures and vanities of this wicked world'.[48] Barret recalls that 'this stinking Flesh (to which this poor Soul of mine is full little beholden) hath sometimes hung back from rising on Winter Lords-Day Mornings'.[49] Temptation for Gervase Disney came from 'unbecoming Dalliances, Glances, and Carriages with young Women',[50] while George Trosse was similarly afflicted, first because of his landlady's daughter in London with whom he 'sought *all opportunities* to be *together* in some Place of *Retirement*', and later in Portugal through another '*Young Comely* but *Wanton*, *Wench*' who supplied 'Fire enough to Kindle my Tinder'.[51] Oliver Heywood found, on the other hand, that living in a worldly household helped to strengthen his faith, because he thereby gained a better understanding of 'carnal pleas and cavils'.[52]

Fourthly, and of more particular significance to a writer, were the events which effected a permanent change in his spiritual

64

awareness. If the outward means were varied, so is the degree of elaboration with which they are treated in different narratives. Vavasor Powell's account of his toothache has become almost the *locus classicus* for showing how physical and spiritual factors could be merged in a Puritan at the most mundane level:

> At this time the Lord visited me with a very sore and great pain of the Tooth-ach, which continued divers days and nights together, in great extremity, so that with the violence thereof, I thought I should have been deprived of my senses, or life; and by another good providence, I met with a little book of Mr. *Perkins*, and in that, with this expression, if the pains of one little bone, or tooth, be so grievous for a few days, what then will the pains of the whole body and soul be in hell for evermore? Upon this my terrour began in Conscience to that degree, that it made the other pain to seem somewhat more easie, and both together, put me upon crying out to *God* with greater sense then before, and between fear and pain, a troubled muddy spirit of prayer began to spring up, . . .[53]

Cause and effect are usually, as here, seen in a simple relationship to each other, though sometimes we are almost given enough evidence to make interpretations which the writer was unaware of. Hannah Allen, in a detailed explanation of her several years' 'deep melancholy and black humour', does not comment on the fact that her troubles began after the death of her first husband and ended when she married again. Only intellectual and reflective writers like Norwood, Baxter, and the Covenanters explore the more complex interactions of human motive and event with spiritual forces. On the whole the external events that stimulated a memorable spiritual reaction were remarkably undramatic. A typical instance is that of the young Robert Blair, who one day looked out of the window to see 'the sun brightly shining, and a cow with a full udder': he remembered that the sun was made to give light and the cow to give milk, but began to realize how little he understood the purpose of his own life.[54]

Fifthly, there is a level at which the writer is aware of a direct correspondence between outward experience and his spiritual condition. Since the verbal communication of inward experience is largely in imagery derived from the physical world, it is not surprising that some occasions were recognized when each seemed to be the expression of the other.

'Having some occasion to undertake a passage on the Sea from *London* to *Newcastle*,' wrote Jane Turner,

> . . . it pleased the Lord to reprove me by the raging waves of the Sea, and tempestuous storms, then began my trouble to increase, but not so much from that which was without, as from something within, the waves of the Sea not beating so fast on the Ship, as the waves of temptations did arise in my heart, being in a very much-troubled dissatisfyed condition, not finding my heart willing to submit to God.[55]

Deliverance from this storm brought some spiritual gain with it: 'then it pleased the Lord to bring us safe to Land, through which mercy I had some little communion with God, being able to speak of his goodness in delivering us from that danger.'[56]

Working on a much more extended scale, Richard Norwood portrays the whole of his early life as the embodiment of a spiritual quest, and he came to see his physical travels as having important spiritual implications:

> But miserable and foolish man, I understood not the many dangers of soul and body whereinto I cast myself, and how every step I went, as it was further from my native country so it led me and alienated my heart farther from God, from religion, and from a desire to return.[57]

The extent to which Bunyan's autobiography centres on his own inner world has often been commented on, and when he does mention his environment it is usually because he has perceived an organic relationship between his state of mind and something in his surroundings: the crows on the ploughed field, the women of Bedford 'sitting at a door in the Sun, and talking of the things of God', the sickness that was doubled upon him when his soul became 'clog'd with guilt'.[58] It is the ability to set up this kind of resonance between the inward and the outward that does most to give significance to the private events of a spiritual autobiography, and those writers whom I shall consider in more detail later on – notably Norwood, Bunyan, Baxter, and the Quakers Fox and Ellwood – are those who do this most effectively.

The projection that is involved in this process becomes even more obvious in the paranoid condition recorded by some writers under the stress of temptations to despair of God's mercy. Bunyan himself felt at one time that the Sun grudged him light, and that the very stones and tiles seemed to 'bend themselves' against him.[59] Hannah Allen feared that the lights of neighbouring houses were the apparitions of devils who threatened her, and many other people recorded encounters with a palpable Satan.[60] The common factor in their experiences was the way they abnormally distorted data perceived via the senses, so that a monomaniac concern with their own doom conditioned every response. When Mrs Allen's aunt complained of how tired she got because her niece insisted on laying late in bed, '*Ah*,' was the reply, '*but what must I do that must have no rest to all eternity.*'[61] There was no end to the tiresome ingenuity of the victim's reactions both to everyday happenings and the words of support offered by friends. All orthodox Puritan writers regarded such happenings as troubles to be overcome as quickly as possible; this dominance of the subject's obsessions, when not demonic in origin, was attributed to wilfulness or emotional disturbance. In this they differed from the vulgar prophets and to some degree from the Quakers also, who were more prepared to take their cue from their feelings, even when this might mean running counter to the Scriptures, common sense, or the consensus of their Christian neighbours: outward signs and outward wisdom might be less reliable, or at any rate less meaningful, than what came by direct revelation.

NOTES

1 Baxter, *Works*, IX. 122.
2 Proverbs, viii. 17.
3 Knollys, pp. 2–3.
4 *Spirituall Experiences*, p. 163.
5 Tryon, p. 8.
6 Evans, p. 8.
7 *Ibid.*, p. 6.
8 Barret, p. 34.
9 Norwood, p. 8.
10 Owen, *A Discourse concerning the Holy Spirit*, ed. cit., pp. 339–45.
11 Halyburton, p. 9.
12 *Ibid.*, p. 12.

13 *Ibid.*, p. 19; cf. Augustine, *Confessions*, tr. William Watts, Loeb Classical Library, Heinemann, 1922 reprint, VIII. 5.
14 Fraser, pp. 11–25.
15 Heywood, p. 155.
16 Martindale, p. 11; cf. pp. 3–4.
17 Cf. *Confessions*, IX. 7.
18 Knollys, p. 3.
19 Disney, pp. 112–17.
20 John Rogers, p. 419.
21 *A Tabernacle for the Sun*, p. 4 (in gathering inserted after p. 412).
22 Goodwin, pp. 6, 11, 13.
23 Newcome, p. 19.
24 *Ibid.*, p. 12.
25 Edward Bagshaw, *The Life and Death of Mr. Bolton*, 3rd ed., 1635, p. 8.
26 Fraser, p. 41.
27 Halyburton, p. 31. Cf. Augustine, *Confessions*, VI. 4, 12, VIII. 7.
28 Shaw, p. 124. Cf. Augustine, *op. cit.*, V. 13.
29 William Hinde, *A Faithfull Remonstrance of The Holy Life and Happy Death, of John Bruen of Bruen-Stapleford, in the County of Chester, Esquire*, 1641, Cf. title page, pp. 7, 13, 15, 19, 43–6.
30 Owen, *Holy Spirit*, p. 346.
31 *Ibid.*, pp. 348–9.
32 *Ibid.*, p. 355.
33 Norwood, p. 61.
34 Bampfield, p. 5.
35 *Ibid.*, p. 11.
36 Bunyan, paras. 265, 268, 271.
37 Kilby, *Burthen of a Loaden Conscience*, p. 31; *Hallelu-iah*, p. 35.
38 Knollys, p. 12.
39 John Livingstone, p. 133.
40 Barret, p. 57.
41 Disney, p. 29.
42 Knollys, p. 17.
43 Pringle, pp. 421, 438.
44 Bunyan, p. 3.
45 *Ibid.*, paras 62, 68.
46 Blair, p. 5.
47 Richard Rogers, *op. cit.*, p. 79.
48 Cf. Halyburton, p. 93; Clarke, p. 3; Powell, pp. 1–2.
49 Barret, p. 50.
50 Disney, p. 34.
51 Trosse, pp. 13–14, 19.

52 Heywood, p. 164.
53 Powell, p. 4.
54 Blair, p. 4.
55 Turner, p. 119.
56 *Ibid.*, p. 121.
57 Norwood, p. 22.
58 Bunyan, paras 92, 37, 257.
59 *Ibid.*, para 187.
60 Allen, p. 34; cf. Powell, Norwood, Bunyan, John Rogers.
61 Allen, p. 27.

Chapter 5

Richard Norwood's 'Confessions'

Richard Norwood was fairly well known in the seventeenth century as a teacher of mathematics, the author of several books on navigation, and the man who surveyed the Bermudas soon after they were settled in 1612. His life story sounds like the plot of a picaresque novel. He was born in Stevenage in 1590 and at fifteen was apprenticed to a fishmonger in London. He ran away to sea, served as a soldier in the Netherlands, and walked to Rome as a pilgrim. Later he made two voyages to the Mediterranean, taught himself enough navigation to instruct his skipper, and had a temporary association with Sir Henry Mainwaring shortly before Sir Henry turned to piracy. He invented and demonstrated a diving bell, and went to Bermuda with some of the early settlers as a technical expert. All this before he was twenty-four. He made two complete surveys of the island and returned to London in 1617. Here he taught for twenty years, published his books on mathematics and navigation, and gave his contemporaries their most accurate estimate of the length of a degree and of the nautical mile. To do this he walked from London to York, measuring the distance by chain and pacing. About 1637 he went back to Bermuda as a refugee from Laud's persecution. He lived there as a schoolmaster and leading planter until his death in 1675.

Norwood had many of the experiences we associate with the adventurous man of his day: shipwreck, attack by pirates, scurvy, the plague, a brief spell in prison. He was marooned for five days on an uninhabited island, and sailed a tiny home-made ship so well in treacherous waters that his skill was attributed to necromancy. As a boy he was good at writing verse; later on, he used to go to the Fortune Theatre, knew some of the actors there, and tried his hand at writing a play himself. He reported to the Royal Society on tidal wells, and they referred to him as 'that intelligent gentleman'.

Until recently we had only the barest outline of his life. Aubrey included some notes on him,[1] and he gets about a column in the *Dictionary of National Biography*, but most of the details I have given come from his spiritual autobiography, which was first published in 1945 by the Bermuda Historical Monuments Trust. It runs to about 45,000 words and it fills some of the gaps in our knowledge of the colony's early years, which were quite eventful ones. His editors have been very thorough in relating the narrative to its historical background, but they feel they have to warn the reader that Norwood is often tedious in the detailed attention he gives to his religious development; they are mainly interested in him as technician and pioneer.[2] Though published as a *Journal*, Norwood himself headed his manuscript with the word 'Confessions', and it is clearly autobiographical in form with a distinctive structural pattern, although drawing extensively on an earlier record of his sins and mercies. Norwood wrote it on some free Saturday afternoons he had in Bermuda in 1639 and 1640, and thus it was produced some years before the other autobiographies I have described. I have left my discussion of it until now so as to show more easily how a work which was clearly not part of the main literary tradition of Puritan autobiography made its own use of a common religious tradition. Knowing the conventions developed by later Puritans in England, we are in a better position to appreciate another direction which the same assumptions and techniques led to under different conditions. For Norwood integrated his outward experience with the pattern of his spiritual life much more closely than anyone else was to do; moreover this life-pattern itself was a remarkable one, not least because of its curious affinities with those of two archetypal figures of later Puritanism: Bunyan's pilgrim and Defoe's Robinson Crusoe.

Puritan values

In some respects there is nothing unusual in the general sequence of Norwood's spiritual experience. He tells us in some detail about his 'childish piety'[3] and how he fell away into a period of carelessness during his apprenticeship, how worldly companions and

F   71

worldly pursuits absorbed him. Then, from time to time over the next few years, he felt the need for a firmly founded belief. He flirted with popery, talked to Puritan pastors in London, battled with temptations, and felt frustrated through a growing sense of sin and the fact that he could not commit himself. Ultimately a great moment of conviction came while he was reading Augustine, though he went through a period of severe depression and temptation when he returned to London in 1617.

And in his record we can identify many of the concepts and values of popular Puritanism: a recognition of environmental factors which prepared him for effectual calling; emphasis on how his unregenerate decisions were shaped by ignorance; orderly summaries at various points in his narrative which imply a sophisticated habit of self-examination. One of these, dealing with the main trend of his self-questioning before conversion, takes the form of an extended internal dialogue.

Here and everywhere Norwood's responses are individual ones, not restricted by conventional Puritan categories and areas of concern. Some of this may have been because as a young man he never stayed long in one place, so had perforce to make his own way both intellectually and spiritually. He tells us himself that through the pastoral concern of Edward Topsall in London he was once almost at the point of full conversion, 'but going presently to sea amongst those which were strangers to these mysteries I soon grew cold and careless' (p. 35). And his subsequent insights came mostly through the private reading of books, notably Augustine and Perkins. He never speaks of any period of 'legal bondage' and his long inability to commit himself came chiefly from a fear of backsliding afterwards, 'and that were worse than not to begin at all' (p. 66). In this procrastination, as in other ways, he resembles Augustine, who had a great influence on both his life and narrative, though it comes out less in particular details than in the general planning and disposition of what he has to say: in the attention he gives to his intellectual development, to his career, and to his relationships with other people, as well as in the way all these are consistently related to his spiritual life.

The summum bonum

Although he nowhere refers to it, Norwood's account as a whole is an exemplification of Augustine's famous assertion at the beginning of his own confessions, 'For thou hast created us for thyself, and our heart cannot be quieted till it may find repose in thee'.[4] The distinctive feature of his life was that it was shaped by a private quest for what he called a *summum bonum*: a search for secret happiness which constantly eluded him because he misread the clues and looked for it in the wrong places. Like Bunyan's Christian, he was delayed by following paths that looked promising but did not lead where he wanted to go to. He does not mention this theme until well on in his story, and even then he does so almost casually, but he says enough to make it clear that this search determined the pattern of his early life.

> For in my youth and childhood I had many childish conceits and fancies: as how far it might be from earth to heaven? Whether there might not be some means devised to go up thither? . . . When I saw rivers they seemed to be as it were some infinite thing, the waters always running and yet remaining full. I wondered whence they came, and thought, when I should be my own man, I would search from whence and whither they were, supposing to find there many rare things.[5]

Already we can see how his bent for scientific enquiry was associated with this spiritual hunger, aroused by the things of beauty in the world. It led him first to be a sailor and then to the study of navigation, for he adds in a marginal note:

> I had from my childhood a fantastical but strong imagination . . . of some great happiness or excellent thing that was to be found out, if men were not negligent or did not so wholly apply themselves to their own particular business. And this I thought was to be found out either by travel or by learning. Now, though I call it fantastical in respect of the conceit it had in me, yet it seems to have been a natural principle in man that [there is] a summum bonum, some great happiness or felicity attainable by men (p. 38).

As a fishmonger's apprentice Norwood talked to sailors, and this led him to think that the East Indies might be where his hopes could be fulfilled. So when an outbreak of the plague caused his

73

master to give up business, he took to travel. But after a year of misadventures he had only reached the Netherlands. Here he served for a few months as a soldier, until peace with Spain in the spring of 1609. He did not want to go back to England, since he saw no chance of getting to the Indies that way, and after some aimless wandering he decided to walk to Rome. For this he needed letters from the English Jesuits at Louvain, and to get them he overcame his Protestant scruples and pretended to be a papist.

So for several more months he lived on the road, sleeping rough, and met up with an English pilgrim named Thomas, who told Norwood that he himself 'travelled with a desire to know what was the true religion' (p. 23). When he reflected later on the discussions they had, Norwood came to realize the complexity of his own motives:

> He persuaded me further of the Popish religion than ever I
> was persuaded before, . . . I conceive it was because I was
> often checked inwardly for dissembling myself to be of that
> religion which I denied in my heart; to avoid which check
> of conscience I was willing for that time of my travel to
> have been persuaded of the truth of that religion, supposing
> ignorance to be a far lesser sin than such dissembling; and
> his reasonings being suitable, prevailed much (p. 23).

Like many other Puritans, Norwood found that ignorance was not so simple a problem as it appeared to be.

When the two pilgrims came to the Alps, Norwood was strangely attracted by them. The succession of peaks drew him on and on, despite the pleas of his companion to turn back, and they almost perished in the cold. He seems to have felt that the mountains somehow embodied the challenge of his spiritual quest, although as the journey went on it involved him in a sense of both physical and spiritual alienation:

> And thus without the special grace and good providence of
> God I had wandered further from home and withal should
> have had my heart more and more alienated from my native
> country, countrymen, and friends, from religion which was
> now as it seemed almost extinct, and from God.[6]

He never considered that Rome would be the end of his quest, and once there even thought of going on to Jerusalem as a pilgrim in the Pope's charge. But he met some friendly English merchants in Naples and they offered him a passage home.

After this Norwood made two voyages to the Mediterranean, but he no longer believed that travel would bring him to his *summum bonum*:

> I began to be something well satisfied with travel, having no such immoderate desire of seeing the world as formerly I had had, and began to conceive well that the world did not in any parts of it abound with those rarities and delights which I had sometimes thought to find (p. 38).

So he now set his hope on learning and intellectual adventure. During these voyages he was 'extraordinarily affected' by the study of Leonard Digges's *Pantometria*, a treatise on geometry first published in 1571. He read this and other books of mathematics by day and night, using every possible minute for the purpose. He even slept on watch so as to have more spare time for study. But although mathematics was to be his calling, which he followed with vigour and distinction all his life, he came to feel that this too was not the answer. He read Cornelius Agrippa of *The Vanity of Sciences*, and this made him aware of the limitations of human learning: 'I began by this to understand . . . that there was no such excellency nor extent in learning as that a man should make it his *summum bonum*, as I was apt to do' (p. 44).

Thus he was baffled in his search for the 'extraordinary and fantastic good' he wanted to enjoy, and he became 'more slack and unsettled' in his studies (p. 44). Both the physical search and the intellectual one had led up blind alleys. There remained only the realm of the spirit, the promises of religion. But these he could not respond to: 'Religion and piety', he said, 'seemed to be a dead, irksome, and unsavoury thing and altogether without delight or relish' (p. 44).

Nevertheless he could not leave it alone, and he struggled for years with fluctuating thoughts, feelings, and convictions. An interesting feature of his speculation at this time was a hankering after a 'middle estate' between heaven and hell. 'I desired to shun the torments of hell but was not much affected with the joys of heaven' (p. 64). It seemed unduly harsh that people who were not believing Christians, but who lived worthy and useful lives, should have gone to hell. If he took no delight in the things of Christ, why should he not be content with the real delights that the mathematics and human learning could bring, while having a life honest enough to avoid provoking God's judgment? But for all his hard thinking he could never convince himself of the reality of this 'middle condition'. In the end he was driven out of even these modest hopes when Satan prevailed through his corruptions to hold him 'in the basest kind of bondage' (p. 68). Though not named as such his chief disturbance seems to have been aroused, as his editors suggest, by his indulgence in masturbation. He refers to it as his 'master sin', though at a later stage he saw its function had been to act as a kind of barometer of his spiritual condition, and so destroy his complacency; with increasing spiritual maturity he could go on to discover that other sins like pride were more deadly and intractable in the long run.

Meanwhile, through reading Augustine, he was developing an entirely new understanding of religion, for it came upon him one day that what he had been looking for all this time was God himself: 'I conceived and understood him to be he who giveth to all things not only their beings, but also their well-beings; . . . who giveth to everything its grace and comeliness.' 'I was as one that had found some inestimable treasure which none knew but myself' (pp. 74, 83). He was at last converted, though he was slow to perceive it, and other people noticed it first. 'And these observations of others, when they came to my notice, were (so far as I can remember) the first thing that moved me to take notice of any change in myself' (p. 72). He thought they had simply drawn over-hopeful conclusions from his reading and conversation, but a little consideration convinced him that his attitudes had fundamentally changed: 'Surely there is a great change wrought in me, or else whence is this heavenly fire in my heart that hath heat and light and motion exciting and carrying me to those things whereunto I was formerly altogether averse?' (pp. 72–3).

Pilgrim and castaway

In his physical search for celestial happiness, Norwood resembles Christian in *The Pilgrim's Progress*. He frequently writes of his experience in the same wayfaring terms. Thus he sees himself as a man 'which so lately was hurried on to final destruction and was come even to the gates of hell, as it were within sight and hearing of that dreadful place' (p. 78). He writes of 'those deep wounds which Satan by his fiery darts had made in my soul', and of the texts of warning and condemnation that stood 'always like a lion in the way' (pp. 103, 36). Spiritual conflict, he says, left so many wounds in soul and body, 'that I am like to bear the marks of it to my grave and to walk feebly and halting all my days' (p. 94). And in the account of the depression he went through after conversion there is more than a hint of Doubting Castle:

> Methought as I looked back I saw myself far entered within
> the gates of hell, and now if the percullus should be let fall
> I should be kept in and could no more return, and I feared
> upon my offer to return the percullis would be presently
> let fall (pp. 94–5).

From this despair Norwood escaped in the same way as Christian did – by remembering the divine promises that he had neglected. So in the details of his experience, as well as in his main quest, Norwood was a forerunner and counterpart of Bunyan's pilgrim.

His life story also resembles that of another archetypal Puritan figure: Robinson Crusoe. Professor Starr has shown how Crusoe's adventures were an expression of spiritual experience, how in fact Defoe used the conventions of Puritan autobiography to structure his plot.[7] Crusoe is shown as a rebellious son, a restless wanderer, and an isolated castaway. In a similar way, Norwood's physical adventures embody his spiritual ones; he too traced his troubles to having forsaken the calling in which his father had placed him; he too had run away to sea and the further he got from home the less he wanted to return. Again like Crusoe, drifting to places more and more remote from home, Norwood was blind to the hand of Providence and he ignored every chance to turn back. Defoe used Crusoe's early progress to show how one sin brings on another by necessity; and Norwood found that by stifling his conscience he had less conscious tension but began to suffer from horrible nightmares. At one time during his travels in Europe he developed a pathological sensitivity to being seen by other people, and felt violently aggressive towards anyone who looked at him. So he took to hiding by day and travelling by night.[8] Now the correspondence between this physical isolation and his spiritual state could hardly be emphasized more dramatically, and it reminds us of Crusoe, whose life on the island has often been interpreted as a symbol of the loneliness that is the price of a developed self-consciousness – a self-consciousness that certainly helped to foster Puritanism, and was in turn reinforced by it.

Norwood's experience was most like Crusoe's in that he was also once cast away on an island. At a time when food was short in Bermuda, he went alone in a home-made boat to get some palmetto berries from an off-shore island. He ran into a storm on the way back, and was weatherbound on another small island for five days:

> This five days seemed to me the most tedious and miserable
> time that ever I underwent in all my life. . . . Yet at other
> times I was apt to retire myself much from company, but
> at this time I thought it was one of the greatest punishments
> in the world, yea, I thought it was one of the greatest
> punishments in hell, and the sense and apprehension of it
> made me to think of hell as of hell indeed, a condition most
> miserable (p. 54).

And we remember that Crusoe's reactions were to be the same, when he found himself 'lock'd up with the eternal bars and bolts of the ocean, in an uninhabited wilderness, without redemption'.[9]

Although Norwood was quite a sociable man, and well thought of by the people he knew, he later saw that he had been much too isolated in his religion. For many years he had what he called a 'monastical conceit' of piety, thinking it involved 'renouncing all the pleasures of the world . . . and a retiring of a man's self to solitariness and prayer . . . and that I must walk it alone, having no company that would do so' (p. 35). Even after conversion he handicapped himself for some time by trying to go it alone: he under-valued public worship and neglected the company of other believers.

Everything in his story, then, shows how a man's personality develops through constant interaction between his inward self and his environment, and each throws light on the other. As we read of Norwood's struggle to unify his spiritual experience and the external pattern of his life, the figures of the pilgrim and the castaway begin to take shape, although not until Bunyan and Defoe were these figures to be clearly defined as characteristic projections of Puritan experience.

A rounded portrait

We also find in Norwood's style links with the Bunyan of *Grace Abounding*. Soon after returning to London in 1617 he despaired of God's mercy and experienced Satan's presence almost physically – leaning, pulling, stifling, stirring up blasphemies, and whispering words of menace that are identical in tone with those of Bunyan's tempter: 'And for thyself, thou art as surely in my hands and power as ever was any man. Well may I give thee leave to wriggle a while this way or that way: better were it for thee to be quiet.'[10] His account brings home very vividly to us the spirit-haunted world of the seventeenth century, the strange horrors of the night that men had to face, and the terrible possibility of Satanic possession. More immediately comprehensible are the paranoid illusions he had in the street:

> It was about two hours after I was up when I set forth to go to Mr. Meacock, at which time I began again to be much troubled with inward terrours and threatenings, and all things seemed in their kinds to be my enemies, and surely going through the streets I escaped the horses and carts but narrowly twice or thrice, which might also be occasioned partly by the present weakness and dizziness of my head and great perturbations, but it seemed then in my apprehension to proceed from indignation, wrath, and as it were a gnashing of teeth against me (pp. 98–9).

Like Bunyan, Norwood attributed much of his trouble to having played into Satan's hands through excessive scrupulosity and by submitting to doubts too inconsiderately. He often speaks of himself as being 'much inclined to a dejected and despairing mind' (p. 45, cf. pp. 7, 12), and he gives a sufficiently full treatment of his early years to suggest some contributory factors: childhood disappointments, a speech impediment, a strict father, and a disparaging schoolmaster.

The whole scope of Norwood's narrative makes us particularly well aware of the culture within which his individuality shaped itself. And there is one episode in particular which is worth quoting because it offers a revealing glimpse of the way in which two Puritan preachers went about their work of counselling.

After his return from Rome, his aunt in London suspected him of being 'infected with popery', and called in the Rev. Edward Elton to deal with the matter. Elton began by sharply rebuking Norwood, and charged him at length with his various disobediences and shortcomings.

> His words though true did touch me very nearly, yet withal I apprehended myself to be contemned of him because I was poor and as it were in a forlorn condition, and so I answered with some stomach and passion . . . more sharply and stiffly than was meet to such a reverend divine. Whereupon after a few other speeches he left me, not desiring (as I remember) any further conference with me, . . . (p. 33).

Fortunately Norwood's father took him shortly afterwards to Edward Topsall, the curate of St Botolph's, Aldersgate, and here his reception was very different:

> When we came he was in his study and my father went in and broke the matter to him, desiring him that he would confer with me. He answered 'Yes', if I would confer, and calling me in though I was in a poor habit, yet he caused me to sit down by him, began at first (as I remember) to confer about my travels in a loving and familiar manner, afterwards touched gently upon religion, etc., and used me with marvelous courtesy and familiarity, . . . When I objected anything of difficulty wherein he thought he could not presently give me a full and satisfactory answer, he would take time, as a day or two, and then resolve me upon such grounds as I could not justly except against. And thus he continued I think a month or near upon, . . . (pp. 34–5).

The records of these interviews, with their precise delineation of the two men's methods and their client's reactions, provide contrasting studies in case-work skill which are as relevant to the modern social worker as to the seventeenth-century pastor.

Norwood shows the same insight in writing of his other relationships, whether it is the ambivalence of his feelings towards a school friend or the complexity of his attitude to his father. And his honesty saves him from tying everything up too neatly. Even after twenty years of reflection he is still not certain whether he has derived benefit or harm from his period of depression: gains and losses are too evenly balanced, and it remains an open question.

Norwood ends his story with this period of trial, which took place before he was thirty, but because of their comprehensiveness his confessions give us as rounded a portrait as we get anywhere in Puritan autobiography outside of Baxter's *Reliquiae*. He saw his life as a unified experience, its unity being derived from his changing relationship with God as his creator and guardian. The process of conversion involved the emergence into consciousness of the fact of this relationship, and then his acceptance of it through the discovery that it was the source of the mysterious and exciting signals that all his life he had been intermittently responsive to: the 'uncertain hopes' of paradise and secret treasure. In this search his physical, intellectual, and social experience were all wide-open territory, and so he saw his spiritual development less exclusively in moral terms than most of his Puritan contemporaries did. Of course, the moral factor is powerfully present, since he used the lens of his mature Puritan convictions to bring his youth into focus; but his story gains immensely through its freedom from any doctrinal pattern of conversion, and because Norwood's own intellect and breadth of experience enabled him to make creative use of the model he found in Augustine.

NOTES

1 Cf. *Brief Lives*, ed. Andrew Clark, Oxford, 1898, I. 124–5, II. 96–8.
2 Cf. Norwood, Introduction, p. xxx.
3 Norwood, pp. 6–14: a section which he calls a 'digression'.
4 Augustine, *Confessions*, I. 1.
5 Norwood, pp. 38–9.
6 *Ibid.*, p. 28. Norwood twice calls our attention to this theme of alienation. Cf. p. 66 above.
7 Cf. Starr, *op. cit.*, ch. 3.
8 Cf. Norwood, p. 22.
9 *Robinson Crusoe*, Everyman ed., 1949, p. 84.
10 *Ibid.*, p. 99. Cf. the passage quoted from *Grace Abounding* on p. 112 below.

Chapter 6

Conservatives and Radicals

One effect of the mutual interaction of doctrine and experience in the believer's life was that each particular work of spiritual autobiography was an expression both of the Puritan tradition in general and of a personal response to it. Of course, Puritan tradition itself was not monolithic. Different views about church government, doctrine, and the Christian life were vigorously explored and articulated; some patterns of emphasis were organized in denominational or party attitudes while ongoing debate produced others for consideration. Any individual seeking to articulate and unify his experience was thus involved in a number of choices, or (since these might not all be consciously made) in a number of possible relationships to the theological and social framework of his environment. These would depend partly on his own temperament and partly on the ideas, opinions, and attitudes which were brought to his attention during his formative years and later. It was during the Commonwealth and Protectorate that the characteristics of the main parties within Puritanism developed and defined themselves. Modern historians refer to 'conservative' and 'radical' wings of the movement, the radicals being identified mostly by their individualism, though any number of intermediate positions were possible and many other factors were involved.

In this chapter I propose to look at some autobiographies in detail to examine how writers with different loyalties shaped their experience, found their identity in relation to the commitment they had, and used their findings as evidence for the truth of their position.

Thomas Goodwin

The Life of Dr. Thomas Goodwin, 'Compos'd out of his own Papers and Memoirs', was first published with his collected works in 1704. It ends with his conversion, which took place when he was a young man at Cambridge, but was written many years later, after he became President of Magdalen College, Oxford. His son, who edited his papers, added details about the rest of his father's life and accurately identified Goodwin's purpose as an avowedly theological one: 'to give from his own experience, a Testimony of the difference between common Grace (which by some is thought sufficient) and that special saving Grace, which indeed is alone sufficient, and always invincibly and effectually prevails, as it did in him' (p. xv).

This is the key to Goodwin's use of his material, beginning with the first note on his childhood in the opening paragraph:

I began to have some slighter Workings of the Spirit of God, from the time I was six Years old; I could weep for my Sins, whenever I did set my self to think of them, and had Flashes of Joy upon thoughts of the Things of God. . . . This shewed how far Goodness of Nature might go, as well in my self as others, to whom yet true sanctifying Grace never comes. But this I thought was Grace; for I reason'd within my self it was not by Nature (p. v).

He saw this misconception as impregnating all his early experience, even though he measured himself rigorously against the orthodox signs of grace and was deeply moved by God's love, the sacraments, and the example of some godly young men at Christ's College: 'and how affected was I, that I should go to Heaven with them!' (p. vi). But these happy sentiments were disturbed when, after having prepared himself carefully to take the sacrament, he was forbidden to do so by his tutor and had to leave the crowded chapel.

Disappointment caused him to fall away. But aspirations revived, and in relating the long process of effectual calling Goodwin analyses with considerable subtlety both his current explanation of what was happening and his mature understanding of it. He consistently defines his problems in doctrinal terms; at one time the new Arminianism seemed to account for his experience, but he had nagging doubts about both the truth of this teaching and the soundness of his own condition, though he could not see where either was defective. When real conviction of sin came, there was a further difficulty: knowing now that no part of his being or experience was untainted by corruption, how could he explain his earlier passionate repentance and aspirations? For he was still convinced 'that whatever is more than Nature must be Grace' (p. ix). And so it was, for this earlier experience had been a work of God, though not resulting in conversion.

> but God was to me as a wayfaring Man, who came and dwelt for a Night, and made me Religious for a Fit, but then departed from me. The Holy Ghost moved upon the Waters when the World was creating, and held and sustain'd the Chaos that was created, and so he does in carnal Mens Hearts, witness their good Motions at times. In a great Frost you shall see where the Sun shines hot, the Ice drops, and the Snow melts, and the Earth grows slabby; but 'tis a particular Thaw, only where the Sun shines, not a general Thaw of all things that are frozen (p. ix).

It was the difference between common grace and saving grace, which he had discovered through personal experience. Such 'slighter Workings' had led him to presumption, but his sincerity was not in question, for his main trouble was ignorance – an inadequate notion of sin and grace.

The turning point in Goodwin's life came through a funeral sermon by Thomas Bainbridge which he reluctantly attended on Monday 2 October 1620. Expecting it to be 'dull stuff' he instead found himself 'to be as one struck down by a mighty Power' (p. vii). A chain reaction followed, and in his narrative he spells out the events in a way that emphasizes his overriding doctrinal purpose. The intellectual process involved was fairly complex, but he sets it out clearly and without too much close argument; and the emotional impact of a number of crucial phases is realized through evocative imagery. Two passages will illustrate this.

The great effect of Bainbridge's sermon (which he had heard once before) was to expose the true nature of sin, and Goodwin explains that this was a 'new sort of illumination' given by light from Christ, which could penetrate infinitely further than that of the natural conscience:

And here let me stand a while astonish'd (as I did then) I can compare this Sight, and the Workings of my Heart rising from thence to be, as if I had in the heat of Summer lookt down into the Filth of a Dungeon, where by a clear Light and piercing Eye I discern'd Millions of crawling living things, in the midst of that Sink and liquid Corruption (p. viii).

And again, as he worked through the implications of this shattering discovery, one thing led to another until his apprehensions were relieved by an act of divine initiative:

So God was pleased on the sudden, and as it were in an instant, to alter the whole Course of his former Dispensation towards me, and said of and to my Soul, Yea live, yea live I say, said God: and as he created the World and the Matter of all things by a Word, so he created and put a new Life and Spirit into my Soul, and so great an Alteration was strange to me.

The Word of Promise which he let fall into my Heart, and which was but as it were softly whisper'd to my Soul; and as when a Man speaks afar off, he gives a still, yet a certain sound, or as one hath expressed the Preachings of the Gospel by the Apostles; that God whispered the Gospel out of *Sion*, but the sound thereof went forth over the whole Earth: So this speaking of God to my Soul, altho it was but a gentle Sound, yet it made a noise over my whole Heart, and filled and possessed all the Faculties of my whole Soul. God took me aside, and as it were privately said unto me, do you now turn to me, and I will pardon all your Sins tho never so many, as I forgave and pardoned my Servant *Paul*, and convert you unto me as I did Mr. *Price*, who was the most famous Convert and Example of Religion in *Cambridge* (p. xi).

Here as elsewhere Goodwin finds his experience confirmed through Scriptural analogies, and he goes on to encourage his readers by indicating their universal validity. His full sense of the wrath of God before conversion lasted only a few hours; and this experience he sees as normative: for God, he says, 'does not often suffer a destroying Apprehension to continue long upon us. . . . I do not speak now of Temptations, but of the just Conviction

85

which many such Souls have, previous to their Believing' (p. xi). Goodwin, then, is concerned to teach from his experience; and much of his language – such as the similitude of the thaw, quoted above – would be appropriate in an expository sermon. At every point his approach is that of the preacher, and he bears out Robert Harris's principle that the preacher had three main fields of study: the Bible, himself, and the people (cf. p. 15 above). Above all, Goodwin wishes to testify that the doctrines he upholds have been proved upon his pulses. Hence his insistence that the war between the flesh and the spirit had been discovered in day-to-day experience: this, he says, 'I found not by reading, or hearing any one speak of it, but (as *Austin* did) I perceived it of my self, and wonder'd at it' (p. xiii). This 'wondering' involved a capacity for disciplined reflection which is perhaps Goodwin's most distinctive quality.

The experience of rebirth, when God spoke the words of life to his soul, was only the most important instance of his perpetual awareness of divine sovereignty. At every stage Goodwin saw himself as responding to an initiative that seemed to come from outside. Conviction of sin, as we have seen, caused him to feel like 'one struck down by a mighty Power', and his account of the ongoing effects conveys how he was overmastered: 'and so the Working began, . . . and I endeavouring not to think the least thought of my Sins, was passively held under the remembrance of them' (p. vii). One reason for narrating the events fairly fully, however, is to show that, despite this element of passivity, the process of effectual calling is not a brutal subjugation of a rebellious will, but involves the liberation of the entire personality:

> I observed of this Work of God on my Soul, that there was nothing of Constraint or Force in it, but I was carried on with the most ready and willing Mind, and what I did was what I chose to do. With the greatest Freedom I parted with my Sins, formerly as dear to me as the apple of my Eye, yea as my Life, and resolv'd never to return to them more (p. xiii).

In a striking image, Goodwin sums up what he thought had been happening to him at this time:

> I remember some two Years after, I preaching at *Ely* in the *Minster*, as they call it, . . . I told the Auditory, meaning my

self in the Person of another, that a Man to be converted, who is ordinarily ignorant of what the Work of Conversion should be, and what particular Passages it consists of, was yet guided through all the dark Corners and Windings of it, as would be a Wonder to think of, and would be as if a Man were to go to the Top of that Lanthorn, to bring him into all the Passages of the *Minster*, within Doors and without, and knew not a jot of the way, and were in every step in danger to tread awry and fall down. So it was with me, . . . And it became one Evidence of the Truth of the Work of Grace upon me (when I reviewed it) that I had been so strangely guided in the dark (p. vii).

In this reference to his sermon at Ely we have a good illustration of how closely Goodwin's preaching was related to his experience. On the one hand, the main emphasis in his autobiography is on the clarification of doctrine rather than on personal confession; on the other, his preaching was derived from his interpretation of God's dealings with him. Though he spoke of his conversion privately to others 'I know not how often' (p. xi), and kept a diary which became a basis for his sermons, he seems to have used such personal material only indirectly in the pulpit, mainly to reinforce his own confidence in choosing Scriptural examples, which could then be more convincingly held out to the congregation 'as Flags of Mercy before a Company of Rebels to win them in' (p. xii).

If Goodwin's spiritual life exemplifies the main intellectual tradition of Puritan doctrine, his outward circumstances show the extent to which he was influenced by a thriving Puritan culture. He went up to Cambridge in 1613 while Sibbes was Lecturer at Trinity Church, when memories of Perkins and Ames were still fresh in men's minds, and the newly converted Preston was rapidly gaining a formidable reputation. Six of the fellows at Christ's were notable Puritans, and Goodwin was also impressed by the bearing and steadfastness of 'several holy Youths' whom he got to know there (p. vi). We hear much of the controversies of his day – including the old debate about plain or witty preaching, and the burning new issue of Arminianism and the Synod of Dort – and he gives us enough brief glimpses of daily routine and interaction with his friends to locate his spiritual development in a precise social context.

His account could, I suppose, be regarded as the most concentrated and consistent record of a man's internalization of the Calvinist doctrine of grace. 'It was this inward sense of things,' writes his son, 'out of which a Man will not suffer himself to be disputed, that establish'd him in the Truths of the Gospel, and possess'd him with a due temper'd Warmth' (p. xv). As I have shown, Goodwin eloquently conveys the affective power of his experiences – the 'Warmth' – while insisting throughout on the need for spiritual development to be underpinned by a right understanding of doctrine – 'the Truths of the Gospel'.

This is characteristic of all the Calvinist ministers. We have seen how Thomas Halyburton deduced his spiritual development in childhood less from his memories than from his theological convictions and analogies with children he had observed. He agrees with Goodwin that to understand his progress it was essential to distinguish between common grace and special grace: 'Common Gifts increasing as Light grew, I took them for special Grace, and thus have taken up, with the foolish Virgins, the *Lamp* of a Profession, *without oil*.'[1] And James Fraser devotes a chapter of twenty-five pages to God's dealings with him 'under some common Work of the Spirit, and not fully converted'.[2]

Ordinary church members of a conservative theology write more briefly than their pastors and are less concerned with fitting their experience into a coherent pattern of doctrine; nevertheless the main tendency of their narratives is to reflect a personal discovery of orthodox teaching and their relief when what seemed to be a unique or eccentric experience was found to be 'such as was incident to the *Saints*'.[3] Those who cannot match their experience to the received doctrine move to a more radical position.

Jane Turner

Jane Turner's chapter headings, which I have already quoted (cf. p. 48 above), suggest a pattern of experience similar to Goodwin's, including a period of formalism during which she nevertheless received some measure of grace: 'there was some change wrought in the whole soul; and every faculty of it; . . . as the understanding was opened, so the will was changed, and made willing to submit to truth.' She was a Presbyterian at this time, 'very cheerful and confident',[4] but her fuller experience of the

88

gospel came from outside this particular tradition. While she was still 'settled upon the Lees of Legal Righteousness' (p. 49) a new preacher came into the neighbourhood and spoke things about 'free grace' and the gospel which had never been heard there before. Mrs Turner borrowed a book by him and was disposed to accept what he said, but the vigorous defence offered by local clergy persuaded her to stick to her old principles. There the matter might have rested if the Presbyterian ministers had not been over-zealous in protecting their people from false doctrine:

> about half a year after, these forementioned Ministers not being satisfyed to speak against those books in private only, . . . brought them into their Pulpits reading particular passages, which as they read and applyed it, was contrary to the sense of it, and sometimes I thought they spake more than was true, which did occasion me to desire the book again for my better satisfaction: . . . and then I found they did not deal faithfully, but did wrest and draw false consequences contrary to the drift and scope of it, all which occasioned serious thoughts in me (pp. 52–3).

So she concluded that what she had been taught all her life did not tally with experience, and it became necessary to relearn the faith. Assurance of a full and free pardon followed, and with her husband she joined a Baptist congregation, 'being sweetly satisfyed and comforted therein' (p. 88).

A feature of the Antinomian theology which Mrs Turner now adopted was its vastly increased emphasis on experience and feeling: believers were encouraged to find spiritual comfort and peace without reference to objective criteria.[5] The focus of interest was less on the truth itself than on the experience the truth produced. It developed largely as a reaction against too much stress by some Calvinist preachers on repentance, humiliation, and self-examination. Antinomian theology, indeed, was an extension – almost a parody – of the high Calvinist plan of redemption. The rallying cry of 'free grace' referred to the conviction that election was free and unconditional, and the elect were held to be justified and reconciled to God *before* they ever came to believe – not simply from Calvary, as the Calvinists affirmed, but from all eternity. The use and purpose of faith was to assure the elect that this was the case with them: if a man could believe he was justified, then he was. Whereas Calvinists insisted that conversion began with repentance, the Antinomians exhorted men to repent after believing, some even claiming that no one could repent until he had received God's forgiveness. The Christian had no need of the law as a standard of conduct; this would trap his conscience into making him act out of fear of hell or the hope of reward, neither of which were proper motives under the gospel dispensation, since one's only motive should be love and gratitude to God. The age of the Law had passed, and the age of the Spirit had come. The Christian life was held to be essentially one of delight and free from difficulties. The believer was urged not to worry about his sins, since it was enough that Christ's righteousness was imputed to him, and faith involved convincing oneself that sin was not present; man had to stop relying on reason, sense impressions, and conscience, and trust wholly in the love and power of God. Assurance came not from examining one's life to see if it measured up to Biblical standards – this was sure to lead to hypocrisy – but from the direct witness of the Holy Spirit convincing the believer that the promises applied to him.

Antinomianism thus offered comfort and peace without the painful Puritan disciplines, and by-passed serious consideration of the wrath, justice, and holiness of God. Faith became largely a matter of feeling and hence allowed for enormously varied individual interpretations of the gospel. And linked with this subjectivism was an ultra-supernaturalism in which the initiative of the Holy Spirit was always and everywhere supreme, superseding human reason and will in everything. The Antinomian preachers were not libertine in intention; they thought they were promoting a new and better way of holiness, but it is easy to see how the spread of this teaching, essentially 'enthusiastic' in the seventeenth-century sense, caused a proliferation of contending sects and individualist prophets, all more or less opposed to established human institutions, all anti-intellectual, and all claiming the immediate authority of the Spirit. The Muggletonians, Quakers, Ranters, and some Anabaptists communities represent the movement at various removes from central Protestant orthodoxy.

Now the commitment of Jane Turner was to a more moderate position, and she explicitly asserts her conviction that 'ordinarily [God] works by means, and leaves no ground in holy Scripture to expect him out of means'.[6] But having rejected the traditional ground of authority she found herself exposed to pressure from those who followed the authority of experience to its logical conclusion: in her case from some itinerant Quakers, who taught a doctrine of an inner Light which entirely of itself would guide men into all truth. She found them attractive and plausible, but ultimately refused to follow them, despite their 'Angel-like appearance', because they obeyed the motions of the Spirit even when these were in opposition to Scriptural precept. Experience of the futility of 'waiting for a power' in time of emergency led her back from this temporary aberration, and she gives us fifty pages of observations in which the snares of the deluders, the causes of her own mistakes, and the steps by which she recovered are exhaustively analysed (pp. 133–79).

The orderly plan of Jane Turner's book – every narrative section being followed by an equal amount of discussion – is reflected in her emotional tone, which is one of composure, almost complacency, despite turns of phrase which identify her with the more radical Puritans. Her habit of reflection evidently prevented her from going more than part of the way with the new teaching.

Anna Trapnel

In contrast to this, much more excited language is used by two of her contemporaries whose theology is hardly any more extreme: Anna Trapnel, a Baptist prophetess, and John Rogers, the Independent minister whose collection of testimonies has already been mentioned.

Anna Trapnel recounts her spiritual experience in three books, all published in 1654. She appears to have come to the notice of the public in January 1653–4 when, having accompanied Vavasor Powell to a meeting in Whitehall, she waited for him in an antechamber and being suddenly seized upon by a strange power was 'carried forth in a Spirit of Prayer and Singing'.[7] When taken to bed she lay there for twelve days uttering prayers and spiritual songs day and night to people of all classes who crowded into the little room. For the last eight days of this happening her prayers and songs were written down by a friend in 'a slow and imperfect hand' and printed the following month as *The Cry of a Stone*, in order to give the world a true record of what had in the meantime been 'deformed and disguised with the pervertings and depravings of the Reporters' (sig. a2v). Her utterances consist of long prayers couched in highly emotional language, alternating with ecstatic hymns in common metre.

It appears that before the Whitehall incident Anna Trapnel had enjoyed the gift of vision and prophecy for a number of years, and had been fighting against a feeling that it was her duty to make it public. Shortly after her recovery she journeyed to Cornwall at the invitation of some friends in order to make known her gifts for the general good of that county. Here, however, she aroused violent opposition from clergy and magistrates, and was arrested, brought back to London, and imprisoned in Bridewell until released by order of the council. The three books already referred to each cover a different part of her life, and their relationship to one another can be deduced from internal evidence. *The Cry of a Stone*, on sale in February, was prefaced with her account of the development of her gift. In July, while she was in prison, her friends came across some papers written a few years earlier in which she described the whole process of her conversion and many early visions. This was published as *A Legacy for Saints*. Finally, on regaining her freedom, she wrote about her journey to Cornwall in *Anna Trapnel's Report and Plea*.

In *The Cry of a Stone* she is concerned to allay fears that she has relapsed into unrestrained Ranterism. She claims to be known to all the Baptist ministers in London as a sober and responsible young woman, and attributes her extraordinary gifts to the fact that her mother, when dying nine years before, cried out, 'Lord! Double thy spirit upon my child; These words she uttered with much eagerness three times, and spoke no more' (p. 3). Visions began when she was recovering from a fever two years later, and she claimed foreknowledge of many public events. Friends told her she was under a temptation for not eating, but she never doubted that the revelations came from God. And except for these phenomena her experience followed a normal course, though with a leaning to Antinomianism on 'the Work of Free-grace and the Testimony of the Spirit', and some admitted signs of emotional instability.[8] From desperate attempts at suicide when signs of grace were lacking, she quickly passed to a condition of ecstasy when convinced of pardon:

I knew not where I was, nor how to get out of the place

92

where I sat, I apprehended nothing but a clothing of glory over my whole man: I never beheld Saints as I did then, I saw their faces like the face of Angels . . . oh how my soul was enamoured with Christ! Earth was now gone, and heaven come; the unclean spirit dispossessed, the pure spirit now possesst . . . but oh now, every bit of bread I eat, how sweet it was to my taste! Christ sweetned every creature to me.[9]

The account of her journey into Cornwall gives an admirably clear picture of the impact of the singing prophetess on both critics and sympathizers, and shows a remarkable freedom from aggressive self-concern. She records the signs and leadings by which she was induced to undertake the adventure and indicates the circumstances that excited her to public prophecy. One such occasion was when she narrated her life story to a critical audience at Truro, and her heart became 'so thorowly heated with discoursing of Gods goodness so many hours' that she broke into singing and had to take to her bed. This had not happened many times before the authorities decided to arrest her, and 'while I was singing praises to the Lord for his love to me, the Justices sent their Constable to fetch me'.[10]

John Rogers

If we compare the testimonies in John Rogers's collection with those in *Spirituall Experiences*, the most obvious difference is in the prominence given to extraordinary phenomena such as visions and voices. An important cause of this must have been Rogers's attitude and example, for his own story is flamboyant in both incidents and language. No one, we feel, could have reacted more desperately to the fear of hell in childhood. At ten years old he fell to duties, heard sermons, read the Scriptures morning and evening, and learnt all the prayers he could. Every night he feared the devil would carry him away if he did not repeat his prayers, the creed, and the Ten Commandments before he went to sleep. It was a kind of charm to prevent the fiends from tearing him to pieces:

> *sometimes* (when I was *sleepy*) to make the more hast I should say *some* of them at least (to be in a *forwardnesse*) in the *Chimney corner* whilest I was *unbuttoning* me, or *untying* my

hose or the like, preparing to goe to *bed*, thinking all was *well enough* so 'twas but done.[11]

And he mentions in particular the 'black gulf of despair' into which he was cast after hearing his father preach on the warning of Matthew v.20. He felt himself to be past all recovery:

the more I *read* the more I *roar'd* in the *black gulf* of *despair*, . . . I have ran into *barnes, stables, house-of office*, any where (pretending as if I had *businesse*) on purpose to *pray*, sigh, *weep*, knocking my *breast*, curse that ever I was born; wishing I were a *stone*, any thing but what I was, for *fear of hell* and the *devils*; whom I thought I saw every *foot*, in severall *ugly shapes* and *formes* (according to my *fancies*) and sometimes with great *rolling flaming* eyes (like *sawcers*) having *sparkling* fire-brands in the one of their *hands*, and with the other *reaching* at me to *tear* me away to torments! O the *leaps* that I have made! the *frights* that I have had! the *fears* that I was in! (pp. 426–7)

These experiences offer an interesting parallel to those recorded by Bunyan a few years later. Like Bunyan, Rogers felt himself condemned by the Scriptures as by a physical presence. Temptations and fantasies took shape in his mind as, 'lying under the *severest* sense and *sentence* of that *Scripture*', he sought desperately for a way of escape (p. 428). He made several attempts at suicide, and had to be tied in bed until the fits were over.

Rogers received his most explicit 'evangelical' call in one of the many dreams he mentions, and his reaction was characteristically excited: 'I said, Lord is this true? say! is it true! if it be so, let it be shewn to me that it is so: So I was *perswaded that the righteousnesse of Christ* was *mine*' (p. 431).

Subsequent afflictions, none of which lose any colour in the telling, included being turned out of doors by his family, poverty and hunger at Cambridge in the depth of winter, and constant harassing from Satan, with further temptations to despair and suicide as well as to work miracles by necromancy. All these trials reached a cliff-hanging climax when he was about to plunge a newly whetted knife into his breast: a fellow student then burst in (through a door Rogers thought he had bolted) with news of a private tutor's post which had just been refused by another member of the college.

Rogers, then, has an eventful story to tell, but though an exuberant writer he is so repetitive and undisciplined that his eye for detail and picturesque exaggeration is not adequately exploited. He has some sense of rhythm, but nearly every sentence has a parenthesis which clogs the flow of narrative, and he perpetually throws off asides and exclamations which add to the confusion.

Comparison with Bunyan shows at once where Bunyan's power lies. The two men's trials correspond fairly closely: they talk of similar hallucinations, fears of damnation, and fervent hopes of deliverance. But Rogers comes through as much more of an 'enthusiast', partly no doubt because of Bunyan's emphasis on the mediation of the Scriptures. Misplaced as Bunyan's intellectual activity sometimes is, his constant worried argument with himself gives a sense of direction which Rogers lacks, concentrating on the lurid portrayal of extremes of feeling. We believe Bunyan when he says that he has tried to be 'plain and simple, and lay down the thing as it was'.[12] We suspect Rogers of exaggeration because he is less critical of himself, and his self-analysis is more sweeping and perfunctory, more tied to pious clichés, than Bunyan's. Rogers is inclined to condemn all his past attitudes out of hand and to conclude that now at last he is entirely right. Bunyan is more careful to trace the hand of God leading him through the years: like the Puritan divines, and unlike most of the radical brethren, he records mercies received while still unregenerate. And the agony of his past suffering is still much too real for him to exhibit it, as Rogers does, with a tone implying amusement and contempt. The later lives of the two men accentuate these differences. It is Bunyan, with 'seven abominations' in his heart, who goes on to consolidate his faith; while Rogers, for all his assurance, leans more and more to extreme religious and political opinions.

The radical experience

Rogers was an Independent minister when he wrote his testimony, having earlier repudiated his Presbyterian ordination. He later became a prominent Fifth Monarchy man and thus, like many of his contemporaries, reproduced in his experience the swing to the left which was a current feature of English radical Protestantism. Of course, the radical Puritan experience was not entirely determined by doctrine or denomination, although Baptist writers in particular shared a common range of attitudes: notably towards politics, church order, religious practices, and paranormal phenomena, and with a nose for any trace of 'legalism'. With Jane Turner and Anna Trapnel we may associate the three ministers Vavasor Powell, Hanserd Knollys, and Francis Bampfield. They all, like Rogers, show a highly charged reaction to circumstances, expressed in characteristic emotive terms, and events undergo a self-conscious dramatization. Rogers, Powell, and Anna Trapnel, for instance, all write of spectacular temptations to commit suicide arising from the sinister fascination of knives, which are flung away in horror at the last moment.

What it all amounts to, and what they have most obviously in common, might be described as a sense of heightened immediacy; for in spite of their normal reliance on the ordinary means of grace the Spirit's guidance comes frequently – and, we are made to feel, most convincingly – through dreams and voices.

Hanserd Knollys claims to have been taught the doctrine of his first sermon in dreams during three successive nights, and he preached it the following Sunday. Earlier in his career he had been guided to a man who helped him, through the words, 'Go to Mr. Wheelwright, . . . but I heard no voice, nor did I see any Vision; only those words were plainly and articulately spoken into my Ears and Understanding.'[13] Strange experiences could also be the ground for claiming freedom from established customs. Francis Bampfield, as well as having interior voices, had a vision of Christ which 'raised him into an higher Way of Later-Day-Glory-hymnifying, than his former way of singing by Mens Forms, read out of a Book, could reach unto'.[14] This kind of illumination, as we shall see, became the authority claimed by all kinds of religious groups, including the Quakers, to replace not only the 'chains of legalism' but many ordinary human disciplines and social institutions.

The witness of the Spirit came to Anna Trapnel in audible form, in an experience something like Thomas Goodwin's in its sense of personal communication; the words, 'Christ is thine, and thou art his', followed her wherever she went for six or seven days:

> sometimes as I have been going along the streets, I have looked behind me, thinking I had heard some locall voice,

96

a voice without me, but sure it was because I was unacquainted with the voice of the Spirit speaking in, or to the soul; I oft-times turned back when I have been going along the streets, to see who it was that spake, taking that for visible which was invisible.[15]

Her language here is as direct and economical as Goodwin's, but an important difference is that Goodwin is consciously figurative, whereas Anna Trapnel is physically involved in the phenomenon. A clearer parallel, in which inward pressure is also projected into an external stimulus, is found in Bunyan:

Now about a week or fortnight after this, I was much followed by this scripture, *Simon, Simon, Satan hath desired to have you,* Luk. 22.31. And sometimes it would sound so loud within me, yea, and as it were call so strongly after me, that once above all the rest, I turned my head over my shoulder, thinking verily that some man had behind me called to me, being at a great distance, methought he called so loud, . . . (para. 93)

Puritan divines always emphasized the importance of the personal, affective element in effectual calling. When depicting the contrast between works and grace, the law and the gospel, they implied that the experiences involved were not simply about different conditions, but were different in kind. Both were intensely felt, both involved the whole being of the subject; but when the gospel broke on a man it brought such a reorientation that all previous understanding appeared to have been inadequate and superficial, to have been going on mainly at an intellectual or 'notional' level only. For all the time the convert was 'under the law' he was certainly hearing about justification by faith and the promises of the gospel – only he did not really apply them to himself! Hence the frequently observed distinction between 'notional' and 'spiritual' knowledge in Puritan experience. Robert Blair discussed this in a forthright passage in his autobiography:

It is one thing to know a truth naturally, . . . or by a gift of common illumination; to know it, I say, notionally, so as to discourse thereof both accurately as to the matter, and elegantly as to the words. This many graceless students and gifted persons attain, . . . A great deal of this brain, frothy, foamy knowledge cometh to little, yea, to nothing; it puffeth up, and is but a witness against him that hath it, . . . This differeth essentially in kind or species, as I may say, from the right, true, and saving knowledge of God. . . . This true and spiritual knowledge is affectionate and practical; as it floweth from the Spirit of grace, so it carries with it a stream and current of holy affections, and stirreth up to endeavours and earnestness in holy practice. A little of this reacheth very far (pp. 23-4).

In the eighteenth century, the 'Private Gentleman' wrote of his own discovery of this in his *Remarkable Passages*. Having complained earlier of his 'want of heart work', he eventually had an experience which changed his whole perception of things:

I saw things quite in a new light . . . : it was light that brought heat; I began to receive the light of the truth in the love of it: I felt the counter part of truths in my heart: I had the practic sense of what I scarce had the notion of before, and that very confusedly. The brightest truths, without a spiritual sensation, are but like beautiful objects displayed before the blind, that make no impression.[16]

And Halyburton, once he felt the invitation to believe in Jesus as a personal one, noted the difference between 'the Discoveries now made, and the Notions I formerly entertained of the same Truths' (p. 70). Not that 'notional' knowledge was to be despised, for although inadequate in itself it formed the essential foundation for the other. Only a year earlier, when already a chaplain, Halyburton had found himself handicapped in disputations because he was 'neither notionally instructed in the Grounds whereon the Scripture is received, nor acquainted practically with its power' (p. 53).

Power, feeling, enjoyment, were key words in Puritan descriptions of spiritual experience, and Jane Turner's definition of it as 'truth brought home to the heart with life and power' would have commanded universal assent (cf. p. 15 above). Disagreement began when people tried to say how this happened. The plain and powerful preaching of Calvinist divines and the quality of life of the local church community were effective agencies for many, but others found these 'legalistic' and so identified the whole orthodox way with 'notionism'. It was not always easy to know whether one had left the law for saving grace, and Hanserd Knollys was surprised to learn many years after his ordination that he was still building his soul on a covenant of works, 'having bin only under legal Convictions, and a Spirit of Bondage' (p. 12). The Quakers and other radicals were much more emphatic: they were convinced that Presbyterians, Independents, Baptists, and all orthodox Puritans had only the knowledge and discernment of the natural man. Richard Farnworth's verdict in 1654 was unanimously supported among the early Friends:

I could not be satisfied with such carnality, and so . . .
Preaching became but as the telling of a Tale, or as a boy
that saith over his weeks work at the School, what he hath
learned all the week, he saith over at once, or one time, and
so did the Priests, they studied out of books, and writ down
in papers, and knew where to begin, and where to end, and
any natural man might do so; but the natural man knoweth
not the things of God, for they are spiritually discerned (p. 4).

To this charge the orthodox retort was that if anyone had not found lasting peace under sound gospel preaching the fault lay squarely with themselves for drifting away too soon – as James Fraser pointed out, commenting on why people turned to the Quakers:

I saw and considered that these that they made their Prey
were ordinarily but only old jaded Professors, that never found
the constant satisfying Sweetness of their own Religion,
and . . . wanting Rest in Christ because never truly united to
him . . . have here at last stumbled (p. 151).

While the disputes were partly over questions of doctrine, then, they seem also to have developed from the radicals' need for a more intense emotional content in their experience. And if conservative Puritans regarded the radicals as being unduly intense about this, we read of at least one Papist who made a similar complaint about the Protestant religion in general: he told Edmund Trench that to take it seriously would make a man far too uncomfortable.[17]

NOTES

1 Halyburton, p. 36.
2 Fraser, pp. 11–36.
3 Mary Simpson, p. 27.
4 Turner, pp. 37, 31.
5 Cf. John Saltmarsh, *Holy Discoveries and Flames*, 1640; John Eaton, *The Honey-combe of Free Justification by Christ Alone*, 1642; John Everard, *Some Gospel Treasures Opened*, 1653.
6 Turner, p. 65.
7 Trapnel, *Cry of a Stone*, p. 1.
8 *Report and Plea*, p. 16.
9 *A Legacy for Saints*, p. 9.
10 *Report and Plea*, p. 20.
11 Rogers, p. 420.
12 Bunyan, pp. 3–4.
13 Knollys, p. 10, cf. p. 15.
14 Bampfield, p. 4.
15 Trapnel, *A Legacy for Saints*, pp. 7–8. Cf. p. 85 above.
16 *An Account of Some Remarkable Passages*, Glasgow, 1765 ed., p. 161.
17 Cf. Trench, p. 25.

Chapter 7

47934

Bunyan's *Grace Abounding*

In a famous passage near the beginning of his autobiography Bunyan tells us how he was convicted of sin while playing tipcat one Sunday in the village of Elstow, where he lived:

> . . . as I was in the midst of a game at Cat, and having struck it one blow from the hole; just as I was about to strike it the second time, a voice did suddenly dart from Heaven into my Soul, which said, *Wilt thou leave thy sins, and go to Heaven? or have thy sins and go to Hell?* At this I was put to an exceeding maze; wherefore, leaving my Cat upon the ground, I looked up to Heaven, and was as if I had with the eyes of my understanding, seen the Lord Jesus looking down upon me, as being very hotly displeased with me, and as if he did severely threaten me with some grievous punishment for these, and other my ungodly practices (para. 22).

At the end of his story, close on a hundred pages later, he reaches the point where he is able in the face of death to commit himself to this same Jesus without fear, without reservation, and if necessary without the assurance he had so desperately searched for:

> Wherefore, thought I, the point being thus, I am for going on, and venturing my eternal state with Christ, whether I have comfort here or no; if God doth not come in, thought I, I will leap off the Ladder even blindfold into Eternitie, sink or swim, come heaven, come hell; Lord Jesus, if thou wilt catch me, do; if not, I will venture for thy Name (para. 337).

What is most apparent in the intervening pages is the strength and cohesion of the narrative. Although Bunyan's purpose is didactic and although his pages are crowded with short episodes and comments (many of which were added at different times) the book as a whole makes an impact essentially as a story, in which the reader finds himself painfully involved to the end. More than with any other Puritan autobiography, with the possible exception of Norwood's, the structure is derived from the line of narrative, and doctrinal points emerge out of the chain of events themselves. These points are not different from those we have noticed elsewhere. The successive phases of conversion, the contrast between law and grace, the moulding of experience by the Scriptures, the manifestation of grace in severe trials, are all matters which are plainly evident in *Grace Abounding*. But whereas most other writers either fit their story into a separately conceived framework or subordinate it to reflective comment (and often they do both), Bunyan presents his spiritual experience as an organic whole. He certainly makes plenty of explicit comments, but the things he wants to teach, and their weighting relative to one another, are effectively communicated precisely as they hang together in his graphically realized narration.

Sequence of events

Two early landmarks of Bunyan's conversion have already been quoted, describing his conviction of sin and the amendment of life that followed (cf. pp. 101, 38 above). He was, however, still ignorant of important matters.

> Thus I continued about a year, all which time our
> Neighbours did take me to be a very godly man, a new and
> religious man, and did marvel much to see such a great
> and famous alteration in my life and manners; and
> indeed so it was, though yet I knew not Christ, nor Grace,
> nor Faith, nor Hope; . . . (para. 31).

The real turning point came one day in Bedford when, in the course of his work as a travelling brazier, he came to where three or four women were sitting at a doorway in the sun, talking about the things of God:

> I drew near to hear what they said; for I was now a brisk

talker also my self in the matters of Religion: But now I may say, *I heard, but I understood not*; for they were far above out of my reach, for their talk was about a new birth, the work of God on their hearts, also how they were convinced of their miserable state by nature: they talked how God had visited their souls with his love in the Lord Jesus, and with what words and promises they had been refreshed, comforted, and supported against the temptations of the Devil. . . . And me thought they spake as if joy did make them speak: they spake with such pleasantness of Scripture language, and with such appearance of grace in all they said, that they were to me as if they had found a new world, . . . (para. 37f).

The security built up by his empty talk and self-esteem was now endangered; he began to read the Bible with new eyes; his mind was seized with the glory of the heavenly kingdom and the new birth, so that 'neither pleasures nor profits, nor perswasions, nor threats, could loosen it' (para. 42).

There is an old saying among Evangelical Christians that the devil does not waste his ammunition: those whom he holds securely within his camp are not often consciously troubled by his assaults until they try to fight their way out. This, at least, seems to have been Bunyan's experience. Now that his heart was 'fixed on Eternity' he became more aware of what it really meant to be a sinner, and he describes this discovery in terms very like those of Goodwin at the same stage (cf. p. 85 above):

But my Original and inward pollution, that, that was my plague and my affliction; that I saw at a dreadful rate always putting forth it selfe within me, that I had the guilt of to amazement; by reason of that, I was more loathsom in mine own eyes then was a toad, and I thought I was so in Gods eyes too: Sin and corruption, I said, would as naturally bubble out of my heart, as water would bubble out of a fountain (para. 84).

Notice how, with the five-times-repeated 'that', Bunyan uses the preacher's dramatic urgency to impress his fascinated loathing on the reader. The more he read the Scriptures, the more convinced he became that his repentance was superficial, that it had come too late, that he had not the gift of saving faith. He was tempted to blaspheme, tempted to work miracles to prove his faith, tempted to give up trying to please a master who must surely reject him in the end. For four or five years abject despair and periods of comfort alternated in his experience as successive waves of fear and doubt surged up within him.

The central part of *Grace Abounding*, more than half of the story, tells of these trials and in particular of two very great storms of temptations which almost overthrew him. They mainly took the form of ferocious and persistent impulses to blaspheme, and culminated in the urge to sell Christ, 'to exchange him for the things of this life'.

> Sometimes it would run in my thoughts not so little as a hundred times together, Sell him, sell him, sell him; against which, I may say, for whole hours together I have been forced to stand as continually leaning and forcing my spirit against it, . . . (paras 133, 136).

After resisting this intolerable barrage for over a year, he became worn out with the struggle and allowed himself to be convinced that he had wilfully betrayed Christ in his thoughts. At once he was plunged into the most fearful despair and there seized upon his soul the words of Hebrews 12.16–17: 'Or prophane person, as Esau, who, for one morsel of meat, sold his birthright; for ye know, how that afterward, when he would have inherited the blessing, he was rejected, for he found no place of repentance . . . .' 'These words', he wrote, 'were to my Soul like Fetters of Brass to my Legs, in the continual sound of which I went for several months together' (para. 143). Indeed, for over two years he had few moments of relief. But he was not passive; his intellectual activity was incessant; he constantly searched the Scriptures for guidance about the nature of his sin and its remedy. He tried to find parallels: David, Hezekiah, Solomon, and Peter were all guilty of terrible things; but his state was most like that of Judas. He had insuperable difficulty in prayer. He was mocked by Satan, who among other things told him that since he had rejected the only mediator with the Father, he must pray for God the Father to be mediator between the sinner and his Son; Christ indeed pitied him but had not died for that particular sin. Such thoughts were no less painful because he was fully aware that they were ridiculous. He was mocked most, however, not by the voice of Satan, nor by the terrible warning passages of Scripture, but by all the promises and most gracious words of the gospel:

> Every time that I thought of the Lord Jesus, of his Grace, Love, Goodness, Kindness, Gentleness, Meekness, Death, Blood, Promises and blessed Exhortations, Comforts and Consolations, it went to my Soul like a Sword; . . . O thought I, what have I lost! What have I parted with! What have I dis-inherited my poor Soul of! (para. 183).

The Scriptures

When looking back on all this trouble Bunyan offered two explanations for it: 'the ground of all these fears of mine did arise from a stedfast belief I had of the stability of the holy Word of God, and, also, from my being misinformed of the nature of my sin' (para. 184). These observations identify for us two of the most important themes in *Grace Abounding*: the relation between experience and objective reality, and the dangers of spiritual ignorance. Let us look at the second point first.

I have already drawn attention to the Puritans' insistence that the Christian life could begin only with knowledge of the gospel and that later progress presupposed increased cognitive understanding at every stage. And Bunyan frequently attributes his troubles to ignorance, although he sometimes uses the word to denote spiritual blindness rather than lack of knowledge. From the time when his interest in religion was first aroused through reading the books of Dent and Bayly with his wife, he shows how his development was hindered through misconceptions and attention to irrelevant matters. For some time he was 'overrun with the spirit of superstition' because of being 'not sensible of the danger and evil of sin; I was kept from considering that sin would damn me' (paras 16, 19). When he began to enjoy reading the Bible, he still despised the epistles, 'being as yet but ignorant either of the corruptions of my nature, or of the want and worth of Jesus Christ to save me' (para. 29). This ignorance, too, led him to think he could please God by living a good life, and as he looks back on his youth – 'poor Wretch as I was' – he expresses something like the compassion that George Fox displayed in reflecting on his own tender years (para. 36, cf. p. 192 below). He took no notice of secret thoughts and, although a 'brisk talker', did not even understand what Satan's temptations were (para. 39). It was only after hearing the poor women of Bedford casually talk of things beyond his understanding that he was awakened to explore further. Even so, it was ignorance again that led him to miss a warning of impending trouble, and to think that the only way to test his faith would be by working a miracle. In these ways, he was constantly 'tossed betwixt the Devil and my own ignorance' (paras 51, 52, 95).

But though this made his progress more painful than it need have been, he records that 'God never much charged the guilt of the sins of my Ignorance upon me' (para. 83). He was able to put it out of his mind fairly easily, and if we can for the most part associate this aspect of his experience with 'notional' knowledge of the faith, we can place his most intractable tensions in the area of striving for genuine 'spiritual' knowledge. This is where his attitude to the Scriptures was so important, and also where his affinity to the radical Puritan heritage is most in evidence.

Bunyan's teacher here was John Gifford, the pastor who baptized him in 1653. Gifford, he said, 'pressed us to take special heed, that we took not up any truth upon trust, . . . but to cry mightily to God, that he would convince us of the reality thereof, and set us down therein, by his own Spirit in the holy Word' (para. 117). The seriousness with which Bunyan responded to this advice, coupled with his 'stedfast belief . . . of the stability of the holy Word of God' largely determined the nature of his temptations and trials. For he could not be satisfied until there was full and lasting correspondence between his emotional experience and objective reality as posited in the Scriptures.

This becomes apparent before Gifford's influence is mentioned, when in spite of being 'troubled and tossed and afflicted' with guilt Bunyan consciously resisted any easing of the pressure on his conscience:

> . . . for I found that unless guilt of conscience was taken off the right way, that is, by the Blood of Christ, a man grew rather worse for the loss of his trouble of minde, than better. Wherefore if my guilt lay hard upon me, then I should cry that the Blood of Christ might take it off: and if it was going off without it . . . then I would also strive to fetch it upon

my heart again, by bringing the punishment for sin in Hell-fire upon my Spirit; . . . for that Scripture lay much upon me, *Without shedding of Blood there is no Remission,* . . . Because I had seen some, who . . . seeking rather present Ease from their Trouble, then Pardon for their Sin, . . . grew harder and blinder, and more wicked after their trouble (para. 86).

His doctrine and his experience thus gave him rational grounds for this attitude, but his need for a full emotional response is the deciding factor at every stage. His depression increased when he could not shed a tear or convince himself that he really wanted deliverance with all his heart; on the other hand, words of Scripture would sometimes generate a warmth in his heart that lasted for days or weeks. One of his first great memories was from a sermon on the words, 'Behold thou art fair, my Love; behold thou art fair.' These words ran through his thoughts and kindled his spirit,

. . . yea, I was now so taken with the love and mercy of God, that I remember I could not tell how to contain till I got home; I thought I could have spoken of his Love, and of his mercy to me, even to the very Crows that sat upon the plow'd lands before me, . . . wherefore I said in my Soul . . . surely I will not forget *this* forty years hence; but alas! within less then forty days I began to question all again (para. 92).

Inevitably his moods oscillated violently and were so intense while they lasted that every one seemed as though it would be permanent. Others had felt the same, Norwood being the most explicit in his observations:

It may seem strange that a man should be so suddenly changed from so much peace and comfort to such perturbations and terrours, and it seemed strange to me even at those times. And when I was comforted and in peace I resolved often I would not be so much moved or dismayed with any terrours. The Lord had abundantly confirmed his mercy and grace towards me, and why should I give place to such temptations and fears? But still when they came they prevailed and I could not withstand them, my comforts being almost wholly withdrawn or rather retired and hidden. And Satan had power to overwhelm all, as it were, with a thick dark cloud and to captivate me in all the powers and faculties of mind and body (p. 100).

So Bunyan often 'lost much of the life and savour' of the gracious words that had seized upon him. At one time, he says, 'my peace would be in and out sometimes twenty times a day: Comfort now, and Trouble presently; Peace now, and before I could go a furlong, as full of Fear and Guilt as ever heart could hold'. Later, though, he had sensible consolations for as long as a year at a time (paras 93, 205, 235f).

His concern involved getting a personal conviction of every facet of the life and work of Christ; 'and truly in those dayes, let men say what they would, unless I had it with evidence from Heaven, all was as nothing to me, I counted not myself set down in any truth of God' (para. 122). By 'evidence from Heaven' Bunyan seems to have meant what Jane Turner meant by her 'truth brought home to the heart with life and power' (cf. p. 98 above). But the importance of this emotional element does not justify Professor Henri Talon's assertion that Bunyan's ultimate standards were as subjective as those of the Quakers. 'Like them,' he claims, '. . . he listened solely to the reasons of the heart and made his feelings the criterion of truth. His final reason for a rejection or denial was if a suggestion was distasteful or unpalatable to his soul.'[1] Bunyan's criterion of truth was the Bible, and all his experience had to be ratified there:

> . . . for this consideration came strong into my mind, That whatever comfort and peace I thought I might have from the word of the Promise of Life, yet unless there could be found in my refreshment a concurrence and agreement in the Scriptures, let me think what I will thereof, and hold it never so fast, I should finde no such thing at the end: *For the Scriptures cannot be broken*, John 10.35 (para. 195).

If Bunyan could not quicken to certain statements in Scripture, or if he felt an active distaste for others, his response was not to reject them but to try to change his own reactions. And we have just seen that he suffered his most severe testing precisely because he could not question 'the stability of the holy Word of God'. It might be argued that Professor Talon is concerned with Bunyan's reactions to fundamental matters such as the unique truth of Christianity and the reliability of the Bible itself. But any man's decision, however rationally taken, about any final authority he will recognize – whether Pope, Church, Bible, Party or anything else – is necessarily subjective and will certainly involve his emotions. He can only be charged with 'making his feelings the criterion of truth' if in practice his allegiance is consistently determined by them rather than by any other consideration. And this was far from being Bunyan's position.

In reconciling himself with the truth he found himself involved in a two-way communication process. The initiative sometimes seemed to come from elsewhere as new considerations burst in to destroy his peace: 'that Scripture did seize upon my Soul', 'These places did pinch me very sore', 'This Scripture also did ... trample upon all my desires' (paras 58, 141, 178). At other times he himself set things in motion as he laboured long and hard to appropriate a text by bringing it to life. The most curious incident of this kind happened in two stages with an interval of several weeks. The words, 'My grace is sufficient', darted in upon him and brought hope for a while; but the utterance was incomplete:

> yet, because *for thee* was left out, I was not contented, but prayed to God for that also: Wherefore, one day as I was in a Meeting of Gods People, full of sadness and terrour, ... these words did with great power suddainly break in upon me, *My grace is sufficient for thee, my grace is sufficient for thee, my grace is sufficient for thee*; three times together; and, O me-thought that every word was a mighty word unto me; as *my*, and *grace*, and *sufficient*, and *for thee*; they were then, and sometimes are still, far bigger than others be (para. 206).

A response was not always long in coming, and on one occasion at least was instantaneous and utterly surprising (para. 188).

Bunyan's awareness of the spiritual forces breaking in upon him with such immense power usually came through the Scriptures, and the resolution of his great crisis occurred when the issues became embodied in two texts – the one about the sufficiency of grace, and the other from Hebrews about Esau's rejection. Peace came and went for him according to which one was uppermost in his mind; then one day he conceived of their meeting in a kind of pitched battle:

Lord, thought I, if both of these Scriptures would meet in my heart at once, I wonder which of them would get the better of me. So me thought I had a longing mind that they might come both together upon me; yea, I desired of God they might.

Well, about two or three dayes after, so they did indeed; they boulted both upon me at a time, and did work and struggle strangly in me for a while; at last, that about *Esaus* birthright began to wax weak, and withdraw, and vanish; and this about the sufficiency of Grace prevailed, with peace and joy (para. 214).

When the great struggle was over he approached the texts as warily as if they were disarmed opponents: 'I came to the sixth of the *Hebrews* . . . trembling for fear it should strike me,' and he found them at times as formidable as a spear, or pikes, or an army of 40,000 men. An encouraging passage, on the other hand, would affect him 'as if one had clapt me on the back' (paras 201, 223, 225, 246, 251).

In Bunyan's story, then, the Scripture is more than simply a medium of revelation; it assumes the role of a protagonist with whom he argues and struggles and which has a complex life of its own: mysterious, powerful, unpredictable, searching him out with desolating efficiency, but ultimately consistent and working for his good. It is a strange, almost personified force, and it is a measure of Bunyan's commitment that his dealings with them are almost as dramatic as those with Satan himself.

Dealings with Satan

For Satan is the third force in the story, and Bunyan's relationship with him shows a clearly perceptible development, from the time when as a child he wished he had been a devil so as to be only a tormentor instead of being tormented (para. 7). Satan is never long absent from what is going on, and his role gradually becomes more complex. Bunyan seems almost to use his relationship with the adversary as one way of portraying his spiritual growth. Successive references to Satan imply a developing awareness and understanding of the way he goes to work, the devil continually finding new and subtler means of attack while all the time persisting in the old ones. So his campaign, and with it Bunyan's resistance, steadily extends to cover more and more fronts. The effect is like different themes entering one by one in a fugue, which steadily swells into a richer contrapuntal pattern. As Bunyan meets his enemy in different forms and becomes alert to different features of his strategy, he tells us about it and how knowledge so gained built up his resources until they were enough to win major battles.

At first, in his adult experience, Bunyan did not recognize that certain thoughts which he attributed to prudence or his own observation were being put into his mind by the adversary, and there is a very effective passage where Satan makes his first appearance as an active participant. He does so by emerging almost imperceptibly from Bunyan's own thoughts as he puzzles over the significance of Romans 9.16:

> Therefore, this would still stick with me, How can you tell you are Elected? and what if you should not? how then?
> O Lord, thought I, what if I should not indeed? It may be you are not, said the Tempter: it may be so indeed, thought I. Why then, said Satan, you had as good leave off, and strive no further; . . . (para. 59f).

It is one of the most effective moments in Puritan literature. After this he is able to see certain things as being presented to him by the Tempter, arising directly out of his natural reflections on matters like the scope of election, the reliability of the Bible, and the possible claims of Jews, Moslems, and pagans to have a true religion.

These were questions that needed careful thought, but Bunyan next begins to mention temptations which he immediately identified as evil and which had to be resisted from the beginning, such as impulses arising from his own heart and ungodly company, and the pressure of distracting thoughts while at prayer. The devil's presence now becomes all too apparent, as an insistent voice which gives him no peace: 'He would be also continually at me in the time of prayer, to have done, break off, make haste, you have prayed enough, and stay no longer: still drawing my minde away.' And it was the interminable '*Sell him, sell him, sell him, sell him,* as fast as a man could speak' that wore him down to the point where he thought he had yielded (paras 107, 139).

Every reference to Satan adds to the portrait as Bunyan gains further experience of his deadly power. Here is an adversary who can instantly block every move he makes, while every attempt at escape is anticipated by his subtlety and resourcefulness. Remembering how his sense of assurance always faded, Bunyan once resolved to exert sustained efforts to keep the flame of faith alive:

> Though you do, said Satan, I shall be too hard for you, I will cool you insensibly, by degrees, by little and little: what care I, saith he, though I be seven years in chilling your heart, if I can do it at last; continual rocking will lull a crying Child asleep: I will ply it close, but I will have my end accomplished: though you be burning hot at present, yet, if I can pull you from this fire, I shall have you cold before it be long (para. 110).

The slow grip of despair induced by these words comes not only from the force of the argument, but from the devil's sinister use of the image of the crying child, emphasizing his ruthless and mocking malignity.

Alongside the growing precision with which Bunyan can identify Satan's tone comes the awareness of him as an almost physical presence: 'In prayer also . . . I have thought I should see the Devil, nay, thought I have felt him behind me pull my cloaths,' and later, 'methought I saw as if the Tempter did lear and steal away from me, as being ashamed of what he had done.' And at the moment of Bunyan's greatest despair we sense the shadow of the implacable hunter: 'Now was the battel won, and down I fell, as a Bird that is shot from the top of a Tree, into great guilt and fearful despair' (paras 107, 140, 144).

As the narrative proceeds, Bunyan uses freer language about Satan, almost as if he were becoming bolder in his characterization. The tempter becomes more outrageous in his suggestions, and his tone more forceful and contemptuous (cf. 181, 184):

> For God (said he) hath been weary of you for these several years already, because you are none of his; your bauling in his ears hath been no pleasant voice to him; and, therefore he let you sin this sin, that you might be quite cut off, and will you pray still? (para. 177).

It is the tone of a malevolent rustic, a projection of his own darker nature. Finally, when Bunyan begins to gain the upper hand, his imagery suggests a more relaxed attitude as they struggle over the application of the promise in John 6.39:

> If ever Satan and I did strive for any word of God in all my life, it was for this good word of Christ; he at one end and I at the other. Oh, what work did we make! It was for this in *John*, I say, that we did so tug and strive: he pull'd and I pull'd; but, God be praised, I got the better of him, I got some sweetness from it (para. 215).

This episode is significant for several reasons. Like most other moments of crisis it is concerned with the appropriation of a Scriptural promise, but here for the first time Bunyan engages in open conflict with Satan on equal terms. We are coming out into the daylight. The image of the tug-of-war, drawn from the sports field which Bunyan had repudiated long before, reminds us of the game of tipcat and suggests how completely his natural desires had been sublimated in this more intense – and ultimately more exhilarating – spiritual contest. And Satan himself has become less terrifying through long familiarity; indeed, Bunyan now feels quite confident that he can interpret his opponent's tactics to us, since a few lines earlier he has even pointed out something Satan failed to do, so well does he now understand him.

Imagery and inward pressures

Thus through the Scriptures and the figure of Satan Bunyan projects and embodies aspects of his divided self which represent the felt tensions of his experience. In fact, the primacy of his inward tensions is apparent in most of his recorded thoughts and actions: his foolhardiness with the adder in plucking her sting out, the way premonitions came as external stimuli, the persistent urge to blaspheme, the apparent triviality of outward afflictions compared with 'the sight and sence and terrour' of his wickedness (cf. paras 12, 86, 93, 103, 293).

Although the action of *Grace Abounding* is located in Bunyan's mind and consists mainly of his encounters with Satan and the Scriptures, there are a number of references to stimuli that came more directly from his Puritan environment. A sermon on sabbath-breaking, a rebuke for swearing, doorstep discussions on personal religion, and popular handbooks of Calvinist doctrine all at various times initiated fresh phases in his spiritual life (cf. paras 15, 20, 26, 37, 41). And the fact that he was such a responsive subject presupposes earlier influences which he does not mention, although their existence is hinted at in some of his early attitudes, such as his sense of dismay when he heard a religious man swear, and his awareness of God's claim upon him as an intolerable pressure (cf. para. 10f). Nor does he pursue his course in complete isolation. Passing references to his friend Harry and the baleful influence of the Ranters, to the ministry of John Gifford, to his own occasional consultation with others, and even the bare location of particular events – on the muddy road to Elstow, 'in a good mans Shop', or at the fireside with his wife – serve with spare strokes to sketch in a physical and social setting (cf. paras 51, 174, 262). Such references probably occur almost as frequently as they do in Goodwin, for instance, but they mean less to us. This is partly because Bunyan is more of an individualist, while Goodwin at Cambridge clearly shared in a powerful group experience. More important is the force of the language in which he portrays his inward life; his imagery of strain and conflict and violence might alone be enough to overwhelm our faint impressions of his outward circumstances. But there is a more cohesive pattern of allusion there which forces another world into our consciousness. This comes from the way Bunyan again and again pictures himself as a man driven by a tempest across a bare landscape. This, we feel, is the world to which he was most alive at this time.

Of course, the comparison of spiritual turmoil with physical storms was the merest commonplace. Bunyan's power to remint the clichés must have come at least in part from his characteristic apprehension of experience; he was hardly conscious of using figurative language at all, but claimed to 'be plain and simple, and lay down the thing as it was' (Preface, p. 3). At all events, his sustained use of the storm imagery provides a dramatic introduction to his first great period of temptations:

> For about the space of a month after, a very great storm came down upon me, which handled me twenty times worse than all I had met with before: it came stealing upon me, now by one piece, then by another; first all my comfort was taken from me, then darkness seized upon me; after which whole flouds of Blasphemies, both against God, Christ, and the

Scriptures, was poured upon my spirit, to my great confusion and astonishment (para. 96).

The rhythm of his prose here follows the buffeting of the storm and he is left cowering. And after these hammer-like blows the rhythm changes a few lines later to reproduce the swirl and drone of the whirlwind:

> These suggestions (with many other which at this time I may not, nor dare not utter, neither by word nor pen) did make such a seizure upon my spirit, and did so over-weigh my heart, both with their number, continuance, and fiery force, that I felt as if there were nothing else but these from morning to night within me, and as though, indeed, there could be room for nothing else; and also concluded God had in very wrath to my Soul given me up to them, to be carried away with them, as with a mighty whirlwind (para. 99).

The storm image has been prepared for by an earlier reference, and by the audible voice which caused him to turn his head, warning that 'a cloud and a storm' was coming (paras 78, 93 – quoted on p. 97 above). The observation that the voice seemed to come from a man 'at a great distance' in an unlocalized setting places Bunyan for us in an empty landscape exposed to the full fury of the elements.

After these sustained allusions, the reader is receptive to briefer references which now come quite frequently. There is the 'noise and strength and force' of the temptations which 'would drown and overflow' everything else, and a sentence that falls 'like a hot thunder-bolt' on his conscience, while he is 'as with a Tempest driven away from God'. He refers to considerations that give him 'shelter' and to short periods of peace in the conscience 'where but just now did reign and rage the Law' (paras 100, 127, 163, 188). At another time, when in headlong flight from God, even the texts that come into his mind are evocative of this inner landscape:

> But blessed be his grace, that scripture, in these flying fits would call as running after me, *I have blotted out as a thick cloud thy transgression, and, as a cloud thy sins: Return unto me, for I have redeemed thee*, Isa. 44.22. . . . Indeed, this would make me make a little stop, and, as it were, look over my shoulder behind me, to see if I could discern that the

God of grace did follow me with a pardon in his hand, but
I could no sooner do that, but all would be clouded and
darkened again . . . (para. 173).

Bunyan's spiritual life is so completely realized in physical terms
here that we see him essentially as a man on a journey, beset by
storm and cloud, rather than as a tradesman going about his work
in a rural community. And as his troubles begin to grow less, there
is still continuity in the allusions: 'And now remained only the
hinder part of the Tempest, for the thunder was gone beyond me,
onely some drops did still remain, that now and then would fall
upon me', while a little later he speaks of being 'torn and rent by
the thunderings of his Justice' (paras 228, 247).

While the storm is thus subsiding he begins to emerge in a new
setting, as a fugitive outside one of the Cities of Refuge, fleeing
from the avenger of blood, and facing the Elders of the City, who
are the apostles and authors of the New Testament, judging him
by the Word (cf. paras 209f, 218, 245, 248).

There are many other images – especially those of imprisonment, conflict, and physical restraint – which bear witness to a
remarkable correspondence between Bunyan's modes of perception and the conventions of allegory which he exploited in *The
Pilgrim's Progress*.[2] But the features of *Grace Abounding* which I
have discussed may help to explain some of the narrative and
dramatic power already present in the autobiography. The figure
of Satan and the half-personified Scriptures supply rudimentary
dramatis personae, and Bunyan's developing relationships with
them represent crucial areas of his subjective experience. The
imagery of tempest and landscape recurs sufficiently often for it
to reinforce the dominant mood of the central episodes, and to
provide a continuity of setting more expressive of Bunyan's felt
milieu than the fragmentary references to his physical environment.

Reliability and motives

Grace Abounding is the most well known of all Puritan autobiographies and the only one to have attracted much critical
comment. Some critics, whilst acknowledging the power of
Bunyan's prose, express doubt about his reliability and deplore
his concentration on his inward life and the 'distortions' induced

both by his theology and by his didactic purpose. This, however, is to ignore what Bunyan set out to do. Since he described his task as a 'relation of the merciful working of God upon my Soul' and it was published 'for the support of the weak and tempted People of God' (para. 1, title page), the limitations are not unreasonable. We know too that every autobiographer selects details from his past life in accordance with principles which may be both conscious and unconscious, and the reader becomes most aware of these when they run counter to his own sympathies. Thus we are told that with Bunyan 'the question of autobiographical reliability arises, *because* the religious propagandist selects and interprets the events of his life according to a scale of values very different from those of the secular historian' (my italics).[3] The naïve assumption that, regardless of purpose, any secular historian's values are intrinsically more reliable than those of a religious writer is perhaps not surprising in someone who patronizes 'poor, ignorant unstable Bunyan' and 'poor gentle harmless Cowper' as victims of a 'savage theology'.[4] But even so discerning a critic as Professor Talon has considered that Bunyan ran the risk of being inaccurate when he attributed certain fortunate incidents of his youth to a providential care which he was not aware of at the time.[5] Now the whole point of Bunyan's narrative was to speak of the undeserved mercies he had received from a God who had always loved him, and his unregenerate years were, by definition, those in which blessings had been unrecognized.

Bunyan has, however, been well served by some of his recent critics, not least by Talon himself who has exhaustively examined the problems of Bunyan's sincerity, of the propriety of his calling himself the chief of sinners, and of the way his narrative was subtly shaped by many pressures. Talon's conclusion is that 'He achieves sincerity in so far as it is compatible with human forces. And although his beliefs are the cause of a slight distorting of his book, they nevertheless guarantee its veracity.'[6] He also makes perceptive comments on Bunyan's psychology with reference to both his experience and his art. 'Truth', he says,

is poetry reborn to existence in a memory that is warmer, intenser and vaster than the reality. The march forward down the course of the years offers fewer surprises than the voyage backwards into the soul where lie the voyager's first horizons. So art flourishes in the story when it grows out of the natural, and everyday life despoils itself so as to rise to the eternal (p. 134).

This last point is also made by Professor Roger Sharrock when he identifies *Grace Abounding* as the greatest of Puritan spiritual autobiographies, 'because its exploitation of the providences behind familiar, everyday things is never trivial'.[7] Sharrock emphasizes too that if we are to understand Bunyan we must begin by accepting him on his own terms; we lose more than we gain if we translate his theological categories into psychological ones and dismiss his religion as a curiosity irrelevant to the twentieth century:

> The saints and mystics are not psychopathological cases, each enclosed in a private universe of illusion, nor even delightful eccentrics. Bunyan's good and evil are our good and evil, however harsh and strange the shapes of damnation and election which his vision assumes. What does mark him off is the plunge into faith that he makes (p. 62).

So if his story is shaped by his unique personality and implies an intensity and heroism shared by very few of his readers, he is nevertheless justified in claiming a universal application for it:

> If you have sinned against light, if you are tempted to blaspheme, if you are down in despair, if you think *God* fights against you, or if heaven is hid from your eyes; remember 'twas thus with your father, *but out of them all the Lord delivered me*.[8]

Some of Bunyan's experiences were like the doubts and depressions of people like E.R., John Rogers, and Hannah Allen: the moods of excessive scrupulosity, the fear of having missed his time of calling, the recurring complaint that of all God's creatures man alone had to endure uncertainty. But there are important differences as well. Bunyan never attempted suicide, as all these others apparently did; and for all his morbid obsessions he shows no trace of the wilfulness and self-indulgence with which they clung to their misery. He never surrendered; he constantly sought, and was ready to grasp, any vestige of hope, though even in his most miserable moments he wanted truth rather than comfort. To label him as a pathological case may not be medically unjustified, but far from discrediting his heroism this would underline it.

> Who so beset him round,
> With dismal *Storys*,
> Do but themselves Confound;
> His Strength the *more is*.[9]

We do not find many understatements in Puritan writings, but Bunyan surely made one when he said of the three or four texts that condemned him, 'I could hardly forbear at some times, but to wish them out of the Book'.[10] Whatever our interpretation of his difficulties may be, he saw himself as consistently searching for an objective basis for reconciliation in Biblical doctrine. It is true that emotional pressures long prevented him from looking rationally at the nature of his sin. But he did eventually do so – and then analysed it with characteristic pastoral precision (paras 220–8, 236–44).

Though this explaining and interpretation was Bunyan's primary concern, we cannot avoid the impression that his strongest motive arose from a need while in prison to assure himself of the pattern and meaning of what had happened to him. 'Bunyan', writes Talon, 'was haunted by the desire to survey his whole life in one glance, to hold his soul in his hands, the better to possess himself.'[11] Puritan as he was, he inevitably (and probably instantaneously) saw such an account as having a 'use' in edification. Hence he explicitly relates how he learnt from his experiences, how these experiences formed the basis of his preaching; and at one point he addresses the reader directly with words of counsel. Some of the things he added to later editions show his desire to reinforce the teaching potential of his book. After having mentioned, for instance, a particularly naïve conviction that he once had, he adds to the third edition the comment, 'This, I then verily believed' (para. 68). Re-reading the episode after a lapse of years he sees it in different perspective, more from the reader's viewpoint, and by drawing attention to an aspect of his own former immaturity he encourages others to admit to theirs, with the implication that they too can overcome such limitations.

This theme of overcoming, of the possibility of progress to final victory, is the great positive message of his experience, and he sounds an unmistakable note of triumph at strategic points in the

I   119

book. It runs through the Preface, where the achievements of Moses, Samson, and David are recalled; and in reviving the memory of his fears and doubts he becomes more aware of how much he has achieved (Preface, p. 3):

> they are as the head of *Goliah* in my hand. There was nothing to *David* like *Goliahs* sword, even that sword that should have been sheathed in his bowels; for the very sight and remembrance of that, did preach forth *Gods* Deliverance to him.

In what are almost his last words he speaks of 'the spoils won in Battel', and the main narrative of conversion fitly ends with the great vision of Mount Zion and 'an innumerable company of Angels', after which, he recalls, 'I could scarce lie in my Bed for joy, and peace, and triumph, thorow Christ'. His tone is that of a man who has come through his doubt and depression and is ready to face whatever comes, whether imprisonment, or slander, or anything else: 'My Foes have mist their mark in this their shooting at me. I am not the man' (paras 339, 262ff, 263, 314, 339).

Most Puritan biographical writings were justified on the grounds that 'Examples are more powerful than precepts'. And if the writer's limitations all too often cause the work itself to belie the axiom, Bunyan's own narrative skill ensures that there is at least one effective vindication of it.

NOTES

1 Henri Talon, *John Bunyan*, 1951, p. 68.
2 Cf. Roger Sharrock, 'Spiritual Autobiography in "The Pilgrim's Progress"', *Review of English Studies*, Vol. 24, April 1948, pp. 102–19.
3 Margaret Bottrall, *Every Man a Phoenix*, 1958, p. 85.
4 *Ibid.*, pp. 106f.
5 Talon, *op. cit.*, p. 20.
6 *Ibid.*, p. 29.
7 Roger Sharrock, *John Bunyan*, 1954, p. 61.
8 *Grace Abounding*, Preface, p. 3.
9 *The Pilgrim's Progress*, ed. J. B. Wharey, 2nd ed., Oxford, 1960, p. 295.
10 *Grace Abounding*, para. 208.
11 Talon, *op. cit.*, p. 132.

Chapter 8

Reliquiae Baxterianae

As the title suggests, the autobiography of Richard Baxter was published posthumously from manuscripts left when he died in 1691. To his friend Matthew Sylvester he bequeathed the task of editing them and supervising publication, a responsibility which Sylvester found heavy indeed, oppressed as he was with ill health, a busy pastorate, and the impatience of Baxter's admirers. However, in 1696 the long-awaited memoirs appeared in a folio volume of just over 800 pages. Interwoven with Baxter's personal narrative and his replies to attacks made on him we find here his record of public events from the beginning of the Civil War until 1685, wide-ranging comment on political and ecclesiastical affairs with elaborate documentation and an almost day-to-day account of the Savoy Conference, characters or 'profiles' of national figures, obituary notices, book reviews, accounts of pamphlet wars and their impact on the public, and summaries of much of the advice on personal problems which he gave to correspondents. Hence we see the aptness of Sylvester's comment that 'the Author wrote this History, *sparsim & raptim*, and it was rather a Rhapsody than one continued Work'.[1] Even after incorporating many letters and miscellaneous papers in the main narrative, the editor found it necessary to relegate others to a bulky appendix. The book in fact contains a great deal of material that Baxter would have found other outlets for had he lived later: in our own day, for instance, we might well have been reading some of it in the Sunday supplements, the weekly reviews, the *British Weekly*, and letters to *The Times*. The folio suffers much from Sylvester's editorial timidity and the true quality of the work was not released for the common reader until J. M. Lloyd Thomas published his intelligent and sensitive abridgment in 1925; this edition (available in Everyman's Library) will undoubtedly remain the standard one for many years to come. However, since Lloyd Thomas had to miss out many good and important things in reducing the narrative to about one-fifth of the original, I have used the folio, and all references are to this edition.

In this chapter I attempt to identify the main strands of Baxter's recorded experience, to consider the style and structure of the work in relation to his themes, and to offer some conclusions on the place of the *Reliquiae* in the Puritan tradition of spiritual autobiography.

Baxter's motives were like those of many of his contemporaries who published their memoirs: to praise God for undeserved mercies, to defend his own reputation from detractors, and to warn young Christians by his mistakes and failings; though here he characteristically adds that he would also like to help them 'to reverence ripe experienced Age, and to take heed of taking such for their Chief Guides as have nothing but immature and unexperienced Judgments, with fervent Affections, and free confident Expressions' (I, 136). Above all he was concerned 'to prevent the defective performance of this Task, by some overvaluing Brethren, who I know intended it' (I, 136).

The greater part of Books I and II was written in 1664 and 1665 and covers the Civil Wars, Baxter's ministry at Kidderminster throughout the Commonwealth and Protectorate, and his work for church unity after the Restoration. Book III was added at various times between 1670 and 1685 and includes the story of his persecution and sufferings in those years.

Spiritual development

As we should expect, it is in the earlier part of the book that Baxter says most about his spiritual development. He was well aware that his readers were eagerly expecting revelations of his 'Soul Experiments' but he may well have disappointed some of them. Concerning detailed accounts of spiritual experiences he says,

I think it somewhat unsavory to recite them; seeing God's Dealings are much what the same with all his Servants in the main, . . . Nor have I any thing extraordinary to glory in, which is not common to the rest of my Brethren, who have the same Spirit, and are Servants of the same Lord (I, 124).

But what he does give us is at once more concise and more comprehensive than the traditional kind of narrative, the 'Actual Motions and Affections' (I, 136), which his admirers may have wished for. The substance of what he has to say on this matter is compressed into fourteen pages of the folio and consists of a review of his changing attitudes.

The process of his conversion is described in the opening pages and is one of the most balanced and sober accounts in the whole Puritan corpus. It bears out Baxter's claim that he experienced nothing not common to his brethren, but his insight, self-analysis, and narrative skill endow the traditional pattern with new power and immediacy. He admits to many common vanities and excesses and to 'Ambitious desires after *Literate Fame*' (I, 5). Other convictions of sin came after he had robbed an orchard with two other boys, and shortly after this, when he was fifteen, he was deeply influenced by 'an old torn Book' which a local labouring man had lent his father. This was *A Book of Christian Exercises pertaining to Resolution*, Edmund Bunny's adaptation of a manual by the Jesuit Robert Parsons, and universally referred to as *Bunny's Resolution*. With this book, said Baxter, 'it pleased God to awaken my Soul, and shew me the folly of Sinning, and the misery of the Wicked, and the unexpressible weight of things Eternal, and the necessity of resolving on a Holy Life. . . . The same things which I knew before came now in another manner, with Light, and Sense and Seriousness to my Heart' (I, 3). We may note in passing how Baxter's cadence here recalls that of Bunyan; more significant is the fact that in these few lines we have the summary of his labour and concern for the next sixty years: the 'folly of sinning' and the 'unexpressible weight of things Eternal' were two convictions which remained fundamental to his whole thought and on which he consistently based his appeals in preaching. Whether or not he could have verbalized his condition in this way when he was fifteen, it is clear that in later life this was the great moment of awakening that he looked back to. From that time he began to live with a 'throbbing Conscience' (I, 3), and through this experience came the first hints of a vocation. But the convolutions of his experience were such that in recording it he was unwilling even here to define the outlines too sharply: 'Yet whether sincere Conversion began *now*, or *before*, or *after*, I was never able to this day to know' (I, 3). This is one of the many places in Baxter's memoirs where we become aware of the fusion of his personal experience with the main Puritan tradition; for all their keen awareness of the utter contrast between darkness and light, sin and grace, the flesh and the spirit, the most articulate of the seventeenth-century Puritans were reluctant to highlight the drama of conversion in a way that would oversimplify the experience. And Baxter had many struggles ahead before he was confirmed in his faith. Chronic ill health and the expectation of an early death were among the first of his trials: 'Thus was I long kept with the Calls of approaching Death at one Ear, and the Questionings of a doubtful Conscience at the other!' (I, 5). The imagery here goes back through Puritan tradition to medieval allegory. This double assault of death and conscience – the physical threat and the psychological one – came at a period when Baxter was having many doubts about his salvation, largely arising from a mistrust of the validity of his experiences, but intermittent reassurances ultimately led to a more settled condition.

Whilst the pattern of Baxter's conversion is basically unexceptional, three features of his account call for comment, particularly as they are prominent throughout the whole of the *Reliquiae*. First is the extent to which his experience was moulded by the books he read; second, his constant awareness of the interpenetration of the divine and the human; third, the central importance he attached to reason in the Christian life.

Books

Bunny's Resolution was only the first of many books which brought him illumination, insight, challenge, and consolation. Other classics of practical divinity came into his hands at an early age – he mentions works of Sibbs, Perkins and Bradford among others. And one of his serious early worries arose directly out of his reading, since he could not reconcile the workings of the Spirit in his own heart with the method described in some of the standard treatises on conversion; however he also derived peace and comfort from the 'Reading of many Consolatory Books'

(I, 9) and the realization that 'God breaketh not all Men's hearts alike' (I, 7). Because of the part played by reading in his youth he could claim that 'thus (without any means but Books) was God pleased to resolve me for himself' (I, 4). The private tutor he had was a man of mean scholarship, 'only', said Baxter, 'he loved me, and allowed me *Books and Time* enough' (I, 4). This was perhaps the best service he could have rendered him, as there is no evidence that Baxter's bookishness hindered his ability to make satisfactory social relationships. His lack of a university education may well have been responsible for the exalted opinion he long had of recondite and difficult writings, but as he became more learned himself he was less overawed by them, 'especially those that think themselves the wisest: And the better I am acquainted with them, the more I perceive that we are all yet in the dark' (I, 129).

The impact of the printed word which he experienced in his youth probably accounts for the fact that of all his labours Baxter attached the most importance not to his direct part in public affairs, nor even to his preaching and pastoral work, but to his writings, to which he gave more and more of his time as first illness and later persecution restricted his other activities. Having accepted this commitment, as one that would make the best use of his talents in the prevailing circumstances, he found himself having to cope with clamouring and multifarious pressures from all sides. His friends wanted more practical directions on the Christian life or the problems of church government; other divines urged him to work at something weightier which would bring him an enduring reputation in theological studies; and remembering the effect on the Parliamentary troops of broadsheets and pamphlets in the Civil War, he felt it impossible to neglect these either. He drafted petitions, argued the non-conformist case repeatedly and at length in voluminous correspondence as well as in print. As the target for attack in over fifty published works, he was obliged to answer in detail as many of them as had attracted significant attention; and when reply was met with counter-reply he carried on the war with vigour, even obtaining his opponents' books in proof from the printers so that his own answers might appear with the least possible delay. It is reassuring to learn that Baxter's energies were not indiscriminately directed. Even when he had overcome misgivings at conspiring to overload the world with books (cf. I, 106), he was not prepared to waste time when his opponent was only prepared to keep the discussion at a superficial level:

> When I perceive People . . . to dispute those things which they never throughly studied, or expect I should debate the case with them, as if an hours talk would serve instead of an acute understanding and seven years study, I have no Zeal to make them of my Opinion (I, 138).

One wonders how quickly social and political issues in our own day would change their pattern if all who influence the public through the mass media became convinced that Baxter's approach was the right one. At all events, both his vocation as a writer and the values which governed his practice derived from the depth of his early reading.

The divine and the human

The second significant feature of Baxter's conversion story is his keen awareness of the baffling interpenetration of the divine and the human in men's affairs. The doctrine of 'common' grace and 'special' grace did not obscure for him the plain fact that God works through natural means. Of course, no Puritan would have denied this, but when in their narratives they attempt to convey the experience of providential care in everyday life we often get the impression of a benevolent puppetmaster at work. With Baxter we feel that the whole process is more organic, more fully integrated into the economy of the universe. One reason for this is that he is more restrained than many of his contemporaries in attributing every incident in his life to God's direct action or unmediated initiative. I do not mean that he was in any way less continuously aware of divine sovereignty over all human affairs, however apparently trivial; it is more a question simply of the way he thought about it and expressed himself. He saw and allowed for the complexity with which the divine purpose works itself out through heredity and environment, as for instance when he described that momentous illumination he had from reading *Bunny's Resolution*: 'Whether it were that till now I came not to that maturity of Nature, which made me capable of discerning; or whether it were that this was God's appointed time, or both together, I had no lively sight and sense of what I read till now'

(I, 3). And a few pages later he commented that '*Education* is God's ordinary way for the Conveyance of his Grace, and ought no more to be set in opposition to the Spirit, than the preaching of the Word' (I, 7). Such an opposition was in fact maintained by many of the more radical Puritans, although condemned by the Calvinists as a practice which 'set the Spirit against the means'. Baxter found grace channelled through natural means in the conversation of 'some Reverend peaceable Divines' (I, 9) in the observation that other men's conditions sometimes resembled his own, in the exercise of proffering spiritual comfort to others ('While I answered their Doubts, I answered my own') (I, 9), and through the actual physical condition of his body. This wholeness of vision enabled him to make distinctions all the more effectively when necessary, as when in the course of his self-review, at the age of forty-eight, he remarked that his tendency in later years to be less emotionally dependent on the way others reacted to him was not necessarily due to growth in grace but possibly because he had at various times received enough applause and public support to meet these particular needs with regard to personal security. In accounting for the successes of his fourteen years at Kidderminster, he lists no fewer than twenty-five factors in the social and economic environment of the place which helped him to further the main aims of his work, and all of which he specifically attributes to 'that Grace which worketh by means, though with a free diversity' (I, 86).

No reader can remain unmoved by Baxter's account of his physical sufferings, whether from ill health or persecution. To these he brought the same amazingly steady acceptance of the ways of providence. Measles, smallpox, catarrh and coughs, indigestion, insomnia, haemorrhages, rheumatism, and fears of a consumption had all left their mark before he was twenty, and he continued all his life to be plagued with tumours, lameness, headaches, and what he called 'vertiginous or Stupifying Conquests of my Brain' (III, 60). But he was never melancholy and seems to have hit upon a combination of dieting and exercise which kept him active, if not free from pain, for well over half a century following his youthful fears of an early death. He complained only of the inroads upon his time which his infirmities and their necessary treatment imposed upon him: an hour to dress, and an hour's exercise before meals were the minimum demands he had to meet before the pressing claims of family, parish, and public duties, so that he counted his greatest external personal affliction to be the little time left for study and writing (I, 84). There were those who said he was a mere 'melancholy Humourist', and as such he found himself 'the Pity, or Derision of the Town' (III, 173), but there is reason to suppose that the published references, harrowing though they are, understate the extent of his physical sufferings. And of course, the effects were felt in every aspect of his life and personality, as he himself recognized when he said, 'the Case of my *Body* had a great Operation upon my Soul' (I, 9). In particular it brought him very early to a serious view of life, made him value his time and so reject all 'pastimes'; it kept him in contempt of the world and so weakened the effect of some temptations; above all it imparted urgency and feeling to his preaching: it 'a little stirred up my sluggish heart, to speak to Sinners with some Compassion, as a dying Man to dying Men' (I, 21).

Indeed, Baxter always worked with serious and thoughtful concern inside what he understood to be the sphere of duty assigned to him. Outside this area, in matters beyond his personal influence, he rested in the same powerful awareness of divine sovereignty. In public affairs he was distrustful of those who found assurance by misunderstanding providence, whether like Major-General Berry they interpreted a victory gained in battle as a sign that God had called them to govern the country, or like the Fifth Monarchy Men they initiated action themselves and attempted 'to set Christ up in his Kingdom whether he will or not' (I, 133, and cf. I, 57). Baxter's attitude was most clearly revealed in his opinion of Cromwell as Lord Protector, whom many found a problem in that he was a usurper who nevertheless promoted the interests of the gospel more than either his predecessors or his likely successors. So the question men asked was, 'Whether they should rather wish the continuance of an Usurper that will do good, or the restitution of a Rightful Governour whose followers will do hurt.' Baxter's solution did justice to both cases without equivocating:

> But for my part I thought my Duty was clear, to disown the Usurper's Sin, what Good soever he would do; and to perform all my Engagements to a Rightful Governour, leaving the Issue of all to God: but yet to commend the *Good* which a

Usurper doth, and to do any lawful thing which may provoke him to do more; and to approve of *no Evil* which is done by any, either Usurper or a lawful Governour (I, 71–2).

We see then how in his personal life, in pastoral work, and in public affairs, Baxter showed a consistent concern to act rightly combined with a relaxed acceptance of the overriding sovereignty of God.

As well as this movement of thought in intellectual and spiritual matters, we get an occasional glimpse of the actual circumstances which helped to mould Baxter's interpretation of the conditions of his day. One example must suffice. We see him hurrying towards Worcester in 1642 to have his first look at an army ready for action. Part of the Earl of Essex's force had come up to seal off Lord Byron in the city, but chaotic communications led them into a series of mistakes and they were surprised by Prince Rupert's cavalry. Baxter's tone as he narrates what follows gives us an extremely vivid impression of his reactions:

> . . . and though the Enemy pursued them no further than the Bridge, yet fled they in grievous terror to *Parshore*, and the Earl of *Essex*'s Life Guard lying there, took the Allarm that the Enemy was following them, and away they went. This Sight quickly told me the Vanity of Armies, and how little Confidence is to be placed in them (I, 42).

The context of this passage suggests that the studious young pastor had been ready to be impressed by the sight of men-at-arms about their business, but the almost contemptuous way in which he records the rout, and the generalization he immediately draws from it, imply that he here found himself seizing upon some evidence in support of one of his basic convictions. He watches in silence and formulates his conclusion. And such impressions as we get of Baxter's physical presence come in hints similar to this one, where his prime concern is to record his intellectual or spiritual development.

'Sober reason'

The third feature of the conversion story which is also a characteristic of the whole book is the value that Baxter places on 'sober reason' in the Christian life. From the moment that *Bunny's*

Resolution convinced him of the 'folly of sinning' he never wavered in his conviction that the way of holiness and humility was the only possible course for a sane and rational man to take: 'no shew of Reason can be brought by any Infidel in the World to excuse the Rational Creature from Loving his Maker' (I, 22). It was chiefly this which made him decide to seek ordination.

> And indeed I had such clear Convictions my self of the madness of secure presumptuous Sinners, and the unquestionable Reasons which should induce men to a holy Life, and of the unspeakable greatness of that Work, which in this hasty Inch of Time, we have all to do, that I thought that Man that could be ungodly, if he did but hear these things, was fitter for *Bedlam*, than for the Reputation of a sober rational Man: And I was so foolish as to think, that I had so much to say, and of such Convincing Evidence for a Godly Life, that Men were scarce able to withstand it; not considering what a blind and sensless Rock the Heart of an obdurate Sinner is; and that old *Adam* is too strong for young *Luther* (as he said). But these Apprehensions determined my choice (I, 12).

Like Bunyan, his great contemporary, Baxter was subjected soon after his conversion to a great storm of temptations. Bunyan's was closely connected with his gift of utterance and fascination with language, and Baxter's also centred on the things he was most sensitive to. Early doubts about his own sincerity were overcome comparatively easily, never to return. But at the time when he was ready to enter the ministry he was assaulted by temptations which were much more insistent and which brought into question the very fundamentals of his faith: 'And these Temptations assaulted me not as they do the Melancholy, with horrid vexing Importunity; but by pretence of sober Reason, they would have drawn me to a settled doubting of Christianity' (I, 21). Baxter's reaction was 'to dig to the very Foundations, and seriously to Examine the Reasons of Christianity, and to give a hearing to all that could be said against it, so that my Faith might be indeed my own' (I, 22). He questioned whether such doubts as he had were compatible with saving faith, but this difficulty was resolved by considerations drawn from his reading

> that as in the very Assenting Act of Faith there may be such

weakness, as may make us cry, *Lord increase our Faith: We believe, Lord help our [un]belief;* so when *Faith* and *Unbelief* are in their Conflict, it is the *Effects* which must shew us which of them is victorious (I, 22).

Although Baxter's struggle was more of an intellectual one, free from the 'horrid vexing Importunity' of Bunyan's, there is a more than verbal parallel here with the passage in *Grace Abounding* where texts of condemnation and promise struggled within Bunyan's mind until 'this about the sufficiency of Grace prevailed, with peace and joy' (para. 213).

Baxter refers frequently to the development of his opinions, especially on the great issues of the day – church unity, non-conformity, and liberty of conscience. In the process of making up his mind he read all the books and manuscripts on the subject that he could obtain, and a feature of the *Reliquiae* is the summaries that he gives of the main points argued by both sides in contemporary religious and political disputes. He places them concisely in their historical context, presents the information dispassionately, and adds the reasons for his own judgments. 'I never thought I understood any thing until I could *anatomize* it', he tells us (I, 6), and the pattern of his summaries probably reflects his habit of mind if not the actual process of his thinking in any particular instance. We certainly get the impression of a man unwilling to commit himself until he has examined all the available evidence, and this meant for Baxter relating his measured opinion of what he read to the circumstances of his time.

Baxter's memory has been chiefly honoured because he consistently used his enormous personal influence to urge the claims of reason and moderation amid the bitter divisions and animosities of his time. The evidence of the *Reliquiae* indicates that this is no more than a just assessment of his principles and intentions. The moral that he never tires of pointing to is that '*Overdoing* is the ordinary way of *Undoing*' (I, 27). He repeatedly draws on incidents from personal life, church life, and state affairs to show that 'rash Attempts of Head-strong People, do work against the good Ends which they themselves intend' (I, 27), and he elaborates on the implications of this with considerable insight and subtlety. The dangers of 'overdoing' impressed themselves on his mind at an early age. Whilst he was living with his tutor at Ludlow he shared a room with a companion whose zeal in reading and devotion far outran his own, who would get up in the night to say prayers and express incredulity that Baxter was not impelled to do the same. But after two years he lapsed from this fervent devotion into equally fervent spells of drunkenness, from which he periodically reacted in revulsion and panic; and when Baxter last heard of him, 'he was grown a Fudler, and Railer at strict men' (I, 4). The important thing about the balance of Baxter's own faith and practice is that while deploring this immoderate oscillation, he did not condemn the intensity of the man's spiritual exercises: in fact, he pays tribute to the stimulus he derived from his zeal and liberality. And towards the end of his life he quoted with approval the example of his mother-in-law who died at the age of ninety-six, having lived 'In constant daily acquired infirmity of body (got by avoiding all Exercise, and long secret prayer in the coldest Seasons, and such like)' (III, 190). We may note that the old lady had the advantage of 'a constitution naturally strong'. But he disapproved of the Quakers when they 'acted the Parts of Men in Raptures', and he mistrusted men like Major Harrison who was 'naturally of such a vivacity, hilarity and alacrity as another Man hath when he hath drunken a Cup too much' (I, 116; I, 57).

Baxter attributed much of the disorder of his times to the unreasoning aggression with which men of all parties reacted to what their opponents said or did. The good that Cromwell did, as well as the evil, was undone merely because he had done it (cf. I, 71); men were ready to embrace as a virtue anything that their enemies reproached them for, and when persecution inflamed the passions of both sides Baxter was appalled 'to observe how dangerously each party of the Extremes did tempt the other to impenitency and further sin!' (III, 40). Friends who visited him in prison tried to work up his feelings against 'the Prelates and their Worship', but he urged them that it was now more than ever necessary not to be carried into extremes: 'If Passion made me lose my Love, or my Religion, the loss would be my own. And Truth did not change, because I was in a Gaol. The temper of my Visitors called me much to this kind of talk' (III, 59). Excessive vehemency, even in the cause of the gospel itself, could defeat its aim, and as he reflected on the way this happened Baxter showed the sensitivity that helped to give him his unique authority both as a pastor and as a spokesman for the moderate party:

And I have perceived, that nothing so much hindreth the Reception of the Truth, as urging it on Men with too harsh Importunity, and falling too heavily on their Errors: For hereby you engage their Honour in the business, and they defend their Errors as themselves, and stir up all their Wit and Ability to oppose you: In controversies it is fierce Opposition which is the Bellows to kindle a resisting Zeal; when if they be neglected, and their Opinions lie a while despised, they usually cool and come again to themselves . . . Men are so loth to be drenched with the Truth, that I am no more for going that way to work (I, 125–6).

It was because of this that 'many honest Men of weak judgments . . . had been seduced into a disputing vein' and others had 'stept further into the contending way, than they could well get out of again' (I, 53).

The main theme of Baxter's labours throughout his life may be summarized as the attempt to bring more order, reason, and unity to human affairs. At the human level this is what the spread of the gospel would achieve, although Baxter discovered that his own efforts often seemed to have the opposite effect. The publication of his *Cure of Church Divisions* merely aroused a 'Storm of Obloquy', while *A Plea for Peace* 'greatly offended many Conformists'! (III, 70; III, 187). It was indeed a long, hard struggle. Many of his critics had not read his books for themselves, but relied on others who interpreted what he said 'by the Spectacles and Commentary of their Passions and sore Conceits' (III, 72). And when he proposed that the basis of church unity should be subscription to the Decalogue, the Lord's Prayer, and the Apostles' Creed, the objection was at once made that a Socinian or a Papist could subscribe to this. Baxter answered, 'So much the better, and so much the fitter it is to be the Matter of our Concord . . . nor must we make *new Laws* as oft as Hereticks will misinterpret and subscribe the *old*' (II, 198).

Changing attitudes

So Baxter came to see the situation of reasonable and moderate men in the Church as necessarily involving friction with both of the major contending parties, namely the forces attempting to impose ecclesiastical uniformity and those who asserted the paramount claims of individual illumination; thus 'The poor Church of Christ, the sober sound religious Part, are like Christ that was crucified between two Malefactors; the prophane and formal Persecutors on the one hand, and the Fanatick dividing Sectary on the other hand, have in all Ages been grinding the spiritual Seed, as the Corn is ground between the Millstones' (I, 103). We can sense Baxter's growing pessimism over worldly affairs as the hopes of reverend and learned men were repeatedly frustrated, sometimes as much by their own pettiness as by their opponents' malice. He seems to have become increasingly depressed at the immense complexity of human needs and behaviour. His awareness of the problems is apparent quite early in the book, particularly in the long passage of self-review which concludes Book I; but it becomes more insistent later on and forms a melancholy refrain to the episodes of his later years. He laments the cost to the nation of learning from the government's mistakes, when many hundreds of ministers lost life, liberty, or maintenance for refusing oaths and subscriptions that ultimately the House of Lords themselves refused: 'But though Experience teach some that will no otherwise learn; it is sad with the World, when their Rulers must learn to Govern them at so dear a Rate; and Countreys, Cities, Churches, and the Souls of Men, must pay so dear for their Governours Experience' (III, 168). And he returns with greater vehemence to another theme touched on earlier when he warns posterity of the unreliability of contemporary historians, 'Lying most impudently in Print, against the most notorious Evidence of Truth. . . . If other Historians be like some of these Times, their Assertions, when-ever they speak of such as they distaste, are to be Read, as *Hebrew*, backward' (III, 187). There is, then, a detectable change in mood as the narrative proceeds, although these sombre reflections on the sins and follies of men are the counterpart of Baxter's serious and compassionate concern for the multitudes of men, women, and children living in ignorance of the gospel – up to 50,000 of them, he tells us, in one parish without a preacher – and this concern too increased with the years and his accumulating experience of their needs. And we must remember that the last pages of his memoirs were written when he had endured over twenty years in the wilderness, during which time he had been debarred from following his vocation as a pastor and preacher.

In his self-review, written in 1664 at the age of forty-eight,

Baxter said that he did not think that his opinions had changed much over the years, although a re-reading of his earlier writings had shown them to have been based at first on inadequate evidence. He notes that he was at one time quicker at grasping new ideas, but is now more alive to 'the ways of Truth and Error . . . because I had only the *Faculty* of Knowing them, but did not *actually* know them' (I, 125) – a development in his experience of the world which corresponds to the spiritual development through which his knowledge of Christian doctrine was augmented by the 'lively sense' of the love of God (cf. I, 3). Baxter, like other Puritans, attached the utmost importance to the integration of these two kinds of knowledge, the knowledge of the head, and knowledge of the heart. One reason why he valued the 'English practical treatises' so highly was that by this means 'my *Affection* was carried on with my Judgment' (I, 6). Baxter's mind was constantly on the move, and although his deepest convictions were unshakeable he never became rigid or complacent. He constantly tested his opinions not only against experience but by being ready to modify them in the light of criticism: the best tribute he could pay his friend Sir Matthew Hale was that 'his very Questions and Objections did help me to more light than other mens solutions' (III, 47).

There is an impressive self-awareness shown in the *Reliquiae* which would alone be sufficient to rank Baxter as one of the most acute and sensitive of all seventeenth-century writers. He values, as one of the marks of growth in grace, an increasingly objective focus in his spiritual life – less concern with his own feelings and penitential tears, and more awareness of the value of love and praise; he places less emphasis on finding the accepted marks of sincerity in his heart and more on the contemplation of Christ's glorious work. How was Baxter able to plot his inner landscape in such convincing detail? The fourteen folio pages of his self-review immediately follow a detailed survey of his writings which he had lately been re-reading, and many of the comments he makes about his changing opinions derive from his reflections on what he had written in the past. But he had published very little before 1658, when he was over forty, and so his analysis must have been based on other records of some kind. It is notoriously difficult for any man to be aware of how his attitudes change unless he has something in writing to refer to. Now we know that when he was younger Baxter wrote 'a daily Catalogue of . . . Mercies and Sins' (I, 21), and that even in subsequent years he kept up a more selective record. It is highly likely, therefore, that he drew on these private notes when he came to plot his spiritual development more systematically in 1664. Not otherwise could he have pinpointed so many factors which were being constantly and insensibly modified in the slow flux of experience.

Influences and style

It is difficult to be certain of what literary influences there were on Baxter's autobiography. His use of *sententiae* may owe something to Bacon, whose essays he quotes on three occasions. There is an echo of Paul's catalogue of trials in Baxter's list of the various men who had written books against him (cf. I, 106), and a fainter echo of the apostle's farewell to the Ephesian elders (cf. Acts 20) in the account of his silencing in 1662:

> Having parted with my dear Flock (I need not say, with
> mutual sense and tears) I left Mr. *Baldwin* to live privately
> among them, and oversee them in my stead, and visit them
> from House to House; advising them, notwithstanding all the
> Injuries they had received, and all the Failings of the
> Ministers that preached to them, and the Defects of the
> present Way of Worship, that they should keep to the
> Publick Assemblies, and make use of such Helps as might be
> had in Publick, together with their private Helps . . . (II, 376).

The fact that his first recorded conviction of sin followed the robbing of an orchard is of course paralleled in Augustine's *Confessions*. Baxter himself remarked on this, and possibly his reading of Augustine caused him like others to throw into prominence this incident rather than any one of a number of others that might have seemed equally significant at the time they happened. What is certain is that the Puritan tradition accounts for much that we find in the pattern of his spiritual life, in his reactions to these experiences, and in the actual phrasing of the narrative. He shared common ground with Bunyan, for instance, in being attracted first to the historical parts of Scripture, in being 'bewitched with a love of Romances, Fables and old Tales' (I, 2), in the way he was influenced by some old practical Puritan writings found at home, and in being subjected in later life to various petty slanders. Like Milton, whom the Civil Wars called from his studies to embark 'in a troubl'd sea of noises and hoars disputes', Baxter felt it his duty to be with the army, although 'I was loth to leave my Studies, and Friends, and Quietness at *Coventry*' (I, 51). And he shares with a number of earlier Puritan writers, notably Richard Kilby, passages of desperate devotional power forged out of the agony of prolonged physical suffering. There is art here, as through the solemn rhythms of his prose Baxter transmutes the sordid and nagging horror of the plan that racked him:

> But God was pleased quickly to put me past all fear of Man, and all desire of avoiding suffering from them by Concealment; by laying on me more himself than Man can do. Their Imprisonment, with tolerable Health, would have seemed a Palace to me; And had they put me to death for such a Duty as they Persecute me, it would have been a joyful end of my Calamity. But day and night I groan and languish under God's just afflicting hand; The pain which before only tired my Reins, and tore my Bowels, now also fell upon my Bladder, and scarce any part or hour is free. As Waves follow Waves in the Tempestuous Seas, so one pain and danger followeth another, in this sinful miserable Flesh: I die daily, and yet remain alive: God, in his great Mercy, knowing my dulness in health and ease, doth make it much easier to repent and hate my sin, and loath my self, and contemn the World, and submit to the Sentence of death with willingness, than otherwise it was ever like to have been. O how little is it that wrathful Enemies can do against us, in comparison of what our sin, and the Justice of God can do? And O how little is it that the best and kindest of Friends can do, for a pained Body, or a guilty sinful Soul, in comparison of one gracious look or word from God. Woe be to him that hath no better help than Man: And blessed is he whose help and hope is in the Lord (III, 192).

There is little direct Biblical influence in the language of the *Reliquiae*. We get a reference to oaths not being 'as easily shak'd off as *Sampson's* Cords' and to the true Church, afflicted by persecutors from above and schismatics from below, being 'like Christ that was crucified between two Malefactors'; but Baxter draws many more of his figures from popular speech. He writes of James Harrington being 'in a *Bethlehem* Rage' and says of the King: 'we . . . do but cut his Throat in kindness; for we pull down the House that he may be Master of it' (I, 64; I, 103; I, 118; I, 71). His most characteristic figure is the aphorism, which he employs very frequently to embody his ultimate comment on a character, an argument, or an incident: 'Soldiers may most easily be had when there is least need of them'; 'Disorderly means do generally bring forth more Disorders, and seldom attain any good end for which they are used' (I, 68; I, 19). Just how integral a part of Baxter's style this feature is can be seen in the fact that two phrases I have already quoted might serve to summarize the essential elements of his life and thought: his central regard for reason and moderation in the watchword, '*Overdoing* is the ordinary way of *Undoing*', and his lifelong passion for the gospel in his concern 'to speak to Sinners with some Compassion, as a dying Man to dying Men' (I, 27; I, 21). These two precepts could easily become incompatible, the one commending prudence, the other urging an almost reckless dedication; it is a measure of Baxter's greatness and sanity that whilst we are convinced of his commitment to both attitudes, we are also compelled to accept that he held them in balance, without compromise, exploring their implications at every stage of his experience.

He makes frequent and striking use of deflating imagery to ridicule his opponents, such as the 'Fanaticks . . . who set up and pull'd down Governments as boldly as if they were making a Lord of a Maygame', and the 'carnal, worldly, proud, ungodly Clergie' who would 'patch up a few good words together to talk the People asleep with on *Sunday*; and all the rest of the Week go with them to the Alehouse, and harden them in their Sin' (II, 214, III, 142, I, 72). He can also be judiciously ironical – 'they were very few of them sick of the Disease called tenderness of Conscience, or Scrupulosity' – and occasionally delights us with a sarcastic thrust such as the comment on William Dell, 'who took *Reason, Sound Doctrine, Order* and *Concord* to be the intollerable Maladies of Church and State, because they were the greatest Strangers to his Mind' (I, 64).

Like other Puritans, Baxter was not greatly concerned to develop a polished style. He laboured primarily with an eye to the needs of the common people whom he wrote for: 'But the

Women and weaker sort I found could not so well improve clear Reason, as they can a few comfortable, warm and pretty Sentences; it is Style and not Reason which doth most with them' (I, 109). Basically he appears to have aimed at the expression of 'clear reason': style (meaning 'Ornaments' and 'Citations of Authors') being added if he had the time. An occasional paromoion (e.g. 'while he *disc*ountenanced them, he *disc*ontented them') (I, 61) catches our attention only because of its rarity. The prolixity which was his chief fault was perhaps encouraged by the needs of the 'ignorant, rude and revelling People' (I, 20), who were his pastoral charge for many years, and of course by his lack of time for revision. As Miss Joan Webber points out, in a fine essay on Baxter's style and personality, 'He is not tedious, but . . . his idea of brevity is unique'.[2] Yet he does vary his phrasing, reinforcing points with examples, comparisons, and effective imagery, and working with an intuitive sense of rhythm which allows him to accumulate a succession of statements before rounding off the period with a more weighty member. In this way he contrives to take us through a great deal of matter in a single paragraph without making us feel that we are reading a bare catalogue. This technique stands him in good stead when, with his lifelong predilection for analysis, he wants to summarize the many factors which contribute to the complexity of a situation, the success or failure of a venture, or the pros and cons of a controversy. The following passage is one of the shorter examples of the kind of sequence that occurs frequently in the *Reliquiae*:

. . . So that if a Man did but pray in his Family, or were but heard repeat a Sermon, or sing a Psalm, they presently cried out, *Rebels*, *Round-heads*, and all their Money and Goods that were portable proved guilty, how innocent soever they were themselves. I suppose this was kept from the knowledge of the King, and perhaps of many sober Lords of his Council: . . . But upon my certain knowledge this was it that filled the Armies and Garrisons of the Parliament with sober, pious Men. Thousands had no mind to meddle with the Wars, but greatly desired to live peaceably at home, when the Rage of Soldiers and Drunkards would not suffer them: some stayed till they had been imprisoned; some till they had been plundered, perhaps twice or thrice over, and nothing left

them; some were quite tired out with the abuse of all Comers
that quartered on them; and some by the insolency of their
Neighbours; but most were afraid of their Lives; and so
they sought refuge in the Parliaments Garrisons (I, 44).

At the risk of indulging in an over-technical digression I should
like to discuss a single paragraph in some detail. It will help, I
think, to sum up the ways in which Baxter's style fits his purpose
so well. The passage which follows describes his early contacts
with nonconformists and immediately follows an explanation
of three matters on which he was even then unwilling to
conform.

But most of this I kept to my self. I daily disputed against
the Nonconformists; for I found their Censoriousness and
Inclinations towards Seperation (in the weaker sort of them)
to be a Threatning Evil, and contrary to Christian Charity
on one side, as Persecution is on the other. Some of them
that pretended to much Learning, engaged me in Writing to
dispute the Case of Kneeling at the Sacraments; which I
followed till they gave it over. I laboured continually to
repress their Censoriousness, and the boldness and bitterness
of their language against the Bishops, and to reduce them
to greater Patience and Charity. But I found that their
Sufferings from the Bishops were the great Impediment of
my Success, and that he that will blow the Coals must not
wonder if some sparks do fly in his face; and that to persecute
Men, and then call them to Charity, is like whipping
Children to make them give over Crying. The stronger sort of
Christians can bear Mulcts and Imprisonments and
Reproaches for obeying God and Conscience, without abating
their Charity or their Weakness to their Persecutors; but to
expect this from all the weak and injudicious, the young and
passionate, is against all Reason and Experience: I saw that
he that will be loved, must love; and he that rather chooseth
to be more *feared* than *loved*, must expect to be hated, or
loved but diminutively: And he that will have *Children*, must
be a *Father*: and he that will be a Tyrant must be contented
with Slaves (I, 14).

Now many characteristic features of Baxter's personality and literary style can be seen here: the tone of moderation which sees the evils of extreme attitudes, the readiness to engage in controversy, imagery drawn from common life (perhaps proverbial), the reinforcement of a point with a preacher's homely similitude, the concern for what is practical for everyone in Christian living, realistic reflection from pastoral observation, the appeal to reason and experience, and the aphorisms which distil his mature conclusion.

The opening sentence would appear to belong to the end of the preceding paragraph, but it gains considerable dramatic effect from being where it is. The linked sentences which follow reproduce the process of Baxter's thought, which is in two movements, elaborating in turn the evils of censoriousness and those of persecution. We are first given the theme and occasion of his experience while the rest of the period specifies the areas of dispute; the two succeeding periods give Baxter's reaction to the nonconformists but without adding any new ideas on the subject. We then move on to the implications of the bishops' persecution, this theme having already been adumbrated. Logically there is nothing to add to the words, 'But I found that their Sufferings from the Bishops were the great Impediment of my Success'; what is important however is the *imaginative* progress in which Baxter illuminates successive facets of the idea, so that the external narrative of the first part of the paragraph is complemented by a process in which the reader seems to be participating in the writer's own reflections as they occur. The four aphorisms which conclude are linked by co-ordinating conjunctions which also have no logical additive force: they again connect successive efforts of the imagination to realize the same idea, though they also serve to modify the abruptness of successive *sententiae* and harmonize them with the flow of the preceding sentences.[3]

Bunyan wanted to be 'plain and simple, and lay down the thing as it was'.[4] Baxter, writing at almost the same time, said that he 'scarce ever wrote one Sheet twice over, nor stayed to make any Blots or Interlinings, but was fain to let it go as it was first conceived' (I, 124). With neither men was the style a considered matter, yet in the work of both of them the reader quickly recognizes a voice related to the personality of the writer. In Baxter's case, the main preoccupations of his life and thought, and the viewpoint he had of them, demanded a style that would move easily from personal to public affairs, from inner experience to outward action, so that each would illuminate the other. And we have seen that the characteristic structure and movement of his prose do this. He exemplified the Puritan concern to see the divine will fulfilled in the 'secular' world. The idea that a man might serve God as well in his worldly employment as in a religious vocation had always been a part of Puritan teaching, and Baxter's attitude implied a development of this principle. The totality of his Christian commitment gave a kind of detachment to his observations on the phenomenal world, which he could describe without constant mention of supernatural reference points. His conviction of God's sovereignty was such that he was not continuously impelled to explain the religious significance of social and political events; he could do so eloquently and effectively on occasion, but much of the narrative of both public affairs and his private life carries implicit rather than explicit overtones of spiritual significances.

He lived and wrote at a time when a polarization of the sacred and the secular was becoming apparent. And this process itself seems to have been part of a wider, more complex movement within the mind and sensibility of Western man. The dichotomy between mind and body, the opposition of grace and nature, the growing self-consciousness of the individual in relation to society, were other aspects of this change that are reflected in Puritanism as in the whole social, cultural and intellectual life of the time. The tone of the *Reliquiae* suggests that Baxter was fully adjusted to what was going on; he was intellectually reconciled to his own age (in a way that Donne and Milton, for instance, were not) however much he might lament its sin and folly and divisions. His attitude to toleration can be taken as an example. Toleration was becoming possible partly because men were ceasing to be identified utterly with the opinions they held, and it is significant that Baxter could complain that the persecuting Anglican bishops most closely resembled the Papists in that 'they agree in destroying Men for their Opinions and Ceremonies sake' (II, 344). We have already seen how in trying to persuade men he thought it best to avoid driving them to 'defend their Errors as themselves' (cf. p. 133 above). Just as the Papists found it reasonable to identify men with their opinions, so Baxter found it reasonable to distinguish them, and in this he was in the van of his age.

And because he put his principles into practice here as everywhere, the total impact of the *Reliquiae* is of a unified sensibility: Baxter harmonized the multifarious tensions between the inner and outer worlds of his experience by the sheer integrity of his faith, subserved by the powers of his formidable intellect. We are made aware, in his record of his life and times, of the growing division between the sacred and the secular but also of constant busy traffic between them. For all its diffuseness this rag-bag of a book gives us a more fully rounded portrait of man as the 'great amphibium', the heir of two worlds, than we get in any other spiritual autobiography of the period. We do not participate in the intense psychological battles which some men, including Bunyan, recorded for us; yet we know Baxter's mind and heart better than any of them, and we know him in a fuller context of relationships.

NOTES

1 *Reliquiae Baxterianae*, 1696, sig. b2. All references in this chapter are to this edition. The pagination of the main sections of the volume is:

Preface   Sig. b recto–d verso.
Lib. I, Part I. pp.   1–138
        Part II. pp. 138–448
Part III.   pp.   1–200
Appendices (not quoted) pp. 1–132

References will be given to part and page.
2 Joan Webber, *The Eloquent 'I'*, p. 144.
3 These features of Baxter's syntax are characteristic of what M. W. Croll called the Baroque style. See 'The Baroque style in prose', *Studies in English Philology in Honor of Frederick Klaeber*, eds Kemp Malone and Martin B. Ruud, Univ. of Minnesota Press, 1929, pp. 427–56.
4 *Grace Abounding*, Preface.

Chapter 9

The Vulgar Prophets

The ordinary Puritan claimed no unique relationship with God beyond the fact that he had experienced a personal call to holiness and could be sure of its effectiveness because the results were the same for him as they had been for other believers. There are, however, many references in the Commonwealth period to vulgar prophets and 'horrid blasphemers' who claimed to be inspired in a special way. These men said they had a public mission and had been driven to their task either by extraordinary visions or by mysterious and irresistible inward pressure. Some eight or nine of them wrote spiritual autobiographies, and these were not intended for the edification of themselves or others, but to give their credentials as seers or prophets, to testify to the authenticity of their visions, warnings, and heterodox opinions. They were emphatically not ordinary converts, but men marked out by God to be a 'sign and wonder' to their generation. Most of them were mentally unbalanced, but they sometimes wrote with a persuasive vitality and intensity.

We can distinguish two kinds of testimonies according to the nature of the prophets' experiences. Some describe in great detail their apocalyptic visions and the peculiar effects which these induced in them. Insofar as any conversion is mentioned it is not from a state of sin to a state of grace, for few of them seem at all concerned with personal sinfulness; it is rather a record of their turning from everyday affairs to a divine mission that overrides every other concern. Others narrate a spiritual pilgrimage, showing how they failed to find satisfaction in any of the existing religious bodies and were eventually brought to the true faith by some form of direct revelation. Here again the writer is concerned to justify himself, and in the record of his wanderings attempts to expose the futility of all accepted forms of belief and worship.

Signs and wonders

The common element in all these men's experiences is an overpowering seizure by some power beyond themselves. George Foster is an early and typical example. His revelations began with shakings, raptures, and groans in the night:

> I was taken in a most pleasant manner, and was forced to lie singing and whisling; And then to rise out of my bed between one and two a clok for to dance; and so continued singing and dancing neare upon two hours by the clock. . . . and why I count it singing, is because I did (as being overpowered with joy) crie *ha ha tall! toll lall derab la loll! la dero tall derall tall toll dero tall aroll atoll loll loll dero* in such a way I did breake forth.

And later:

> I desired my brother that lay with me, to lie upon me, and so he did, to try whether I should then shake, and I did tatter him up and down and shake so much, that he could not make me lie still: . . . I shoke him as if he had been in a cradle.[1]

He had visions of armies, angels, fantastic beasts, temples, and chariots in heaven, which he explained as foreshadowing the destruction of Parliament, the purging of all forms of religion, and the coming of universal liberty. Reading Foster's fifty pages of apocalyptic nightmare, and others like it, we get a sense of how the political upheavals of the time unleashed enormous psychological unrest. These prophets usually describe their experiences in terms of their physical effects, which authenticate them by their very strangeness:

> the manner of the comming of the Spirit of the Lord Jesus upon me, was by touching lightly the haire of my head, so soaking down into my head, it made all my necke and shoulders to rise; after two hours, it entred into my soul.[2]

The most colourful and notorious of these figures was Abiezer Coppe, whose writings provoked two ordinances against blasphemy, in May and August 1650. Coppe belonged to a licentious group known among themselves as 'My One Flesh' who represented the extreme antinomianist position.[3] In *A Fiery Flying Roll* (1649) he aggressively defended his habit of 'base hellish swearing, and cursing' and in *A Second Fiery Flying Roule*, published in the same year, claimed that although the precisian must 'howl in hell' if he dares to think of darting one glance with one of his eyes at his neighbour's wife, 'yet I can if it be my will, kisse and hug Ladies, and love my neighbours wife as my self, without sin' (p. 9, second paging).

Amid his warnings and prophecies Coppe gives us some vigorous autobiographical fragments, beginning with an account of his mystical death and rebirth:

> First, all my strength, my forces were utterly routed, my house I dwelt in fired; my father and mother forsook me, the wife of my bosome loathed me, mine old name was rotted, perished; and I was utterly plagued, consumed, damned, rammed, and sunke into nothing, into the bowels of the still Eternity (my mothers wombe) out of which I came naked, and whetherto I returned again naked.[4]

The incidents here are not arbitrarily selected, but through their Biblical associations with the sufferings of God's servants subtly reinforce Coppe's claim to be a true prophet. The highly charged rhythm and over-emphasis are characteristic of all that he wrote, and in particular of his dramatic self-portraiture. When he tells us how he went among the crowds in the city to make known God's demands for social justice, the emphasis falls less on the divine word than on the part played by himself in proclaiming it:

> Wherefore be it knowne to all Tongues, Kinreds, Nations, and languages upon earth, That my most Excellent Majesty, the King of glory, the Eternall God, who dwelleth in the forme of the Writer of this Roll (among many other strange and great exploits) hath i' th open streets, with his hand fiercely stretcht out, his hat cockt up, his eyes set as if they would sparkle out; and with a mighty loud voyce charged 100. of Coaches, 100. of men and women of the greater ranke, and many notorious, deboist, swearing, roystering roaring Cavalliers (so called) and other wilde sparks of the Gentry: And have proclaimed the notable day of the Lord to them, and that through the streets of the great Citie, and in

Southwark; Many times great multitudes following him up and down, and this for the space of 12. or 13. dayes: And yet (all this while) not one of them lifting up one finger, not touching one haire of his head, or laying one hand on his raiment.[5]

Coppe's expectations here seem to have been remarkably modest: so far was he from expecting any real response to his message that he is satisfied with having escaped molestation! He repeatedly displays an energy and extravagance that we associate more with the Elizabethan stage than with Cromwell's London, and he thrusts his book towards the reader with a flourish that might have come from Ancient Pistol himself: 'Read it through, and laugh not at it; if thou dost I'l destroy thee, and laugh at thy destruction.'[6]

A year in Newgate seems to have sobered him a little, and in May 1651 he appealed to Parliament for release, signing himself, 'Your humble, faithful servant, and very, very poor prisoner.' A complete recantation accompanied the appeal, which was published later in the year as *Copp's Return to the Wayes of Truth ... And the Wings of the Fiery Flying Roll Clip't.* He also gives us more light on his earlier spiritual experience; a subdued and repentant Coppe emerges, though still, he assures us, 'With a little t'uch of what he hath been, and now is; sparkling here and there throughout these Lines.'[7]

An anonymous broadsheet, entitled *Divine Fire-works*, and published in January 1656–7, almost certainly gives us further light on Coppe's prophetic experiences. The midnight revelation which it records bears all the marks of his style and shows that some years after his chastening in Newgate he could still exhibit more than 'a little t'uch' of what he had been. There is a fantastic vein of poetry here, though the sound and fury of his voice all but drown whatever mystical impulse he had, and his eccentricities soon become monotonous.

Like most of his fellow prophets, Coppe reaches us most effectively not in direct accounts of spiritual experience but in the way he shows himself in action. Perhaps he does fuse inner and outer experience in the account of his meeting in the country with an old deformed beggar, which must be quoted in full:

1. Follow me, who, last Lords day Septem. 30. 1649. met him in open field, a most strange deformed man, clad with

patcht clouts: who looking wishly on me, mine eye pittied him; and my heart, or the day of the Lord, which burned as an oven in me, set my tongue on flame to speak to him, as followeth.

2. How now friend, art thou poore?

He answered, yea Master very poore.

Whereupon my bowels trembled within me, and quivering fell upon the worm-eaten chest, [my corps I mean] that I could not hold a joynt still.

And my great love within me, (who is the great God within that chest, or corps) was burning hot toward him; and made the lock-hole of the chest, to wit, the mouth of the corps, again to open: Thus.

Art poor?

Yea, very poor, said he.

Whereupon the strange woman who, flattereth with her lips, and is subtill of heart, said within me,

It's a poor wretch, give him two-pence.

But my EXCELLENCY and MAIESTY (in me) scorn'd her words, confounded her language; and kickt her out of his presence.

3. But immediately the WELL-FAVOURED HARLOT [whom I carried not upon my horse behind me] but who rose up in me, said:

Its a poor wretch give him 6.d. and that's enough for a Squire or Knight, to give to one poor body.

Besides [saith the holy Scripturian Whore] hee's worse then an Infidell that provides not for his own Family.

True love begins at home, &c.

Thou, and thy Family are fed, as the young ravens strangely, though thou hast been a constant Preacher, yet thou hast abhorred both tythes and hire; and thou knowest not aforehand who will give thee the worth of a penny.

Have a care of the main chance.

4. And thus she flattereth with her lips, and her words being smoother then oile; and her lips dropping as the honey comb, I was fired to hasten my hand into my pocket; and pulling out a shilling, said to the poor wretch, give me six pence, heer's a shilling for thee.

He answered, I cannot, I have never a penny.

Whereupon I said, I would fain have given thee something if thou couldst have changed my money.

Then saith he, God blesse you.

Whereupon with much reluctancy, with much love, and with amazement [of the right stamp] I turned my horse head from him, riding away. But a while after I was turned back [being advised by my Demilance] to wish him cal for six pence, which I would leave at the next Town at ones house, which I thought he might know [*Saphira* like] keeping back part.

But [as God judged me] I, as she, was struck down dead.

And behold the plague of God fell into my pocket; and the rust of my silver rose up in judgement against me, and consumed my flesh as with fire: so that I, and my money perisht with me.

I being cast into that lake of fire and brimstone.

And all the money I had about me to a penny [though I thought through the instigation of my *quondam Mistris* to have reserved some, having rode about 8. miles, not eating one mouth-full of bread that day, and had drunk but one small draught of drink; and had between 8. or 9. miles more to ride, ere I came to my journeys end: my horse being lame, the waies dirty, it raining all the way, and I not knowing what extraordinary occasion I might have for money.] Yet [I say] the rust of my silver did so rise up in judgement against me, and burnt my flesh like fire: and the 5. of *James* thundered such an alarm in mine ears, that I was fain to cast all I had into the hands of him, whose visage was more marr'd than any mans that ever I saw.

This is a true story, most true in the history.

Its true also in the mystery.

And there are deep ones couch't under it, for its a shadow of various, glorious, [though strange] good things to come.

7. Wel! to return – after I had thrown my rusty canker'd money into the poor wretches hands, I rode away from him, being filled with trembling, joy, and amazement, feeling the sparkles of a great glory arising up from under these ashes.

After this, I was made [by that divine power which dwelleth in this Ark, or chest] to turn my horse head – whereupon I beheld this poor deformed wretch, looking earnestly after me:

and upon that, was made to put off my hat, and bow to him seven times, and was [at that strange posture] filled with trembling and amazement, some sparkles of glory arising up also from under this; as also from under these ashes, yet I rode back once more to the poor wretch, saying, because I am a King, I have done this, but you need not tell any one. *The day's our own.*[8]

Professor Crofts pointed out the Wordsworthian quality of this encounter,[9] and certainly Coppe brings the solitary old man before us with a seer's insight and seems almost as he writes to be probing after the burden and mystery of divine love and human pity. Moreover, his prose here has a sustained rhythm that he only fitfully achieves elsewhere: his ear for dialogue – both external and internal – is faultless, and although the prophet is in the cloudy grip of his wild mythology, the old man is seen with a marvellously clear eye.

Men with a message

Another outstanding individual in this goodly fellowship is the Welshman, Rhys (or Arise) Evans, who, while he shared Coppe's megalomania, was at least on the side of the Anglicans. In 1651 he published *A Voice from Heaven to the Church of England*, in which he urged the restoration of Charles II to the throne, and claimed among other things that the Church of England was the only true church, that he alone had the spirit of illumination, and that the words 'Smite the lintel' in Amos 9.1 were a command to attack the Speaker of the House of Commons. The following year, in *An Eccho to the Voice from Heaven*, he attempted to deal with the inevitable objections:

> And to satisfie men in this point, I intend to inlarge my self, and give a full account, . . . For so indeed I am sent before *King Charls* to prepare a people to receive him, as S. *John* was sent of old to prepare the way of the *Lord Jesus*, the case is the same: But I suppose such an account as S. *Paul* sometime gave to the people, is expected from me, that is in some measure a *Narration* of my whole *life*, & specially of my calling to this work, *Acts* 22. *Acts* 27. wherein you shall finde Gods *special purpose* in me, preparing me from my infancy.[10]

This programme he faithfully carries out, beginning with a genealogy that goes back to 'the Lion and the Ren'. Evans has no difficulty in producing the evidence that God's hand was upon him throughout his childhood. In due course he was apprenticed to a man named Hugh Jones, and whenever anyone called Evans by his Christian name, 'Rhys', Jones would tell them that they should know the English meaning, which was 'Arise'. Thus, says Evans, 'the sound of this word Arise had such an operation upon me that my ear was always attentive to it.'[11] So it came about that he felt called to go to London when he heard one Oliver Thomas preach on Cant. ii.10: 'Arise up my love, my fair one, and come away.' He went there in 1629 and prospered at his trade until four years later he discovered his gift for prophecy after hearing a preacher urge the congregation to wrestle with God for spiritual gifts. His calling was confirmed by visions, as well as by texts picked at random from the Bible, and when an angel appeared in his shop he became convinced that he had to tell the King that he and his kingdom was to be destroyed. The King accepted the paper Evans gave him, but Evans was turned out of his lodgings when his land-lord heard what he had done. He was treated no better when he went home again, for his parents were persuaded by neighbours that he was mad, and confined him to his room. His subsequent career was one of disputes, tumults, visions, and imprisonments; he records them in detail, along with the divine judgments executed on those who opposed him.

Evans's great merit is that he keeps his narrative moving, and like Coppe can bring himself vividly before the reader's eye when he portrays himself acting out his prophetic commission. In the accounts of his two visits to Greenwich Palace, for instance, we see him all too clearly as a lurking menace, ready at the slightest cue to unburden his life-history on the passer-by:

> . . . hearing the King was at *Greenwich*, I went my way there, and when I came into the Hall among the guard, I asked where the King was, and they looked upon me, seeing me, having my Bible under my arm, said, what will you do with the King, I told them that I had a message from God unto him, they laughed, saying, when did God speak to you? and I shewed them how I was called, and all the passage from the time of my calling to that time . . .

L

151

I went to *Greenwich*, and staid there two days, declaring
publickly to all the people in and about the Court, what
destruction was coming upon them, and when I saw a Bishop
or a Doctour passing by, I followed them to their chambers,
intending to deliver my minde in a sober way to some of
them, but they run from me and their servants kept me out
of their chambers by force.[12]

For all his hot-eyed, garrulous enthusiasm, however, Evans does
leave us with the impression that he wished his hearers well,
though he succeeded only in antagonizing them. He was well aware
of this, for he was sensitive to the reactions of others to a degree
which they probably did not suspect, and he offers by way of
explanation an apology that has become increasingly popular in
all kinds of situations in our own day – that it was simply a failure
in communication:

> . . . though I do seem to examine and reprove you, know that
> if I had learning and choice of expressions, I had done it
> in such words that it should not offend any of you, and
> therefore bear with me in what I say by this book, for my
> want of expressions makes me seem as if I fell into passions,
> but it is not so, for my desire is to declare the truth in all the
> ways of love.[13]

The only one of all these prophets to have an organized band of
followers was Ludowick Muggleton, who with a companion named
John Reeve founded the sect of the Muggletonians, which lasted
until well into the nineteenth century. Reeve and Muggleton
claimed to be the two Witnesses of the Spirit spoken of in
Revelation 11, and both recorded their experiences. Reeve appears
to have been the initiator of the enterprise, since he relates how a
voice came to him in February 1651, saying:

> I have given thee understanding of my mind in the
> Scriptures, above all men in the world. . . . I have chosen
> thee my last messenger for a great work, unto this bloudy
> unbeleeving World. And I have given thee Lodowick
> Muggleton to be thy mouth.[14]

Muggleton himself tells us that Reeve did not at this time know
what his message was to be: '*But*, said he, *if God do not speak
unto me the next morning, I will come no more at thee.* . . . Which

I was in good Hopes he would not, for I was willing to be quiet.'[15] It is clear that Muggleton was a resourceful barrack-room theologian, well suited to his role as Reeve's spokesman. He claimed no direct revelation for himself, and whilst his theology was eccentric he insisted on a strict moral code being observed by his followers; the movement in some ways anticipates the Mormons. Muggleton summarizes his teaching in his accounts of disputes and interviews, and though his style is prolix and unsuited for exposition his book contains a number of lively anecdotes.

Spiritual pilgrims

All the men mentioned so far begin their stories with the revelations they had, and then go on to describe their reactions. A second kind of autobiographical record concentrates more on the writer's experiences in seeking the truth, so that the crucial moment of discovery comes at the end of the story rather than at the beginning.

One of these is the recantation written by Joseph Salmon after being imprisoned for blasphemy. Salmon is said to have 'sowed the seeds of ranting familism',[16] and his behaviour appears, like Coppe's, to have been not only blasphemous but disorderly. The ordinance of 1650 condemned the Ranters both for their 'monstrous opinions' and because they 'tend to the dissolution of human society'. They were looked upon with loathing even by the most tolerant men. Cromwell, who would grant an interview with Arise Evans and talk to him for several hours, cashiered an army officer in October 1650 for asserting that 'sin was no sin'.[17]

Salmon was released on condition that he publicly disowned his former conduct and opinions. 'Truly,' he says, 'I would very willingly say nothing, & yet at present I am forced into a freedom to speak my mind.'[18] But though apparently an unwilling autobiographer, he writes with a facility and self-conscious extravagance that belie his disclaimer:

> After a while posting most furiously in a burning zeal towards an unattainable end (my manner of walking being adjudged by those in power contrary to the peace and civill order of the Commonwealth) I was justly apprehended as an offender . . .
> Being now retired from the noyse of the world, and cloystered up from the usuall society of my friends, having

> my grates on the one side for a defence, and my doore fast
> bolted on the other, I had time enough afforded me to
> ponder my state and condition (A3v–A4).

It is difficult to tell whether this naïvety is genuine or assumed;
Salmon is certainly a born journalist, and takes care to present his
case in the most engaging manner possible.

His path led from episcopacy to Presbyterianism, thence to
Independency and Anabaptism, and then right out into pantheistic
antinomianism. Among the Baptists he had been eminent 'in the
hottest time of Persecution', but though tempted to settle with
them the inexplicable restlessness common to other prophets
would not allow him to do so: 'Then came that voice from the
throne of the heavenly Almightiness: Arise and depart for this is
not your rest' (p. 12). Salmon interprets all his progress up to that
point as a groping after shadows, following Christ only 'in the
flesh'. He was now stripped of his glory, left 'weeping with *Mary*
at the Sepulcher', and found nothing in formal religion but a few
marks of mortality, 'a few grave clothes, or such like stuff' (p. 13).
But when his three mystical days were expired, the grave stone was
rolled away and heaven opened upon him, an experience he
recounts in terms suggesting that there was an authentic mystical
impulse here:

> I can give you no perfect account of that glory which then
> covered me; the lisps and slipps of my tongue will but render
> that imperfect, whose pure perfection surmounts the reach of
> the most strenuous and high flown expression.
>
> I appeared to my selfe as one confounded into the abyss
> of eternitie, nonentitized into the being of beings; my soule
> spilt, and emptied into the fountaine and ocean of divine
> fulness: expired into the aspires of a pure life:
>
> In breife the Lord so much appeared that I was little or
> nothing seene; but walked at an orderly distance from my
> self, treading and tripping over the pleasant mountaines of
> the Heavenly land, where I walked with the Lord and was
> not (pp. 15–16).

Salmon deals exclusively with inward experience, the external
world impinging on his consciousness only as the bars and bolts of
his prison cell which ensure that his introspection will not be
interrupted. Like the others, he presents himself with a dramatic

flourish, though as the centre of the field of battle, the scene of the struggle, rather than acting in the world as the agent of Omnipotence. His flow of eloquence never ceases, moving with a kind of loose-limbed, puppy-like uncertainty, perpetually hovering between the felicitous and the ludicrous. His allegorical conceits are appropriate enough, since he does not perceive the supernatural only in extraordinary manifestations, but through an interpretation of the Scriptures by which he finds a parallel for every stage in his own pilgrimage.

A pilgrimage with a different destination is recorded by Richard Coppin in *Truths Testimony; and a Testimony of Truths Appearing in Power, Life, Light & Glory*. Coppin was one of the first men in England to preach universalism, but his main concern here is to defend himself against his opponents, and most of the book deals with his trials for blasphemy and his defence of what he taught. His career was as stormy as those of the other prophets, and he started disputes wherever he went, including Rochester Cathedral, where he succeeded Salmon as an incumbent in 1655. Coppin also knew Abiezer Coppe, but he was no Ranter, and despite his antinomianism no accusations were made about his moral conduct, and there was never enough evidence to keep him long in prison. In much of his experience and teaching he resembled the Quakers, especially in his internalization of the Last Things:

> I having had the experience of it all within me . . . saw, as
> to my self, a death of the one part, as of the Devil, hell
> and damnation, with all things, at the left hand of God; and
> a living of the other part, as of God, Christ, Heaven and
> Salvation, with all things, at the right hand of God; . . .
> which was to me the day of the Lord, and a restauration of
> all things to God (p. 14).

Alone of all the prophets Coppin claims to write for his readers' guidance; he puts his life forward as a standard for others, 'that you by comparing it with the manner and course of your life, and the dealings of God with you, may see how near a progress you have made to . . . the fathers Kingdom, and end of your journey, God himself, attainable in this life' (pp. 9–10).

The outrageous individualism characteristic of all these men is apparent throughout Coppin's career. An even more eventful story is told by Lawrence Clarkson, or Claxton, a follower of

Reeve and Muggleton, who in a period of rebellion against his leader wrote a spiritual autobiography to prove that he was 'the onely true converted Messenger of Christ Jesus, Creator of Heaven and Earth'.[19] He tells of wandering through seven churches before finding rest in the gospel according to Muggleton, and then relates his adventures as an itinerant preacher. He spent one winter in confinement for 'dipping' and on his release became first a Seeker and then a Ranter: 'Now observe at this time my judgment was this, that there was no man could be free'd from sin, till he had acted that so called sin, as no sin.'[20] A pamphlet published in 1650 speaks of the notorious indecency of the proselytes of '*Cop* and *Claxton* and the rest of that infernal gang which have been the dispencers of a Diabolicall opinion that there is neither heaven nor hell'.[21] Clarkson tells us that he went up and down the country with a Mrs Star, travelling as man and wife, 'spending our time in feasting and drinking, so that Taverns I called the house of God; and the Drawers, Messengers; and Sack, Divinity'.[22] He practised astrology with some success, then returned to preaching, with a benefice of £100 a year in Norfolk. While here he met Reeve the prophet and was convinced by his writings. In the introduction to another book, published in 1659, Clarkson speaks of the moral struggle he had when it became clear that he could not both follow Muggleton and retain his living:

> the more I labored to preserve my self under that goard of above an hundred pounds *per annum*, the more the beams of the eternal God did scorch and wither my shadow of rest [until] . . . many . . . refreshings did arise from my seed spring within me, that I was made willing to disown all.[23]

The main interest of Clarkson's accounts lies in his frequently changing opinions and the incidental details of his narrative, especially his examinations before the justices. If these are to be trusted he had a quick wit and a ready tongue; they also show his ability to write realistic dialogue, as can be judged from part of his wife's cross-examination, where she is being questioned about the method of dipping:

> What were you plunged over head and ears? So saith the Scripture. What Mr. *Claxton*, did you go with her into the water? No I stood on the bank side. Mrs. *Claxton*, were you not amazed, or almost drowned? No Sir, the obedience

to the Command of God did shut out all fear and cold.
What did not you go to bed after dipped? I had a warm bed
with dry linnen provided. Did not your husband lodge with
you that night? There is no such wickedness among us. . . .
Till we were [married] publickly before witness, we had no
such custom, and let me tell you, if it be the practice of your
Church, it is not so in ours. Nay woman, be not angry, I
do not say you did so, for truly I am as much against sin
as you are.[24]

Clarkson was always interested in any new ideas that he met, and
he seems to have been a persuasive preacher of whatever doctrine
he adhered to at the moment. Like Chaucer's Pardoner he had all
the more dubious tricks of the preacher's trade at his finger-tips,
and makes unashamed confession of his chequered career.

The appeal to experience

All these men, then, were primarily concerned with self-justification either to authenticate their prophecies or in reply to attacks
made on them. Their appeal to personal experience was made
not to encourage others in a similar condition but to emphasize
their own authority. What strikes us most forcibly is the extreme
narrowness of the criteria by which they repudiated everyone else's
position. Evans would allow only one kind of revelation, 'which
is by a laudable [*sic*] voice directing a man to the Scripture'.[25]
Reeve and Muggleton uttered a solemn 'curse to Eternity' on all
who in any way opposed them. Clarkson explicitly claimed to be
'the onely true converted Messenger of Christ Jesus'[26] and when
Coppin invited his readers to measure their experience against 'the
race that I have won . . . and the price that I have won' he obviously considered himself ahead not only of them but of the apostle
whose language he borrowed – and who claimed merely to have
finished the race, and not yet to possess the promised reward.[27]

Unlike the orthodox Puritans, they did not write out of systematic self-examination, nor was their experience interpreted by
means of an accepted theological framework, though they made
constant use of theological vogue words in their attacks on Puritan
religion. These attacks showed a development from the moderate
radical position and at many points coincided with the views
of the Quakers. Coppin's complaint against the prelates and

Presbyterians was that their God was afar off, and not within, and they could not guarantee freedom from sin in this life.[28] Clarkson ridiculed the image of God he was taught as a child: a grave old man on a chair of gold, 'with variety of rooms suitable for Himself, and his Son Christ, and the Holy Ghost'. This, he thought, was still all the bishops' men themselves knew, and the Presbyterians were little better, being 'ensnared in the land of *Egypt*, burning Brick all the day'.[29] They drew sweeping generalizations from their individual experience and showed little evidence of inward conflict except when resisting the urge to preach; in general they placed unquestioning confidence in an experience which was completely self-authenticating without rational justification; they did not 'try the spirits' in the Puritan manner, and had no intellectual problems or doubts concerning their personal destiny. Muggleton said, 'I never had no Guilt of Actual Sin that did ever trouble me.'[30] They were concerned with immediate contact with the divine will, leading directly to action in the world.

This delight in their prophetic role colours all the narratives. Consequently, whilst the element of spiritual autobiography provides us with interesting data on the psychology of religious enthusiasm, their most effective passages are those which describe what they did. Most of them write lively and evocative summaries of their sufferings, disputes and petty exasperations. Muggleton on Reeve, for example: 'I could not follow my Business quietly for his asking me Questions, for if I went out of one Room into Another, he would follow me to talk to me.'[31] And the quotations from Coppe, Evans, and Clarkson will have illustrated their ability to achieve a personal narrative style.

For the visionary prophets the thing which has come upon them has, as it were, swamped the imagination, and in solidifying has taken the form of what was already there. The process of communicating it to the reader consists in disgorging it just as it stands, in a form which to the writer represents divine truth exactly as it was given to him, but which to the reader is apt to appear as an inconsequential collection of familiar images. Others of these men are more active and inquiring in their search, and their possession by the Spirit takes a less spectacular form than the voluptuous inbreathings enjoyed by the visionaries who were the penmen of an angelic power; hence their narratives are more deliberate in tone and more immediately comprehensible to the ordinary reader. Nevertheless it is the Ranters, Coppe and Salmon, who come closest to linking up the spiritual and material worlds and throwing off some 'sparkles of glory'. They must both have been uncertain at times whether they were walking the streets of mystical Babylon or seventeenth-century London, and it is to their credit that the reader is often not quite sure either.

NOTES

1 Foster, pp. 9–10, 12.
2 Nicholas Smith, p. 5.
3 Cf. *D.N.B.* s.v.
4 Coppe, *A Fiery Flying Roll*, 1649, Preface, sig. A2v.
5 *Ibid.*, pp. 14–15.
6 Coppe, *Second Roule*, p. 1.
7 *Copp's Return to the Wayes of Truth*, 1651, Preface, sig. B2, and title page.
8 Coppe, *Second Roule*, pp. 4–6.
9 Cf. J. E. V. Crofts, *Wordsworth and the Seventeenth Century*, Warton Lecture on English Poetry, 1940.
10 Evans, 'To the Reader', sigg. Bb7v–Bb8.
11 *Ibid.*, p. 11.
12 *Ibid.*, pp. 25, 27–8.
13 *Ibid.*, p. 66 (second paging).
14 Reeve, p. 5.
15 Muggleton, p. 41.
16 Cf. C. E. Whiting, *Studies in English Puritanism, from the Restoration to the Revolution, 1660–88*, 1931, p. 277.
17 Cf. Rufus M. Jones, *Studies in Mystical Religion*, London, 1909, p. 478.
18 Salmon, p. 7.
19 Clarkson, *Lost Sheep Found*, title page.
20 *Ibid.*, p. 25.
21 *The Ranters Ranting*, 1650, p. 5.
22 Clarkson, *Lost Sheep*, p. 28.
23 Clarkson, *Look about You*, Epistle, sigg. B2, B3.
24 Clarkson, *Lost Sheep*, pp. 16–17.
25 Evans, p. 102.
26 Clarkson, *Lost Sheep*, title page.
27 Coppin, p. 9. Cf. 2 Timothy iv. 7–8.
28 Cf. Coppin, p. 13.
29 Clarkson, *Lost Sheep*, pp. 6–7.
30 Muggleton, p. 19.
31 *Ibid.*, p. 35.

Chapter 10

Quaker Testimonies

In 1691 the spiritual journey of a Quaker pilgrim was described by Stephen Crisp in an allegory called *A Short History of a Long Travel from Babylon to Bethel*. It is a story of a man who was desperately concerned to find the House of God, so he set out with some other seekers in the company of a man who offered to be their guide in return for payment. But their leader's qualifications were very soon put in doubt: 'Before we had gone one whole Days Journey, I saw my *Guide* sometimes stand still and look about him, and sometimes would pull a little Book out of his Pocket, and read a little to himself; which made me begin to mistrust, that *he knew the Way no better than I*.'[1] Then he met a man who said he knew the way because he had been there, and after a long journey they crossed a river and came to the house. But it was dirty and the people were quarrelsome. 'I spoke to them, and told them, Such kind of Doings as this, did more resemble a Place in the World called *Billingsgate*, than the *House* of GOD.'[2] So he left them and was guided by a small light to a house of great beauty and peace which he knew at once to be the true House of God.

The heart of the Quaker message concerned the discovery of this light. It was an inward power that convicted a man of sin, showed him the truth, and gave him power over evil. It was identified with 'the true light, which lighteth every man that cometh into the world',[3] and the early Friends called it by various names: 'the seed of God', 'the righteous principle', 'the witness of God in me', or 'the inner Light'. As soon as a man submitted himself to it, all evil in him was destroyed and a life free from sin became possible. The attractiveness of this possibility, the simplicity of the idea, and the vigour with which it was promulgated won many converts, and it has been estimated that the Society of Friends had between 30,000 and 40,000 members by the time of the Restoration, some twelve years after George Fox had begun to attract followers.[4]

The conversion they spoke of involved a turning inwards, since all guidance came from the power within and final authority was to be found not in the teaching of the Church, nor in the Bible, but only through this personal experience. So it is not surprising that from 1652 onwards, when the first Quaker pamphlets were published, the written testimony was a popular weapon of evangelism. It was simple, practical, and involved no 'windy doctrine'. The writers spoke of nothing but what they knew, and claimed authority to direct others into the way of peace because they had found it themselves. 'What I have seen and known I testifie for the relief of others', said Isaac Penington.[5] They wrote 'for the simple ones sake, who are groping in the dark, whether in forms, or out of forms'.[6]

Some wrote their stories without knowing that many similar accounts were being spread abroad, either in print or as spoken testimonies. 'Truly,' said Alice Hayes, 'I have thought, that if I had met with the like Account of any that had gone through such Exercise, it would have been some Help to me.'[7] Thomas Thompson, on the other hand, spoke of 'reading such Books as were publish'd of the Experience of those that had any openings of the way of Life.'[8] Evidence that narratives of conversion formed part of Quaker preaching is found in George Fox's *Journal*. He tells us that Thomas Taylor, two days after he was convinced, 'began to declare how he had been before he was convinced'.[9] And one writer specifically states that his confessional tract, addressed to 'The *Tender*, *Sober* and *Conscientious Professors* amongst the People call'd *Independents*, in the County of NOTTINGHAM', was based on his earlier public testimony: 'And this is the Sum of the Confession which I was not ashamed to witness in your publick Assemblies, both at Nottingham and other places, in the year 1668.'[10]

The pattern of convincement

Crisp's allegory of the journey from Babylon to Bethel summarizes the most noticeable features of the early Quaker conversion stories, which identify three stages of searching: growing dissatisfaction with orthodox Puritan teaching, a period of fruitless seeking for true religion among the sects of the time especially the Anabaptists, and finally submission to the inner Light.

All the writers begin with a quest for lasting peace of heart, and all of them assert that neither a pious upbringing, nor fervent prayer, nor powerful preaching heard with reverence and attention did anything but make them more restless and frustrated. They particularly resented the Puritan's dependence upon the Bible – the little book that Crisp's guide pulled out of his pocket:

> . . . and I ran to the highest of Mountains and Hills, and heard Sermons from them, three in a day, and . . . I did encrease in the old wisdom, and I was tossed up and down in that wisdom, like a wave of the Sea, . . . and when I came to the Mountains, I see they were at a losse as well as I, for they would say, such an Author saith thus of such a saying of Scripture, and such an Author saith thus, and a third thus, and then the people must have his meaning also; and then he saith, I take it thus; And this was all that ever I learned from them, even setled upon their deceitful meanings, and that I was to believe upon Christ that died without the Gates of *Jerusalem*, and then all is well.[11]

They lost faith in 'formal' religion, for in spite of believing all the articles of faith required of them they could not really understand how outward baptism, outward observances and a Christ who died at Jerusalem 1600 years earlier could free them from the bondage of an inward corruption. No one could tell them where God was to be found; all whom they asked either confessed their ignorance or else repeated the empty words of the priests, who were 'physicians of no value', 'blind guides', and 'daubers with untempered mortar'. Moreover, since they took a stipend, they were 'hireling shepherds'.

As a result, the seekers either abandoned themselves to the pursuit of pleasure or vainly tried to find the way to God by associating in turn with the Presbyterians, Independents, Anabaptists and other less reputable sects:

> Then there appeared more beauty in them called Independants, and I loved them, and so joyned my selfe to

them, and all the money I could get I purchased books with, and walked with (and owned) them as more separate from the world; and they prest separation, but at last I saw it was but in words, that they would doe things . . .

Then they whom they called Anabaptists appeared to have more glory, and walked more according to the Scripture, observing things written without; and I went among them, and there was something I loved among them; but after they denyed all but such as came into their way, as out of the fellowship of the Saints and Doctrine of Christ, I saw the ground was the same . . .

Then some preached Christ within, but they themselves were without, had but words, and yet they said all must be within (unto which my heart did cleave) . . . But still I saw though they spoke of all things within, and of a power to come, that they enjoyed not what they spoke.[12]

But at last, when they heard the Quaker message, the perplexed seekers understood that by thinking of God as being 'at a distance' they had been following a false trail. They then submitted themselves to the light of God within and waited for this to show itself in its own time. It revealed the indwelling principle of evil more and more clearly until the dreadful judgment of God came with great turmoil and distress to destroy evil at the root.

. . . I turned my mind within to the light of Jesus Christ wherewith I was enlightned, which formerly had reproved me for all vanity . . . and all things was brought to remembrance that ever I had done, and the Ark of the Testament was opened, and there was thunder and lightning and great haile, . . . and the dreadful power of the Lord fell upon me, plague, and pestilence, and famine, and earthquake, and fear, and terror, . . . and in the morning I wished it had been evening, and in the evening I wished it had been morning, and I had no rest, but trouble on every side; . . . and as the Judgement was pronounced, something cryed, *Just art thou oh Lord in all thy judgements*; and as I did give up all to the Judgement, the captive came forth out of prison and rejoyced, and my heart was filled with joy, . . . and the new man was made, and so peace came to be made, and so it pleased the Father to reveal his Son in me through death.[13]

It is interesting to notice that, unlike orthodox Puritans, Quaker writers do not dwell long on any struggles they may have had with blasphemous thoughts or the sin against the Holy Ghost. Because of their belief in perfect sanctification they did not need to place much emphasis on what was no longer felt to be a serious menace.

Individual variations

Although they all had practically the same story to tell, every man had to speak honestly of his own experience; and since no two lives are completely alike, every memoir shows an awareness of individual problems which the common pattern does not entirely obscure. Spiritual progress is usually related to some particular issue which provides a kind of inner framework for the narrative.

For some writers the centre of interest is determined by the nature of their first religious crisis. Thus Edward Burrough, one of the first to publish a testimony, says that when he was seventeen he often heard a voice in his prayers saying, *'Thou art ignorant of God, thou knowest not where he is, nor what he is; to what purpose is thy Prayer'*.[14] And this conviction of ignorance forms an undercurrent to his short memoir, for the thing he wishes most to emphasize is the contrast between the 'notional' knowledge of the head and the 'spiritual' knowledge of the heart which, as we have seen, is spoken of by other Puritans. For many years Burrough thought the first was sufficient for salvation: 'I lived pleasantlie, for I had the true God, and the true Truth in my comprehension, which by my wisdom in the light I had comprehended, and I had the world in my heart, Pride, Covetousness, and the earthly spirit ruled.'[15] George Fox taught him the higher sort of knowledge, which leads to separation from the world, and Burrough writes to testify that ordinary religious teachers knew nothing about this.

Other writers interpret their spiritual life as a prolonged search for purity of heart or for something that might enable them to overcome the power of indwelling sin, a power they identify with any or all of the forces of evil in the Bible: the Harlot and the Beast of the Apocalypse, the Dragon, the House of Saul, the chaff to be burnt with unquenchable fire, or the darkness of Egypt, 'where darknesse is so thick, that if yee wait but diligently to see your selves, you will feele it also.'[16]

164

Confessional narratives sometimes subserved the purpose of longer tracts in which they were incorporated, or themselves made a plea for a particular Quaker concern. William Britten wrote his *Silent Meeting a Wonder to the World* as a witness to the value of waiting upon God in silence because he himself had been converted by this distinctive Quaker practice after being first in the episcopal church and then a Baptist.

> And as one alone from the Tumult, or outside of a Wood,
> can easily hear the Clamours and Out-cries within; so I
> being come forth of the Forms and Forests of the World,
> unto a holy Silence, by the Power of Jesus Christ within me,
> could the better discern to see and view the various sects and
> Forms in their Congregations[17]

John Mulliner's *Testimony against Periwigs and Periwig-making* reflects the Quaker's rigorist attitude to all forms of pleasure and finery; he relates how he gave up his employment after burning a wig in the presence of his two apprentices, and turned to more serviceable work. A special purpose is also apparent in Humphrey Smith's two autobiographical pamphlets, one of which was written to justify leaving his outward employment to become an itinerant preacher, and the other to warn parents by the example of his own childhood not to mislead their children with 'devised fables and evil examples'.[18]

As might be expected, the three main stages of conversion already mentioned do not always receive equal attention, since a man's main problems might have lain only in one or two of them. There is therefore some variation in the emphasis given by different writers to their reaction against the orthodox clergy, their search for a genuine people of God, or their inward battle against the power of evil.

While George Fox was seeking for the truth he was always disappointed when he tried to get help from ministers of religion. 'I thought them miserable comforters,' he said, 'for they could not reach my condition.'[19] It was not long before he stopped going to them at all and withdrew with his Bible into the orchards and fields instead of going to church. Richard Farnworth, in one of the very first confessions to be published, says of the Puritan 'priests': 'So I have cleared my conscience, in declaring part of my experience of them, and not by report nor opinion of others.'[20]

And his whole story is centred on his interactions with the representatives of orthodoxy. A more sustained and abusive attack on the clergy as 'Messengers of Satan' is found in Thomas Rawlinson's testimony.

There were four chief complaints against the Puritans. They preached a false doctrine which 'blasphemed the light within';[21] they had no divine authority but followed only the traditions of men; they did not practise what they preached, for despite their boasts of 'experiences and comforts and assurances' they were 'not yet redeemed from foolish Jesting, from Idle Words, from Anger and Passion'[22] and finally the salvation offered by these hireling shepherds was incomplete, it was a 'miserable salvation' because 'all of them cryed out, *No Freedom from Sin on this side of the Grave*'.[23] Fox had many encounters with those who 'roared up for sin in their pulpits', and the possibility of attaining perfection on earth was universally accepted among the early Friends; 'Oh! beleeve not those that say, The best of Gods Children cannot be free from sin in this life', said Thomas Forster, and he speaks for an entire generation of Friends.[24]

Other writers spend less time on their rejection of Puritan teaching and portray their experiences mainly as a journey towards union with God. Francis Howgill was spiritually 'tossed from mountain to hill' in his pilgrimage,[25] which was also a literal one for him and many others,[26] who like some of the vulgar prophets relate their movement from one denomination to another and their dissatisfaction with each of them in turn ('We looked into the Independent way, but saw death there, . . .');[27] they relived the historical development of Protestantism. As late as 1717 Samuel Keimer was writing of the 'hankering desire after being fix'd upon a Rock spiritually'[28] which led him to Quaker sympathies after he had been brought up a Presbyterian, had leanings towards popery, and relapsed into following the then notorious French prophets, who gave their followers a written pardon from Jehovah and a green ribbon a yard long 'as a Mark for the destroying Angel to know us by'.[29] The temporary satisfaction gained in joining one of the Puritan sects was interpreted as a 'false peace' or 'false rest', usually induced by trusting in the signs of election:

> . . . then would I try my self in their Measure, and weigh my self in their Balance, and so gather up a little Peace to

my self, finding such things in me as they spoke of for Signes; as, *a desire against Sin, a loathing my self for Sin, a love to them that were counted the best People, a longing to be rid of Sin,* &c. But alas! Here was yet but the blind leading me poor blind Soul: This was not the Ballance of the *Sanctuary.*[30]

Frequent references to a 'wilderness condition' are a reminder that ever since apostolic times conversion had been compared to leaving slavery in Egypt and travelling to the Promised Land. The Quakers also used this language: 'no way to *Canaan,* but through the *Red Sea,* and the *Wilderness*; no way to enter the Kingdom, but *through many Tribulations.*'[31] And Thomas Forster refers to his spiritual development almost entirely in these terms:

> ... the Lord God ... mercifully brought me out of *Egypt,* and delivered me from those cruel *Taskmasters & Builders* of Confusion, and set me at liberty to travel towards the *Holy Land*: for in all the Land of *Egipt* I found no outward Guide to lead me out of my *Egiptian* darkness, ...
>
> ... being delivered out of *Egypt,* and journying towards *Canaan,* I met with divers sorts of *Travellers,* with whom I had converse & acquaintance:

(Here he discusses the Independents, the Baptists, and 'those called Notionists'),

> ... and being now come to the red Sea, I had a lingring and secret longing to the *Garlick and Onions of Egypt* again, yet the Lord kept me from going back into *Egypt* (where was no *light* at all) but I walked in the *Wilderness* to and again for many yeers together, filling my head with Notions, and comprehending of Mysteries, which were very pleasant and delightful unto me.
>
> ... and though the Spirit of innocency often cryed in me Return, return, and come into the narrow-way which leads to life; yet I flattered my self that I had been there already, and that now I was come to the Borders of Canaan.[32]

Those who concentrate on the third and final stage of convincement speak less in terms of pilgrimage and make more use of the imagery of spiritual warfare. And their interpretation of past events tends to be more influenced by their mature opinions.

M   167

Every seventeenth-century Christian thought of his life as a sustained conflict with the devil, but unlike the Puritans, for whom the holy war began only at the moment of regeneration, the Quakers claimed that the seed or witness of God was in all men from their birth and continually struggled for supremacy in spite of being oppressed by the principle of evil. The only Quaker writer who appears to retain the Puritan outlook is an Anglican convert, John Jeffrys, who says that although he had detested immorality all his life, he was thirty-eight years of age before he entered into holy warfare against his soul's enemies. All other writers of the earlier generation speak of a struggle from their childhood which was intensified as they grew up, but which they clearly did not regard as changing in nature, even though they did not understand it until later:

> Now I can look back again, and see how the Lord was all along present with me in the light and holy seed, and the contrariety and varience grew more and more between these two seeds, though I was very weak of understanding, to discern or make a true separation between the precious and the vile in me.[33]

Thomas Symonds relates how before he understood the nature of the conflicting motives in his soul he attempted to find relief by enlisting as a soldier in the Civil War: 'I entred into the war without me, thinking therby to be beloved of God for my forwardness in that work, and the war within me did somewhat cease but not wholly'.[34]

It is William Ames the first Quaker missionary to Holland, who sees his conversion most consistently in terms of inward warfare. From his youth he was aware of something within which condemned him when he did wrong:

> But as I grew in years, I grew in *wickedness*, and the *wicked one* grew *stronger and stronger* in me, and the *just* grew *weaker and weaker*. So that I came to delight more & more in sin, and that, which before reproved me, I found to be *dead*.[35]

The strategy of the enemy was to direct his attention outside himself to rules, Scriptural promises, or to the fact that Christ died for his sins at Jerusalem: '. . . and always, when the *witnes of God convinced me of Sin in my Conscience*, the *deceit* drew out my mind from it, to looke upon a *Christ without me*: and to mind the *Scripture* to be my *rule*.'[36] Thus his religion was only an outward profession, and his soul was occupied by an enemy who blinded his eyes to the real nature of sin by turning his attention outwards:

> Then, as I grew *higher* in my *wisdom*, I began the *more to conform to the Letter of the Scripture*. For the Scripture declared against *anger*, then I began to abstain from it *outwardly*, and from uncleanness, filthyness, and deceit *outwardly*, and from pride *outwardly*, and so many of the *branches* of Sin were cropt off. But the *Root* and *ground* from whence it proceeded, was not removed.[37]

The enemy was defeated when he identified the light in his conscience which convicted him of sin with the power of Christ to save and heal; his attention was thereby directed inwards to where the enemy also was, and in a riot of apocalyptic language he describes how the army of God destroyed his corruption.

After conversion

When a Quaker came to write of the sufferings or persecution endured after accepting the Truth he sometimes spoke of it as an extension of the inner conflict leading up to convincement, for conversion had itself been a reproduction or foreshadowing of 'the *Enmity* of those of the world against those who are not'.[38] One of the commonest trials to be undergone was the hostility and ridicule with which the news of convincement would be received at home. Not only was the Friends' teaching unpopular, but their peculiar social customs of plain speech and refusal of hat honour were even more instrumental in creating domestic tension. When Fox held meetings at Malton in 1651, 'several people would have come but they durst not for their relations'.[39] Alice Hayes's husband threatened to leave her and 'grew unkind and contemptuous' until he himself was convinced.[40] Richard Sommerland relates that when his wife frequented Friends' meetings after reading some testimonies he was greatly troubled and 'had rather have suffered Death, than to have been called a *Quaker*':

> Then . . . the Enemy of my Soul, seeing that his Kingdom

169

began to be weakened, to the end that it might be destroyed, then did he begin to Rage, and to stir me up to take those Books which my Wife was formerly reading: and I hid them, with an intent that I had to burn them, if my Wife would not go with me on the next First Day unto the World's Worship, so great was my Rage against Truth in that day.[41]

There are many detailed accounts of how Friends were despised by their acquaintances, derided in the street, attacked by parents or employers and turned out of home.[42] When these troubles had been overcome, the need to witness against oaths, tithes and military service brought further persecution and the renewal of inner turmoil. When, for instance, the commander of a man of war saw that he could no longer with a clear conscience stir up his men to killing and plunder he found that 'the good Spirit strived on the one hand, and my place of honour, and my livelihood, and families, and being counted a fool on the other hand'.[43] So as early as 1656 Fox was instructing his followers that they had still to endure many spiritual trials and temptations: 'And Friends, though you may have tasted the power and been convinced and have felt the light, yet afterwards you may feel winter storms, tempests, and hail, and be frozen, in frost and cold and a wilderness and temptations.'[44] Two years later he was still warning, 'Take heed of destroying that which ye have begotten.'[45]

This reiterated advice was prompted by the tragic example of James Nayler, one of the most gifted and eloquent of the Quaker preachers, who in June 1655 allowed himself to be led into Bristol on an ass followed by a small group of devotees who hailed him as the Messiah, singing, 'Holy, holy, holy, Lord God of Israel'. He was arrested and tried for blasphemy, and his answers at the trial gave the impression that he had voluntarily accepted this worship and saw himself as God incarnate; but his behaviour seems mainly to have resulted from the very imperfect doctrine of human nature held by Friends at this time, and their lack of clarity regarding the exact nature of the indwelling divine presence which their teaching proclaimed. Nayler was savagely punished by Parliament, and during his imprisonment in Bridewell wrote a few words of confession and explanation in a tract called *To the Life of God in All*, showing 'how the innocent, Just and Holy Life came to suffer in me and be betrayed, and I to lose the light thereof, so far as to be taken captive again under the power of darknesse'. This occurred when he gave way to 'the reasoning part, as to some things which in themselves had no seeming evil', but which 'by little and little drew out my mind after trifles, vanities'.[46] A few years later, in his treatise *What the Possession of the Living Faith Is*, Nayler made a unique and interesting attempt to generalize this experience by omitting all external details and deriving each stage of his argument from a corresponding stage in his own experience of conversion, backsliding and restoration. The result cannot strictly be called a spiritual autobiography, but it links up with the other testimonies in that Nayler used his personal experience as the basis of his teaching and as proof of its validity. Other Friends related their story and then exhorted the reader to follow their example. Nayler fused these two elements of the personal confession in an attempt to cover more ground and to offer a more reasoned argument for the Quaker faith.

Thus at a very early date in Quaker history we have a recognition that the inner Light did not inevitably ensure security from sin, and gradually the outright demand for immediate perfection, which was such an important matter for the first apologists, becomes less noticeable in the autobiographical records. In 1671 Francis Lea, writing from the Fleet Prison, claims no more than 'some measure of victory',[47] and by the end of the century it is common to find records of the 'subtle workings of Satan' after convincement. Richard Claridge relates how he was tempted to re-entangle his soul, to doubt the truth; to mistake his true place of rest, to exalt his mind, to despise the Scriptures, and to judge others;[48] Joseph Pike compares the soul to a garden, which continues to produce weeds even after being cleaned,[49] and John Kelsall admits that trespasses and offences are sometimes unavoidable.[50] So in the eighteenth century William Crouch can specifically deny having reached the Land of Rest; it is necessary to continue to travel, he says, because 'a Distance is set betwixt Seed-time and Harvest'.[51]

Apart from Nayler's, however, the only detailed confession of a falling away from the truth appears in Anthony Tompkins's *Faithfull Warning to all Backsliders*, published in 1669. Like Nayler he attributes his fall to 'the reasoning part' which in his case led him to persuade himself by a number of ingenious arguments that he might properly pay tithes to the parish priest. He is careful to point out that there were few outward signs of his apostasy: 'as for my dealing amongst men, I have very little to charge my self with, but can truly say, as to that point, I kept my self very much unspotted of the World'.[52] But it would appear that Tompkins's experience was not an uncommon one at this time: 'the Devil', he says, 'drew me to acquaint my self with those that did also flee the Cross',[53] one of whom was a Friend who rebuked him when all the time 'he was worse than he should be as well as I'.[54] And the pamphlet hints at many others, since it is addressed to 'all backsliders Who hold the *Truth* in *Unrighteousness*'.

Anti-Quakers

Not all backsliders were restored. Some wished to show that their acceptance of Quakerism had itself been a fall from grace, and there are six or seven narratives which record such a lapse in order that 'others may heare, and feare, and take warning'.[55] The virulence of Quaker teaching was exposed in confessions of the delusions and irrational conduct that followed uncritical acceptance of the Light within. They are remarkably like the extravagances of the Ranters already described. Fox was often interrupted at meetings by the aberrations of enthusiasts, and Friends lost no time in condemning such conduct, since they seemed to confirm only too clearly all the popular prejudices against the new movement. So Friends were quick to take up the challenge with printed replies and there ensued pamphlet wars of answers and counter-charges in which each contribution was longer and more abusive than its predecessor. The original narratives make very little criticism of Friends' morals or conduct, but are more concerned to point out the dangers inherent in their principles, such as the setting up of George Fox in place of the Spirit of Christ.[56] In fact, the writer sometimes cannot avoid giving the impression that Friends behaved with considerable sympathy and common sense towards their misguided brethren. One such case was that of John Toldervy, who had hallucinations after submitting to the Light and tried to perform miracles. A long period of mental disorder ended one night when he impaled his thumbs and attempted to re-enact the crucifixion, after which he ran 'fiercely' to the meeting house saying that Christ had risen,

shewing the Holes that were made in my Thumbs with the

Needle: upon which, I was looked upon with a strange hasty look; and charged to be silent, for I was in Darkness; the Witnesses of God were slain in me. So there being many there, and all of them judging me with one Consent, I was silenced: Upon which they spake lovingly to me and bad me to sit down; and put on my Shoes.[57]

A more reasonable anti-Quaker confession grew out of the intellectual problems of William Dimsdale, who after owning allegiance to the Society for some time began to have doubts about perfectionism: 'I saw evil motions no longer as only the temptation of the devil, but as actual sin arising from the flesh', and groaning under this burden prayed both 'to Christ in me, and to Christ in the Heavens'.[58] He achieved peace of conscience through faith in the imputed righteousness of the historic Christ who had perfectly fulfilled the Law, a conviction which came 'not by the Light which every Man hath, but by a Light which every Man hath not'.[59] Such a return to orthodoxy did not pass unnoticed, and Dimsdale was branded by the Quakers as 'a *Judas* to that Truth which once he tasted', and his book dismissed as a 'washpot, which is filled with the Filth of Scoffs, Slanders, Falsehoods, Contradictions and Confusions'.[60]

Their place in Puritan tradition

Looking back over three centuries on the dust and heat of these controversies it is easier to be aware of what all the disputants had in common than it would have been at the time, and the Friends' debt to mainstream Puritan tradition is everywhere apparent in their testimonies. Even when they react most violently against their religious environment it is usually to take hold of some principle of Puritan teaching and apply it more rigorously. A comparison of the early Quaker autobiographies with those of their Puritan contemporaries helps to show where Quaker behaviour and doctrine came closest to Protestant orthodoxy and in what ways they departed from it.

The accounts of childhood and youth are particularly illuminating in this respect; the fullest are those of Humphrey Smith and Stephen Crisp, but nearly all the confessional writers have some significant reference to the habits of their early years. Most of them were brought up in a nominally Puritan home and so were imbued with Puritan standards from the beginning. Some of them speak slightingly of their parents as being, like William Edmundson's father, 'Religious in what he knew'.[61] They were serious children who eagerly followed preaching and disputes, mourned for their sins in solitary places, and anxiously studied their lives for the marks of election. Like Thomas Thompson, who was called 'a hopeful Boy' by his parish priest,[62] they behaved as models of Puritan piety. And when conscience was thoroughly awakened, the misery of their soul's condition might find expression in the widespread contemporary feeling that man alone was vile and out of harmony with creation: 'Oh that the Lord had made me a frog croaking in some stinking Ditch, yet happy and free from the just Judgment and Indignation of God.'[63]

So their youthful sins are not the 'gross pollutions' of the world so much as 'lightness of spirit' and 'outward prophaneness': there is only one reformed drunkard among them all, and no such sensational transformation as that of a swearing Bunyan or drunken Perkins. John Crook's catalogue of transgressions includes idle talk, keeping vain company, wasting time, pride in apparel, wearing long hair, and spending money in vain. This is a typical catalogue, and it is to be condemned all the more since at the same time he was much admired for his gift of prayer. Dancing, bellringing, card playing and music-making also caused great pangs of conscience even when, as was sometimes the case, parents encouraged these activities as antidotes to religious melancholy. Whilst this condemnation of pastimes is a logical outcome of Puritan teaching on the necessity to live as always in 'the great taskmaster's eye', the Quakers were much more severe in their condemnation of activities such as music-making; and Puritans like Bunyan, who made himself a flute from the leg of a chair in prison, and Cromwell, who employed forty-five musicians at his daughter's wedding, would have regarded the wholesale burning of musical instruments as the fruit of an overscrupulous conscience. For John Mulliner, the ex-wigmaker already mentioned, not only deplores his own 'Playing on Instruments of Musick' but also condemns it 'among CHRISTIANS, or any other in the days of the Gospel'.[64]

Much, indeed, of the sobriety of clothing and gravity of bearing associated with the Puritans belongs more properly to the Quakers.

Fox and others are continually complaining of the 'lightness' and 'chaffiness' of the clergy, and there is no reason to suppose that the sober customs of a Quaker household would have been commended by all the spiritual brotherhood. Fox once met a captain who was 'the fattest, merriest, cheerfulest man and most given to laughter that ever I met with', so he admonished him in the power of the Lord, and 'before he got home he was serious enough and left his laughing . . . and became a serious and good man'.[65] What is interesting about this incident is Fox's implication that the man's cheerfulness itself, without any qualification, was justification for the rebuke. The Quaker was always 'a serious and good man', and one epithet implied the other. 'Grave', 'solid', 'weighty', are the tributes paid to the pioneers in posthumous testimonies.

Poetry is the only art that escapes unreserved condemnation. It is true that Samuel Wilde burned his 'vain and ungodly writings', but he does not say what they were.[66] Both Thomas Ellwood and John Kelsall, on the other hand, reproduce passages of their own verse in their autobiographies. Kelsall does so apologetically, admitting that 'very few have made use of Poetry to a right End'. Nevertheless 'some have a Gift that way (and I believe too of the Lords giving) and as they use the same only to the Honour of the Giver (mark that) it may be of service'.[67]

This is entirely in the Puritan tradition. Wherever the early Friends do differ from accepted Puritan standards it is to demand a more rigorous enforcement of them. Some even claim to trace their dissatisfaction with orthodoxy far back into childhood before ever they heard of the Quakers. Elias Osborn spoke about the 'pride and covetousness' of preachers and says that his father 'would seem to be struck with Admiration, and say, *Lord! What will become of this Boy?*'[68] And Humphry Smith, even more precociously, had a theological objection: 'I . . . did speak against their way of sprinkling Infants, and said I should never stand as a God-father for any (nor never did) whereat a man swore at me, and said, it was a pitty any one did it for me.'[69]

This brings us to the question of Friends' doctrine and how it affects their conversion stories. As far as conviction of sin is concerned we have seen that as with so many Puritans this came first through an incident or a text that disturbed their complacency. This is well illustrated in Josiah Langdale's manuscript, where he writes of an experience closely resembling Bunyan's:

175

One Time when I was about 9 Years of Age, it being a hard
Frost and but little Snow on the Ground, I and another Boy
of my Years were playing at Foot-Ball, and eagerly meeting
left the Ball to Try our Strength; we closed very fiercely and
I being strongest took him up on my Breast so fell a Top of
him, & his Head first coming to the Ground with Violence
was sorely bruised—When I perceived how ill he was, and
being cooler in my Spirit, I heard a Voice sound aloud in
me saying . . . 'If he had been killed how wouldst thou have
answerd for it before the Lord in the Great Day?' The
Words that I heard thus sound in me did so pierce my
Heart, and had such an Influence upon my Spirit, that I
immediately left Playing and went aside out of the Croud in
a By-place where I wept much, seeing plainly by the Light
and Spirit of Christ Jesus (tho' at that Time I did not know
that it was the Light of Christ which did shew me) that
those Games that stirred up Men & Boys Spirits to such
Wantonness, Wrath & Violence; were all wrong, and not
becoming Christians.[70]

It will be noticed, however, that whereas Bunyan while playing
tipcat sensed a voice 'dart from heaven' and 'the Lord Jesus
looking down upon me',[71] Langdale significantly 'heard a Voice
sound aloud in me'. Thus the same experience came to be interpreted differently in the light of the two men's mature theological
assumptions: Bunyan normally to an external reference point,
Langdale to an internal one.

There are three main features of Quaker teaching which affect
the narratives. Firstly, the Quakers postulate an original innocence,
children not being born with a nature completely subservient to
evil but able to please God until the desire of evil sprang up and
innocency was lost: '*in many tender Babes and young Children,*
there is a meek, innocent, harmless principle of God, . . . and by
the violent, fierce, wrathful nature that ruled in others, was my
quietness disturbed.'[72] 'As I grew in years I grew in wickedness'
is the general theme, and if they had had Traherne's eloquence
they might have spoken with him of the 'angelical and wholly
celestial' felicity of that time. Only William Dewsbury confesses to
having been 'conceived in sin and brought forth in iniquity',[73]
and that was in a pamphlet published in the very early years of

Quakerism. It is interesting to notice that 'birthright' Friends of the second generation, i.e. those whose parents were convinced, did not come to enjoy the peace of the inner Light without spiritual turmoil: 'But though I was educated under the Profession of Truth, yet the wild Nature was apt to appear in me, till Truth took hold of me and opened in my Understanding.'[74]

Secondly, even after this falling away from childish innocency, they were aware of a 'pure witness' within them which never consented to any evil and would sometimes overcome evil impulses. It was not recognized at the time as the source of divine power, but it was afterwards identified as the Spirit which, according to the Quaker principle, dwelt in every man from his birth. Thomas Goodwin, as we have seen, spoke of it as 'common grace', and Francis Howgill's Puritan teachers told him that it was 'a naturall conscience that kept from sin, and did restraine it, and said, he had but restraining grace, (as they called it) he was but a tame Devill'.[75] Friends rejected the distinction between common and saving grace, and moreover their inner Light seems to have performed the function of both the Law and the Grace of Puritan theology: 'I found an Accuser near me: Yet also I found, that he that reproved me for Sin, and shewed me the *Deceit of my Heart*, the same also counselled me to embrace *Truth* and *Righteousness*, and was always with me, to instruct me, and guide me in the Way of Holiness.'[76] Compared with the Puritans, however, they have much more to say about the power of sin over themselves than about their guilt before God and the need for atonement.

The first generation of Quakers shocked and alienated their contemporaries by the claim to possess the same Spirit as that which inspired the Scriptures. In the excitement of their discovery of the power of the Spirit in every man they abandoned the customary means of grace, such as Biblical exposition, the sacraments, and regular prayers, and even appeared to disparage the revelation that came through the Scriptures. But the great strength of the movement, which prevented it from degenerating into the vicious enthusiasm of the other illuminated sects, was the supremely practical way in which mysticism was tested by its outcome in everyday life, notably by whether it gave a clear condemnation of evil and brought men together in peace and fellowship. Although the Spirit was not tested by the written Word as in orthodox Puritanism, the inner Light was nevertheless known as such by its power to generate the standard of conduct demanded in the New Testament. Their memoirs testify that the Quaker leaders were, in fact, so immersed in the Scriptures as a result of their Puritan upbringing that the manifestation of the Spirit to which they bore witness was tested by the written Word in a way they were not conscious of.

Thirdly, other doctrinal differences affect the form of the Quaker confessions as much as their content. Since release from the burden of sin rested on the single issue of the inner Light, the pattern of Quaker experience was correspondingly simpler than the Puritan one, with less place for individual variation in the actual process of conversion. This may account for their striking uniformity of language and the similarity of the events related. And Quaker spiritual autobiographies are usually shorter than those of the Puritans because Friends were not so anxious about the ultimate destiny of the soul and the search for assurance. The doctrine of immediate perfection also made the pattern of regenerate life less eventful. Sanctification was complete at conversion, the struggle was short and fierce, and any details which a Quaker's life story gives of his adventures after convincement are mostly concerned with the services to which he was directed by the indwelling power, or with the sufferings that resulted from allegiance to the Society.

But in spite of these contrasts in the personal histories of Quaker and orthodox Puritan, it is still apparent that both grew out of the tradition of heart-searching and diary-keeping of an earlier age. They both find that as they reconsider the events of their lives a pattern emerges which was not of their own design. They come to see their conversion to God less as a conscious search for Him, although it seemed that at the time, than as something that happened to them. The initiative came from a power other than themselves, however it may have expressed itself through their faculties; they were taken up into a larger plan and guided by the will of an unseen power to purposes of good which they did not then understand. I have already quoted the tribute of Goodwin, the Independent divine, to the way God's unacknowledged mercy guided him through the intricate perils of his youth.[77] With this should be compared the testimony of Elizabeth Stirredge, a humble Quaker woman, to her own discovery of the mysterious ways of Providence: 'I little thought he looked so narrowly to my ways; but since the Lord hath been pleased to open my eyes, I can look back and admire his goodness, . . . he took me by the Hand, and led me when I knew not of it, in the days of my tender years.'[78]

On the larger issues, then, all the testimonies reflect a preoccupation with ideas and problems that are characteristically Puritan. But while even the most radical Baptists remained in the essential points satisfied with the answers and techniques worked out by their fathers, the Quakers felt these to have grown sterile and so they explored other channels of experience. The social and political upheavals of the Commonwealth and Restoration were symptomatic of the spiritual restlessness of the period, and it is impossible not to feel in the Quaker confessions a more dynamic though certainly more perilous apprehension of the sources of divine power. The massive structure of Puritan theology gives more steadiness to the reflections and reminiscences of the other writers, but the openings into splendour which they would have us share seem to take on a sombre and almost ominous tinge from the black horrors of sin of which they were always conscious. The ardour of the convinced Friend burns with a whiter flame, although in all the early testimonies there lies never far below the surface the hint of a wilder, self-consuming passion such as possessed the ranting monomaniacs who were unchecked by the sanity and genius of George Fox. It must be left for historians to determine why the Friends failed to develop the possibilities which their first flashes of insight opened up.

NOTES

1 Crisp, *A Short History* . . . , 1711, p. 5.
2 *Ibid.*, pp. 11–12.
3 John i.9.
4 Cf. W. C. Braithwaite, *The Beginnings of Quakerism*, London, 1912, p. 512.
5 Penington, *Babylon the Great Described*, 1659, sig. A4v.
6 George Whitehead, *Jacob Found*, p. 10.
7 Hayes, p. 29.
8 Thompson, p. 14.
9 Fox, p. 124.
10 Jackson, pp. 3, 7.
11 Strutt, pp. 6–7.

12 Howgill, pp. 8–10.
13 *Ibid.*, pp. 11–13.
14 Burrough, p. 32.
15 *Ibid.*, p. 33.
16 Howgill, p. 5.
17 Britten, p. 3.
18 Smith, *To All Parents*, p. 4.
19 Fox, p. 6.
20 Farnworth, p. 13.
21 Bennet, p. 10.
22 Stephen Crisp, *Memorable Account*, p. 9.
23 Baker, p. 8.
24 Forster, sig. A3.
25 Howgill, p. 8.
26 Cf. Andrews, Blandford, Forster, Green, West.
27 Mary Penington, p. 12.
28 Keimer, p. 86.
29 *Ibid.*, p. 26.
30 Stephen Crisp, *Memorable Account*, p. 6.
31 Whitehouse, p. 37.
32 Forster, sigg. A5–A6.
33 Patrick Livingstone, p. 24.
34 Symonds, p. 2.
35 Ames, p. 4.
36 *Ibid.*, p. 7.
37 *Ibid.*, pp. 6–7.
38 John Whitehead, p. 1.
39 Fox, p. 84.
40 Hayes, p. 38.
41 Sommerland, p. 2.
42 Cf. Baker, Gratton, Ellwood, Davies, Osborn, Richardson.
43 Strutt, p. 11.
44 Fox, p. 283.
45 *Ibid.*, p. 340.
46 Nayler, *To the Life of God in All*, p. 2.
47 Lea, p. 14.
48 Claridge, pp. 22ff.
49 Pike, p. 362.
50 Kelsall, p. 147.
51 Crouch, p. 6.
52 Tompkins, pp. 2–3.
53 *Ibid.*, p. 2.
54 *Ibid.*, p. 5.

55 Gilpin, p. 3.
56 Anon., *A Short Account of the Life of Mr. John Pennyman;* . . . *The Second Edition*, London, 1703, p. 7.
57 Toldervy, p. 38.
58 Dimsdale, p. 7.
59 *Ibid.*, p. 13.
60 J. Crook and W. Bayly, *The Counterfeit Convert Discovered*, 1676, sig. A.2.
61 Edmundson, p. 1.
62 Thompson, p. 13.
63 Wilde, p. 6. Cf. *Grace Abounding*, paras 88, 104, 149.
64 Mulliner, title page.
65 Fox, pp. 232-3.
66 Wilde, p. 2.
67 Kelsall, pp. 128, 94.
68 Osborn, p. 18.
69 Smith, *To All Parents*, p. 10.
70 Langdale, p. 1.
71 Cf. *Grace Abounding*, para. 22.
72 Smith, *To All Parents*, pp. 3, 5.
73 Dewsbury, p. 12.
74 Whiting, Sig. A4v. Cf. J. Dickinson, J. Barcroft.
75 Howgill, p. 6.
76 Gratton, p. 2.
77 Cf. pp. 86-7 above.
78 Stirredge, pp. 13-14.

Chapter 11

Quaker Journals

Most of the early autobiographical pamphlets were published in the hope of convincing the world of the reality of Friends' experience and hence of the truth of their teaching. They were not complete life histories, but conversion stories with just enough detail of the writer's outward life to explain his inward development.

Purpose and content

In the year 1689, however, there was published in London *A Journal of the Life of that Faithful Servant and Minister of the Gospel of Jesus Christ Will. Caton. Written by his own hand.* Caton had died in 1665 and the manuscript was now published on the recommendation of Fox himself:

> In the Year 1663. *William Caton* went to *Holland*; and not long after he had finished his Testimony there, he Died, and soon after that, his Wife Died, and he left this Journal of Passages behind him, which was sent to me, which I thought fit to put in Print, and Recommend to all them that knew him.[1]

It will be noticed at once that Fox does not seem to have regarded the book primarily as an instrument of evangelism, but recommends it specifically 'to all them that knew him'. One of his reasons for arranging the publication would have been to help younger members of the Society of Friends to understand the achievements of the first generation of preachers at a time when many of them had died and were in danger of being forgotten. It is tempting also to link up Fox's belated decision to publish this twenty-five-year-old manuscript with the growing tendency of Friends in general to acknowledge the need to supplement the guidance of the inner Light with writings designed to consolidate the faith of those already convinced. But in any case the habit of keeping a journal was well established soon after the start of the movement and there must by this time have been dozens of them in various stages of development. So it was inevitable that some would eventually find their way into print.

Caton had been a servant in the Swarthmore household and was one of Fox's own converts. He was the pioneer Quaker missionary in Holland and Germany. The journal begins with a detailed account of his conversion and goes on to relate his call to the preaching ministry and his subsequent travels, sufferings and imprisonments. Many other journals were published in the years that immediately followed, most of them a year or two after the writer's death, and they follow the pattern of Caton's.

The literature of sufferings was almost a separate class of auto-biographical writing. Practically everyone who maintained the Quaker witness against tithes and the Conventicle Acts suffered fines, imprisonment and distraint of goods, often much in excess of the law, and the fact that Friends would not swear in a court of law made it extremely difficult for them to obtain redress when unjustly imprisoned by magistrates or persecuted by brutal gaolers. They therefore tried to enlist public sympathy by publishing the relevant details with all the documents involved. Such accounts vindicated the ways of the Society in the face of charges of sedition and fanaticism, and also called attention to the harshness of the law and the way it was administered. Many hundreds of pamphlets of this kind were published, some running to book length, mostly taken up with petitions, lists of names and reprints of legal documents. Published journals drew on this material as well as on the conversion stories and logs of travels.

Although afflictions of the outward man frequently tested a man's faith severely enough, we have already seen that Quaker thought left at first little room for wide fluctuations in spiritual life after the rigours of convincement. The biggest religious crisis which the ministering Friends had to face was the call to public testimony, a costly and difficult duty which was resisted to the utmost by the natural man's plea of weakness, his fear of ridicule, or his concern for the welfare of his family. Once again the uniformity of Friends' experience is striking, and they narrate in almost identical terms their resistance to the tyrannous pressure of conscience and duty, their apprehensions of becoming 'a Common Mock to Drunkards, and a Taunt to Fools'.[2]

The earliest testimonies described in the last chapter were written and published soon after convincement and conclude with a note of finality after the agonies of conversion. The experience had been so overwhelming, and the power of the new life was felt to be so complete, that the writers could hardly consider the possibility of further spiritual progress, even if the doctrine of immediate perfection had not made that impossible. But when they came to look back over their lives twenty or thirty years later the change in perspective led some of them to feel that growth in grace had in fact taken place. John Banks, whose withered arm was cured by Fox, says that six years after receiving the Truth he made a 'godly resolution' to rely on the sufficiency of God's power, and that as he grew in experience, so the enemy grew in subtlety.[3] And John Burnyeat, in a journal published very soon after Caton's, acknowledges that even after becoming an itinerant preacher he still had 'great exercise of spirit' because he was 'not yet deeply acquainted with the way and work of the Lord's Power and Spirit'.[4] The astonishing vehemence of their own excuses when they felt called to preach forced others to admit that their souls' enemies were not yet all destroyed.[5] It appears, however, to have been no part of their plan to record their spiritual development from this stage onwards, and later pages of the journals are concerned with external adventures in the service of Truth.

The record of travels is sometimes little more than a list of the places visited by the writer. Charles Marshall records 400 meetings attended during the first two years of his preaching ministry and then ceases to keep such a careful account. And few of the others show any trace in the journal proper of the elaborate introspection of their conversion narrative. The most interesting and well written of the records of ministering Friends are the journals of Stephen Crisp, John Crook and John Gratton.

Lives and times

The tendency to neglect inner personal details after the time of convincement is carried furthest in a number of journals which partake of the nature of a 'Life and Times' of the writer. William Crouch's *Posthuma Christiana*, published in 1712, was the first of these, and incorporates 'a Narrative of the Beginnings and Progress of TRUTH'.[6] Crouch had died in 1710, but John Whiting in 1715 broke with tradition and himself issued *Persecution Expos'd, in Some Memoirs . . . of John Whiting* in an attempt 'To do Justice to my self and my Friends; and to Commemorate the Lives, and Noble Acts, of many renowned Worthies, as well as the Lamentable Ends of many Persecutors'.[7] This inclusion of his autobiography was an innovation that had to be justified:

> It may be some may say, *It is not usual for any to publish* Journals, *or* Memoirs of their Lives *in their Life time.* To which I answer, Neither is this but in Part; and it is usual to publish Parts, so far as relates to some particular Sufferings, Tryals or Travels, as I could instance in several (known to Men of Books) and this is no more than a Part at most, therefore called SOME MEMOIRS: So that Objection, I hope, is easily removed.[8]

There were two other works of this kind: a massive folio of Thomas Story 'bestowed upon the Publick as the AUTHOR'S LEGACY' in 1747, and the 700 pages of *The Christian Progress of George Whitehead.* Story wrote for the 'profitable Entertainment' of his readers.[9] He was Penn's deputy in Pennsylvania from 1700 until 1705 and he gives a fluent and readable account of the events of his time. Here is his description of how the Papists celebrated the birth of an heir to James II in 1688:

> And, when the News came of his Birth, they made another great Fire in the same Place; where they drank Wine, till, with that, and the Transport of the News, they were exceedingly distracted, throwing their Hats into the Fire at one Health, their Coats at the next, their Waistcoats at a third, and so on to their Shoes; and some of them threw in their Shirts, and then ran about naked, like Madmen: Which was no joyful Sight to the thinking and concern'd Part of the Protestants who beheld it.[10]

Lively detail of this kind is, however, quite missing from George Whitehead's account. He was active in the Quaker movement from

1650 until his death in 1723, and gives a survey of its development during his long life, a task he should have been qualified to perform because he knew everybody who was ever at all prominent in the Society. His method of writing was to collect 'divers *Papers, Notes* and *Memorials*' and to 'digest the same into such a plain Method as briefly as I well could'.[11] He writes of travels, messages and chance meetings; of disputes in streets, houses, inns, churches, court rooms and prisons; of illnesses, arrests and imprisonments; of dealings with criminals and drunkards; of persecution at the hands of soldiers, priests, magistrates and gaolers. But the events of these crowded years are not digested well enough to make a satisfactory narrative. The insertion of many general and private letters, of petitions, warnings, and records of disputations, and of legal documents such as orders for release from prison intolerably slacken the pace of a not very lively narrative and dissipate the interest of the modern reader – although it is easy to understand the importance of such papers to Whitehead and his contemporaries, since they represented the very milestones of their progress. His life story, like those of all the Quaker preachers, is a record of his public service and contains hardly any reference to family and personal relationships. And the national life as a whole is referred to only when it impinges on the activities of Friends, mainly in times of persecution. A Quaker historian has described Whitehead as 'the embodiment of worthy and drab respectability', and if this does less than justice to him as a man, it is a verdict that readers of his memoirs are all too likely to confirm.[12]

Sources and motives

Apart from letters and other documents inserted in the journals, material must frequently have been drawn from a private diary begun by the writer after finishing his account of convincement. For whilst the early pages are retrospective it is apparent from specific details in later parts of the narrative that some kind of written record had been kept at the time of the events described. John Kelsall and John Whiting each refer more than once to their diaries as giving further details of matters mentioned in their autobiographies. When Thomas Rudd died in 1719 his journal could not be found and an account of his travels and sufferings was compiled from his letters to his wife and friends.

Journals were evidently written with little thought of publication. What the writers hoped to derive from them was a better understanding of the ways of God; and many wrote for their children's benefit also. They were published posthumously at the discretion of surviving Friends who submitted it to the Morning Meeting for approval and censorship. This is probably why all the journals published in the seventeenth and early eighteenth century are those of 'public' or 'ministering' Friends who would have been well known up and down the country. Few organized groups of men can have travelled so extensively in Britain before this time. From about 1650 until after the turn of the century there was a constant interchange of preachers between most towns and villages in the kingdom. Once a meeting was established it would be visited at frequent intervals. The journals show that most of those who had received the call to preach travelled very widely in the course of journeys that were undertaken between spells of work at home following their trade. Thus anyone who was at all prominent in the Society would be known personally to the majority of members, and this gave the preachers an interested public for their memoirs. The journals of more obscure men and women were not published because there was much greater interest in those of people more widely known.

The appearance of these works at this time offers a further example of the central importance of personal experience in Quaker doctrine and organization. Just as the short conversion stories of the early days had interpreted the doctrine of the inner Light in terms of individual lives, so for the next generation the journals of leading members helped to increase the cohesiveness of a community that had been built up and maintained largely by personal contacts.

Foreign travel

As the Quaker movement gathered momentum during the early fifties the message was preached not only throughout Great Britain but also beyond the seas. As early as 1654 William Edmundson settled in Ireland, and his journal records his work there and three subsequent journeys to America. Caton and others tell of preaching expeditions to France, Germany and the Netherlands, but few of them write much more than a log of their travels with notes on their reception at different places. The place names are often the only indication that the travellers are not in England.

William Penn, in his *Account of . . . Travails in Holland and Germany* in 1677, goes beyond the others in giving character sketches of some of the people he met, and although the narrative is frequently interrupted for the insertion of epistles and tracts he does manage after a somewhat cursory start to convey his concern for the men and women he describes. The journal as a whole suffers from his complete silence about his companions and about the purpose and results of the mission; consequently the journey is not fully realized and the book remains a fragmentary work which is superior to the chronicles of his contemporaries only as and when it bears the marks of Penn's more interesting mind.

Several parties of Friends set out for the Mediterranean and had adventures in Malta, Rome and parts of the Turkish Empire. George Robinson reached Jerusalem in 1657, in spite of active opposition from friars, Turks, and English consuls and merchants. His adventures were published with those of Katharine Evans and Sarah Chevers, who had been imprisoned by the Inquisition for three and a half years at Malta. In 1661 a group of four men set out for the East with letters from George Fox for the King of Spain, the King of France, the Magistrates of Malta, the Great Turk, the Emperor of China, and Prester John! Mary Fisher gained an audience with the Sultan. John Perrot and John Luffe got as far as Rome, where Luffe was hanged after seeing the Pope and Perrot was put in the madhouse. The published records of these journeys are mostly compiled from the letters sent home by the travellers and are sometimes rambling if not incoherent. That of Sarah Chevers and Katharine Evans was greatly improved when reissued in 1715 with the narrative parts condensed and rewritten by an editor.

By far the most readable of all the Quaker journals of travel is found in a manuscript by Edward Coxere (pronounced, and sometimes spelt, Coxery) which came to light only in 1940 and was edited for publication by E. H. W. Meyerstein. This is not a Quaker journal at all in the accepted sense, since four-fifths of it concerns Coxere's adventures as a merchant seaman before he was convinced by Edward Burrough and Samuel Fisher at Dover in 1661. But the vigour, humour, and integrity of his character are as obvious from his seafaring exploits as from his later sufferings for Quakerism. 'From the first picture he draws of himself,' says his editor, 'in his ignorance of French, shutting his eyes and laying his head on his hand when he would go to sleep . . . his reader . . . is kept in the presence of a vivid, resourceful, quick-answering individualist.'[13] Sent to France to learn the language at the age of fourteen he was soon able to give a good account of himself, and later went to sea in default of finding congenial work ashore. His adventures cover voyages to Africa and Newfoundland, five months in an Algerian prison as a slave, and capture by the Spaniards. Twice he arrived home in disguise to escape the press gang, once so effectively as to deceive his own mother, who approached him in the street to see if he brought 'some news of Ned'.[14] But tired of hiding indoors he and his brother volunteered for service in a frigate.

> As I was at first with the Hollanders against the English I continued in this frigate in the wars against the Hollanders till about the peace. I had not been long in this ship but I was made coxswain: so that I served several masters in the wars between King and Parliament at sea. Next I served the Spaniards against the French, then the Hollanders against the English; then I was taken by the English out of a Dunkirker; and then I served the English against the Hollanders; and last I was taken by the Turks, where I was forced to serve then against English, French, Dutch, and Spaniards, and all Christendom. Then, when I was released from them, I was got in a man-of-war against the Spaniards, till at last I was taken prisoner by the Spaniards (pp. 25–6).

With a sharp eye for foibles of character and in breathless syntax he carries the reader through a realistic account of these changes of fortune, and of the Moorish oppressors and whimsical captains under whom he worked. A snatch of dialogue or an ironic comment is sufficient to fix a situation clearly in the mind: 'I was not long at home but the old tiresome tone was sounded in my ears again: "What trade now?" ' (p. 5). A drunken captain was lame in the shoulder from an injury received 'by laying ashore in a French house, where the bed was suddenly pulled from under him, and he hove on the floor by an evil spirit' (p. 30). Coxere's abrupt prose

189

is that of a sharp-witted seaman who wastes no words, but he can fill out an episode occasionally with welcome touches of realistic detail.

His command of languages earned him favourable treatment and he won high opinions for his skill as a seaman and for his personal character. The last twenty pages of his story are concerned with his imprisonment and suffering in the Quaker cause, but even this is a straightforward narrative of his adventures and not a justification of Quakerism. A few references to the slighting of divine mercies are the only explicit comments he makes on his unregenerate years, and a brief sketch of his own character at the time of his marriage in 1655 is characteristically uncoloured by his later beliefs.

> For what I undertook, although I was young and had spent my time amongst the wildest people a-man-a-waring and with other nations, few young men more of my age, yet I think I was as just in my undertakings and as honest to those I served, of what nation soever, and as real to those I had to do with on any other occasions as most young men in my condition, though I confess I was too wild, being left to my own range amongst other nations and people besides my own. I being most of the time on one design or other, seldom out of employment, I was never inclinable to lay at home spending my time idle and my money sottishly in alehouses (pp. 32–3).

Like Thomas Lurting, with whom he served in a Quaker ketch, he had to debate long and anxiously the lawfulness of bearing arms at sea, but 'the Lord let me see that fighting, killing, and destroying one another was of the Devil and not of Himself' (p. 88).

Although faced with this and other challenging moral issues Coxere does not delve into introspective detail. His feelings and personality in general emerge from the story itself: a tough, nimble and resourceful Kentishman, quick to seize the initiative and shrewd in making a bargain. His professional competence and reliability won the confidence of the most unlikely and temperamental masters, while his candour, sociability and high spirits retained the respect and affection of his fellow seamen. His scruples of conscience are at the farthest remove from eccentricity or fanaticism, but are the outcome of a plain and practical concern 'to be true to God and man and not deceive my own soul' (p. 89).

Coxere's *Relation* was almost certainly not written as a Quaker testimony and we may doubt whether it would ever have been passed by the central committee for publications even with drastic curtailment. But his natural gift for racy narrative and the evocative phrase gives us a picture of seventeenth-century life which is within its limits unsurpassed by any of his Quaker contemporaries. Some of the chroniclers who undertook to narrate the progress of Truth in the soul tended to neglect the more homely details of their lives and so did not always avoid the danger of making their religious experience seem like an exotic growth. It has already been mentioned, for instance, that most of the preachers' journals are concerned only with the 'labours for the Truth' and tell us nothing about how they earned their living or about their life at home between preaching journeys. Coxere's passing references to his trading ventures, or to his thoughts for his young wife at home without news, are sufficient to place his life story more securely in the everyday world and to complete as refreshing and attractive a self-portrait as anything in seventeenth-century autobiography or the novels of Defoe.

George Fox

The most widely read of the journals has of course been that of 'the great Quaker of England' himself. Fox founded Quakerism, says Dr Nuttall, 'by the sheer force of personality and of faith in his mission',[15] and these are the qualities that are most apparent in his journal.

It was the preaching of George Fox, begun in 1648, that gathered scattered seekers together to form the Society of Friends, and his was, in a sense, the archetypal Quaker experience. But this experience, at least as recorded in his journal, does not entirely conform to the common pattern. Apart from telling us that he 'knew pureness and righteousness' as a child,[16] he says little about his religious development before the age of nineteen. He makes no mention of ever having followed Puritan teaching and unlike most of his followers confesses to no heavy burden of sin in the conventional sense. Fox's attitude to his own youth was a sense of compassion for an innocence exposed to the hypocrisy and wickedness of the world. The key to the understanding of his early life – and, indeed, of the whole early Quaker movement – is found in the word *tender*. He constantly emphasizes his timidity and lack of experience. At the age of twenty, when his family would have him marry, 'I told them I was but a lad, and I must get wisdom' (p. 4); and three years later, 'I durst not stay long in any place, being afraid both of professor and profane, lest, being a tender young man, I should be hurt by conversing much with either' (p. 10). He found those who professed orthodoxy 'miserable comforters, . . . for they could not reach my condition', and 'I was afraid of them for I was sensible they did not possess what they professed' (pp. 6, 4). These sickly fears of contamination were not caused by self-righteousness but rather by a disenchantment that obsessed him as he came to feel that other men cared nothing for his own passion for purity of conduct. This was the shock that precipitated his first religious crisis when he was nineteen, and it was followed by a long period of isolation and despair as he searched for human and divine guidance. He records many contacts with 'tender people', but insists that deliverance came ultimately from the voice of God speaking directly to his heart 'without the help of any man, book, or writing' (p. 11). His omission of all reference to the Puritan influences of his childhood may have been the result of this experience:

> And when all my hopes in them and in all men were gone, so that I had nothing outwardly to help me, . . . then, Oh then, I heard a voice which said, 'There is one, even Christ Jesus, that can speak to thy condition', and when I heard it my heart did leap for joy (p. 11).

A new note of confidence is sounded as he responds to promptings to 'wait patiently upon the Lord', and his experience from here onwards is more like that of his followers. The Light of God appeared in him to expose evil, and there was a fierce struggle because of 'the groans of the flesh (that could not give up to the will of God)' (p. 14). This is all that Fox has to say concerning his battle against the power of indwelling sin, and from that time on his assurance never wavered, 'For I had been brought through the very ocean of darkness and death, and through the power and over the power of Satan, by the eternal glorious power of Christ' (p. 21).

Fox does not analyse his experience so closely as some of his associates did, nor does he attempt to work out any clearly defined stages in his conversion. As far as this part of his life is concerned we have the story of an untidy and spasmodic progress from fear and obscurity to the certainties that gave such immense power to his subsequent preaching. And while in broad outline it resembles the story of other Quaker pioneers, it is always apparent that 'as to man he was an original, being no man's copy'.[17]

Fox evidently regarded the account of his convincement as no more than the necessary introduction to the main part of his narrative. 'I think fit', he says, '(before I proceed to set forth my public travels in the service of Truth), briefly to mention how it was with me in my youth, and how the work of the Lord was begun and gradually carried on in me, even from my childhood' (p. 1). The whole book is, in effect, the record of how 'the work of the Lord' was 'carried on' in him, but his theology did not allow for growth in grace after convincement and so it is only in the opening section that any sort of spiritual progress is recorded. Fox's journal, like the rest, thus falls into two sections. Throughout the book he frequently gives summaries of his preaching at various places. This remains substantially the same throughout his career and is based on his own early experience. The reader is thus constantly referred back to that experience, and the power of Fox's conviction allows him to say the same thing again and again without it becoming stereotyped. From the reader's point of view these résumés are a constant reminder of Fox's own inner life and thus to some extent they take the place of the details of growth in grace that would be found in an orthodox Puritan's life story. The narrative is also interspersed with exhortation to the reader and expositions of doctrine which in some cases may have represented his developed views on the subject under discussion rather than what he actually thought at the time. The journal was not published until 1694, but the insertion of such advice was in accord with the earliest Quaker practice of using spiritual experience as a testimony to the reality of the inner Light. Bunyan and the other Puritans could rely on their readers knowing their theological assumptions and so had less need to incorporate teaching of this kind into their narratives. Since Fox was undoubtedly writing for the convinced Friend as much as for unconverted readers he was probably also concerned in these passages to give an account of the genesis of his own teaching.

If in the early pages of his book Fox emphasizes his timidity, nothing is more apparent later on than his authority. It is the authority of a religious genius whose words and deeds have the power to move profoundly even those who have found themselves out of sympathy with his teaching. Some extraordinary power was unmistakably present with him to an overwhelming degree. 'The most awful, living, reverent frame I ever felt or beheld, I must say, was his in prayer', said Penn.[18] Men looked upon him with awe as one who could read their thoughts and perform super-human deeds: 'Have a care of him, he is a princely man' (p. 561). When he was detained at Ulverston one night sixteen men kept watch over him, and some of them sat in front of the fireplace because they were afraid he would go up the chimney. Rumour invested him with the trappings of a sinister figure out of North country folk-lore when an Independent preacher spread stories

> that I carried bottles and that I made people drink of my
> bottles, and that made them to follow me, and that I rid of
> a great black horse, and that I was seen in one country upon
> my black horse in one hour and in the same hour in another
> country three score miles off (p. 101).

His followers sometimes addressed him in language that was Messianic in its adulation, but there are few traces of this in the *Journal*. Fox always claimed to be bringing the power of Christ with an authority that had been lacking since the apostle's days, and his own language reflects this belief in his unique mission. The response to his message, for instance, often recalls the divisions caused by the preaching of Christ; 'Some heard and others said that I was mad', and on one occasion, 'Some said I was mad and spoke to my outward relations to tie me up.' In 1652 a woman at Holderness said she could have left all and followed him, and years later the Mayor and officers of Shrewsbury 'took counsel together to imprison me' (pp. 91, 48, 90, 515). Because it was a conscious attempt to revive primitive Christianity it may well have been inevitable that Biblical allusions and comparisons like this should have dominated the saga of Quakerism and they must have led weaker brethren towards Messianism. Fox also finds that the scholars at Cambridge 'raged as bad as ever Diana's craftsmen did against Paul' (presumably for the same reason), and he can list the perils he has survived and the troubles within and without that 'could not be uttered', although in the latter case he characteristically modifies the Pauline allusion to make it clear that his own troubles within had been overcome before the outward persecutions began (pp. 219, 661, 277).

Penn feared that Fox's language 'might sound uncouth and unfashionable to nice ears' (p. xliii), but its rustic vigour and occasionally startling imagery put the modern reader sharply into Fox's situation and convey his feelings with more precision than a polished style might have done, as, for instance, in the famous description of St Mary's, Nottingham:

> when I came on top of a hill, as I looked upon the town the great steeplehouse struck at my life when I spied it, a great and idolatrous temple . . . And when I came there, all the people looked like fallow ground, and the priest, like a great lump of earth, stood in his pulpit above (p. 39).

At Kingsbridge in Devon he had been preaching to his fellow guests at an inn, 'And the innkeeper stood uneasy, seeing it hindered his guests from drinking, snatched up the candle. "Come," says he, "here is a light for you to go in to your chamber" ' (p. 234). Whether by design or not, the abruptness of the syntax reinforces the impact of the innkeeper's impatience.

Fox had a good ear for dialogue and could write it convincingly. When he describes a court scene or a cross-examination he is, of course, primarily concerned to repeat the arguments he had used, but the relation rarely degenerates into a quasi-catechismic style. The words are the words of real men, not prototypes, and he writes with the particular scene clear in his mind. The accounts of his examinations at Holker Hall and Lancaster in 1664 are particularly successful in sustaining the dramatic tension of these encounters with legal authority. This is achieved not only through closely worked argument, but also with unconscious artistry by effective transitions between direct and reported speech and by an occasional forceful reference to the tone or gesture of a speaker.

Penn commended Fox as 'a discerner of others' spirits' (p. xliii), and time and again the journal gives convincing evidence of his ability to see through to the heart, especially to sense what a man's attitude to him was. He can convey this relationship with remarkable economy, as when he elicits grudging admiration from an opponent: 'if he would but come to the church now and then, he would be the bravest man that ever was' (p. 531). The 'now and then' effectively typifies the religious complacency that Fox so persistently disturbed. When John Wilkinson's entire congregation deserted him for the Friends' meeting at Pardshaw Crag, Fox tells us that 'he would come and walk about the meeting on First-days like a man that went about the commons to look for sheep' (p. 314). And the account of his first interview with Cromwell shows a quality in the Lord Protector that is nowhere hinted at in Baxter's more acid portrait:

> And many more words I had with him. And many people began to come in, that I drew a little backward, and as I was turning he catched me by the hand and said these words with tears in his eyes, 'Come again to my house; for if thou and I were but an hour in a day together we should be nearer one to the other', and that he wished me no more ill than he did to his own soul. And I told him if he did he wronged his own soul (p. 199).

But hand in hand with this insight and particularity there goes a tendency to relapse into a kind of jargon or catch-phrase formula to describe more routine matters. Meetings are recorded as being 'blessed' or 'precious' so often (sometimes several times to a page) that the adjectives lose all significance, except when there is an exceptional outpouring of the Spirit and the gathering is described, adequately enough, as 'a blessed, heavenly, powerful and thundering one' (p. 637). People whom he meets are classified according to the Quaker formulae. If friendly, they are 'convinced', 'tender', 'loving', or 'satisfied'; opponents are 'rude and vain', 'chaffy' or 'high', and their reactions indiscriminately levelled to a 'rage'. No reader of the early Friends' publications can fail to be impressed by the emotive power with which they can endow such harmless words as 'priest' and 'reasoning', and in a similar way Fox can find no stronger way of condemning the men who sent James Parnell to prison than to brand them contemptuously as 'a kind of Presbyterian Independent justices' (p. 213). The depth of feeling that comes through such apparently clumsy abuse is analogous to that of Milton's 'blind mouths'.[19]

As this last example testifies, it would be mistaken to condemn

Fox out of hand for working these clichés so hard. They were in any case part of the technical vocabulary of the readers for whom he wrote, and their own experience as witnesses to the inner Light would engender full realization of Fox's reactions. In fact, writing as he was of some thousands of public meetings and personal encounters many years after they took place, it is not surprising if he fails to bestow particularity upon them all. He presumably thought that nothing less than a detailed narration would satisfy his readers, and so had perforce to include much that could otherwise have been omitted. Except for the pages describing his journeys in America we do not have a day-to-day record of his activities. He often gives us the subsequent history of people he met, and occasionally turns aside from personal narrative to record his pride in Friends' achievements: their honesty in trade, their courage under persecution, their loyalty to the Truth. His book reads like the reminiscences of an established leader of men. The perspective of this later knowledge makes the impact of the book less immediate than that of a journal proper; on the other hand the lack of any formal structure prevents it becoming an autobiography. Many other Quaker journals are of this kind – life stories written up from diaries with little attempt at anything more than a chronological summary.

Fox dictated the central account of his convincement, travels and suffering to his son-in-law in 1675, and in spite of many terse and moving passages he cannot avoid the monotony that comes from accumulating many short episodes with only a chronological sequence. We do not know whether he referred to a diary or notes of any kind, or how much he relied on his memory. The fact that he dictated so much of it would certainly have made cohesiveness less likely. The reader who knows the journal only from the passages most frequently quoted by its admirers must, then, be prepared to find its total effect less than he might have supposed. The best sections of any length are those which have unity imposed on them by the events they describe, notably the opening narrative of convincement, the many extended accounts of disputes, trials, and imprisonments, and the log of the American travels of 1672–3. Most diaries and journals are difficult to read for long at a time, and Fox's stands up to random dipping as well as most. In spite of all its unevenness it is impossible to read it without being impressed by his genius both as a pioneer of mystical experience and as a leader of men. If it cannot without reservation be called a great book, it is unquestionably a book written by a great man.

Thomas Ellwood

The only other Quaker autobiography of this period which has been widely read outside the Society of Friends is that of Thomas Ellwood, and this is in every way a remarkable contrast to Fox's: the more so in view of the contemporary uniformity of Quaker principles and practice. Fox is the religious leader of genius, his faith puts him indisputably in command of every situation, and the force of his personality is apparent in every paragraph he wrote. Ellwood is the loyal and self-effacing convert, he starts with no greater mystical faculty than the rest of us, and his religious experiences are inextricably associated with his response to external events. Fox fought out his spiritual battles alone and then emerged to initiate a deliberate campaign against the forces of darkness in this world. The crises of Ellwood's faith arose from his circumstances, when he had to face domestic tension or imprisonment or some other personal difficulty.

The intimate scale of his religious experience can be illustrated by an incident that took place shortly after he had become a Quaker. He was visiting Oxford on business for his father and despite much trepidation had come through a meeting with some old school friends without removing his cap to them or using any of the customary forms of polite address. A further trial was in store for him, however, from which he did not emerge so well:

> But when I was ready to take horse, looking out into the street, I saw two or three justices standing just in the way where I was to ride. This brought a fresh concern upon me. I knew if they saw me they would know me; and I concluded if they knew me, they would stop me and inquire after my father, and I doubted how I should come off with them.
>
> This doubting brought weakness on me, and that weakness led to contrivance how I might avoid this trial. I knew the city pretty well, and remembered there was a back way, which though somewhat about, would bring me out of town without passing by those justices: yet loth I was to go that way. Wherefore I stayed a pretty time, in hopes they would

have parted company, or removed to some other place out of my way. But when I had waited until I was uneasy for losing so much time, having entered into reasonings with flesh and blood, the weakness prevailed over me, and away I went the back way, which brought trouble and grief upon my spirit for having shunned the cross.[20]

Now this is a trivial matter, and might serve as an example of the needless misery inflicted by an over-scrupulous conscience. But the fact that such Quaker idiosyncrasies appear illogical and absurd is irrelevant. Ellwood gives a sensitive account of a psychological crisis which is not even confined to Puritanism, but can occur whenever a man's supernatural loyalty leads him into difficulties which would never have occurred in his unregenerate experience. And the importance of these scruples in building up Quaker character must not be underestimated, for in the stamina which they developed lay the secret of their steadfastness under persecution. Ellwood himself says that only a generation later some Friends were

apt to account this testimony a small thing to suffer so much upon, . . . yet they who, in those times, were faithfully exercised in and under it, durst not despise the day of small things, as knowing that he who should do so would not be thought worthy to be concerned in higher testimonies (p. 37).

'I found,' he says, 'that home was . . . a school in which I was to learn with patience to bear the cross' (p. 39). He is referring here to his estrangement from his father who, while at first taking no offence at his son's association with Friends, was outraged when he took the final step and discarded the traditional marks of respect towards him. Ellwood suffered the contempt and blows that followed with the peculiar quality of Christian patience which often arouses incredible fury in the ungodly and even in many otherwise easy-going men. And whilst there is something in his language that could lend colour to the charge of self-satisfaction, the superhuman frenzy of religious persecutors is only partly accounted for by the so-called obstinacy and sanctimoniousness of their victims. If St Stephen had been only the brash young man that Bernard Shaw found him to be, he might have provoked something less than the murderous wail of outraged

o   199

prejudice that was the final harbinger of his doom. At all events, the Quakers were neither the first nor the last to discover that even a soft answer does not always turn away wrath. As always, Ellwood conveys the quality of his own religious experience by a careful and detailed account of the external events, the behaviour and changing human relationships, to which it gave rise; and he is sufficiently objective to make us realize his father's sense of disappointment and frustration at his only son's perversity. Ellwood's experience, then, is that of the common man in the everyday practice of his religion, and he does not try to inflate it into anything more sensational.

It is in the recording of these incidents, with a novelist's eye for significant and unlaborious detail, that his narrative justifies itself. The following account of one of his first visits to a Quaker meeting will give some indication of what he adds to the traditional record of the process of convincement.

I had a desire to go to another meeting of the Quakers, and bade my father's man inquire if there was any in the country thereabouts. He thereupon told me he had heard at Isaac Penington's that there was to be a meeting at High Wiccomb on Thursday next.

Thither therefore I went, though it was seven miles from me, and that I might be rather thought to go out a-coursing than to a meeting, I let my greyhound run by my horse-side.

When I came there, and had set up my horse at an inn, I was at a loss how to find the house where the meeting was to be. I knew it not, and was ashamed to ask after it; wherefore, having order'd the ostler to take care of my dog, I went into the street and stood at the inn-gate, musing with myself what course to take. But I had not stood long ere I saw a horseman riding along the street, whom I remember'd I had seen before at Isaac Penington's and he put up his horse at the same inn. Him therefore I resolved to follow, supposing he was going to the meeting, as indeed he was.

Being come to the house, which proved to be John Raunce's, I saw the people sitting together in an outer room; wherefore I stept in and sat down on the first void seat, by the end of a bench just within the door, having my sword by my side and black clothes on, which drew some eyes upon me. It was not long ere one stood up and spoke, whom I was afterwards well acquainted with; his name was Samuel Thornton, and what he said was very suitable and of good service to me, for it reached home as if it had been directed to me.

As soon as ever the meeting was ended and the people began to rise, I being next the door, stepped out quickly, and hastening to my inn, took horse immediately homewards, and (so far as I remember) my having been gone was not taken notice of by my father.

This latter meeting was like the clinching of a nail, confirming and fastening in my mind those good principles which had sunk into me at the former (pp. 14–16).

The circumstantial details are not irrelevant. They convey the quiet atmosphere of a country town and Ellwood's half ashamed eagerness to learn more about a despised sect as well as the palpable isolation in which he pursued his enquiries. And this was the characteristic condition of the seventeenth-century seeker after truth. The same precise and quiet realism is found throughout the whole account of his convincement and of his experiences in Bridewell and the Fleet Prison.

None of the itinerant preachers who were persistently harassed by soldiers and watchmen up and down Britain relate their adventures with half so much realism as this retiring scholar, whose travels were restricted to a small area in the home counties, with an occasional excursion to London and beyond. The preachers were so taken up with the urgency of their mission that the more intimate details of their journeys and misadventures pass unrecorded. Ellwood writes his story in a more detached state of mind and this, combined with the 'great strength and plainness of speech' commended by his editor,[21] sustains the interest of his narrative as a whole and makes the individual episodes more significant. For he wrote with a more self-conscious literary purpose than any of his brethren, as is suggested by the title of his book, *The History of the Life of Thomas Ellwood*. It is not a journal and it bears no obvious traces of having been based on one; it is a highly selective account of his life, and the episodes chosen are narrated in full with a large proportion of dialogue. Of the few pages that describe his life before meeting the Quakers half are devoted to a single incident – a roadside encounter in his father's company with a pair of ruffians, during which, in his 'youthful heat', he narrowly escaped running a man through with a rapier. The incident is well told and it suffices to demonstrate the temper of his early years, for he adds that he had no regret for what he had intended to do, 'but went on in a sort of bravery, resolving to kill, if I could, any man that should make the like attempt or put any affront on us; and for that reason seldom went afterwards upon those public services without a loaded pistol in my pocket' (p. 8). But it does more than this. It establishes his relationship with his father as one of comradeship. Throughout the episode we feel the bond between them in their common danger: when in the course of the struggle his father 'turning his head to me, said, "Tom, disarm them", I stood ready at his elbow, waiting only for the word of command' (p. 7). Their relationship is the central theme of the first part of the book. The breaking of this bond, the necessity laid upon Tom to become a Quaker in defiance of his father's commands, provoked his first major trial and was the most painful experience of his life. This dispute, as we have seen, figures largely in the later narrative, and although Ellwood says that he mentions the episode of the skirmish because of 'the effect it had upon me afterwards' (p. 5), it is tempting to suppose that there was some artistic consideration involved as well.

At school he was frequently birched for 'waggish pranks' (p. 3). In later life his bearing became properly grave and sober, although we are told that 'his countenance was manly and cheerful' (p. xxxii). And from time to time in his writing there appears a pleasantly caustic humour, a little reminiscent of Baxter. A watchman who stopped him in Beaconsfield caused unnecessary trouble 'being both weak-headed and strong-willed' (p. 83). Of John Perrot, whose adventures in Rome have been noted, he says, 'being, though little in person, yet great in opinion of himself, nothing less would serve him than to go and convert the Pope' (p. 156). And his comments on the behaviour of a sympathizer who had accompanied him to a meeting at Isaac Penington's house show the delicacy of feeling that lifts his book above those of the journeyman chroniclers.

The meeting was scarce fully gathered when [the soldiers] came; but we that were in the family, and many others, were settled in it in great peace and stillness, when on a sudden the prancing of the horses gave notice that lightening was at hand.

We all sat still in our places, except my companion, John Ovy, who sat next to me. But he being of a profession that approved Peter's advice to his Lord, 'to save himself', soon took the alarm, and with the nimbleness of a stripling, cutting a caper over the form that stood before him, ran quickly out at a private door, which he had before observed, which led through the parlour into the gardens, and from thence into an orchard; where he hid himself in a place so obscure, and withal so convenient for his intelligence by observation of what passed, that no one of the family could scarce have found a likelier.

By the time he was got into his burrow came the soldiers in, . . . (pp. 76–7).

The contrast between Ellwood's autobiographical method and Fox's appears the greater when it is remembered that Ellwood prepared the first edition of Fox's journal for the press, and in accordance with contemporary standards this involved him in some rewriting of Fox's work. He cannot have failed to come deeply under the influence of the other's forceful personality. Yet when he came to write his own life story he approached it in a different way. We must remember, of course, that the two men differed very greatly in their social and educational background. His chief claim to notice by literary historians has been the few pages where he records his acquaintance with Milton, and no doubt his wider reading freed him from exclusive reliance on Quaker literary models. Human learning was looked upon with great suspicion by the early Friends, and there is a note of apology in the preface by Ellwood's editor (who was Joseph Wyeth, the son-in-law of Edward Coxere): 'The judicious reader', he says, 'will easily observe that his method and style do denote him to have been a scholar'; and he finds it advisable to add: 'and yet not farther so than the simplicity and purity of the truth whereof he made profession would permit him' (p. xxxii). Ellwood's published works include numerous controversial treatises undertaken on behalf of his friend William Penn, the Sacred Histories of Old and New Testaments, and an epic poem on the life of David.

In some ways Ellwood seems to be a little out of place amid the 'surge and thunder' of seventeenth-century Quakerism and to anticipate the quieter and more cultured Friend of a later age. But the modest way in which he relates his imprisonments is to some extent misleading, and the emotional fervour which his contemporaries poured into their preaching and pamphlets was not lacking in him. He narrates the crisis of his convincement with much of the traditional prophetic imagery and at least one of the verse profusions in the autobiography was composed under great stress of temptation. In 1660 he wrote *An Alarm to the Priests* at the dictation of the Divine Spirit. Quite apart from the esteem in which he was held there can in fact be no question of his whole-hearted identification with the Society of Friends as he found it, and the quieter tone of his autobiography may owe something to the more settled age in which it was written. It is significant in the Puritan autobiographical tradition for two reasons. In the first place it is of all the seventeenth-century records of the common man's religious experience one of the most worthy to stand alongside those of the great leaders, Bunyan, Baxter, and Fox. Secondly, its narrative method is more like that of *The Pilgrim's Progress* than of *Grace Abounding*; it anticipates to some extent the tone and structure of those fictitious autobiographies which form a high proportion of early eighteenth-century novels.

Quaker and Puritan life-patterns

The unique contribution which the Quakers made to the Puritan autobiographical tradition was the expression of a powerful mystical experience which was associated with a passionate concern for purity of heart. The mysticism links them with the vulgar prophets, while the ethical concern belongs more to the central Puritan position. They wrote because they felt they had to, and this guaranteed freedom from one kind of dulness, although too often it led in the first place to an intolerable profusion of extravagant language; but the fact that they were striving to express a first-hand experience that was essentially worth communicating sometimes caused them to triumph over sectarian jargon, overworked imagery, and an all but fatal disorderliness of sentence structure. But even Fox's most perceptive and moving passages remain tantalizing fragments, and there is no single work which gives a complete and convincing portrayal of Quaker life in the way that either *Grace Abounding* or *The Pilgrim's Progress* can be said to delineate Puritanism, the one by sheer coherence of forceful narrative and the other by its unique exploitation of universal symbols. Ellwood comes nearest to doing so, but just fails to give adequate expression to the exhilarating and authoritative manifestation of the Spirit which was the essence of the whole movement.

We might say that in Quaker and Puritan writings we are conscious of slightly different relations to eternity. An unmediated irruption of divine power and light floods the foreground of the Quaker's field of vision and we miss the dimension of hope and striving and expectation which gives a continually expanding horizon to the Puritan way of life. In the language of *The Pilgrim's Progress*, Quakers have already entered the Celestial City, which for them lies on this side of the River of Death. The imagery of spiritual conflict is no longer applicable, except with reference to 'trials in the outward', and the language of mystical union becomes more common. This is in marked contrast to the Puritan's continuing battle with indwelling sin, over which he is indeed assured of ultimate victory, but of which the fruits are yet to be fully enjoyed. For even after Friends come to acknowledge the fact that they have not reached the end of their spiritual journey, the general view of life embodied in their memoirs remains unaltered.

But even though there is this sharp division in the journals between the introspective opening pages and the subsequent external narrative, there is still after convincement a recurrent call to bear witness to the light which has to be acknowledged, and which clearly shows the Quakers fighting on the spiritual battlefield of Puritanism, albeit with different weapons. We have seen that Friends continually found themselves called upon to act in a way contrary to worldly prudence and natural desire. The use of plain language, the witness against tithes and 'hat honour', the summons to public ministry, and the suffering of fines and imprisonments were not accepted without deliberation and inner turmoil. Next to the actual conversion story these provide the most dramatic scenes in the journals, although they are often cursorily written. The most fully realized passages are those that relate the writer's call to preach and his sufferings in prison. The first of these was a less heart-shaking matter than the upheaval of convincement, but it did lead to a radical change in the convert's way of life as it meant giving up a trade and trusting his family to Providence. And imprisonment left a deep mark on the memory, so that in describing it the writer had the help of more than usually vivid impressions. These might take him some way towards lifting the narrative level above that of a chronicle, but they are not enough in themselves to produce effective writing. Now when a man came to write down the events leading up to his convincement, the experience of which he was writing lay at the heart of the Quaker faith and was the burden of every spoken testimony; it was the basis of his interpretation of Scripture and he might have heard or read many accounts which directly or indirectly covered the same ground. Thus his strong recollection of a unique and overwhelming experience could be reinforced by scriptural imagery and the vocabulary of his brethren. Personal experiences of the outward life could not so easily be brought into correspondence with a familiar pattern without losing particularity; they had to be literally described, and this made more demands on his powers of self-expression. Hence the conversion story is usually told with more precision and confidence than subsequent episodes.

Another factor which limits the literary impact of the journals springs from their portrayal of a closed world; the writers look outward on unregenerate society and their whole perspective comes from the beliefs and practices of the group. Only Ellwood and Coxere set their stories in the life of society as a whole, and so they go further than the others in the direction of the novel. Without this wider context, this capacity still to identify with those outside one's own circle, we get a tract rather than a novel. Putting the contrast in another way, we can say that Fox dominates his material with his message, while Ellwood submits himself to it and tries in some measure to elucidate its social significance.

Any assessment of these 150 autobiographies must take into consideration the fact that they were not written to entertain the judicious modern reader, but to convince men and women in their own day of the reality of the experiences described or to edify the convinced Friend with the achievements of his leaders. The rapid growth of the Society in its early years indicates that the former aim was being achieved somehow (and no doubt the confessions played their part) while the steady flow of these publications throughout the whole of our period is evidence of their popularity. And some of them do contain things of permanent literary value. The vast majority of writings in any literary form are virtually unreadable after a century or two, and if the early Quaker autobiographies are nearly all pedestrian and stereotyped the fact that at least three of them have been reprinted in the twentieth century and can still be read with pleasure should be enough to justify the tradition as a whole. Coxere, Ellwood and Fox produced contrasted and lively works which show the Quaker journal to belong to no mere backwater of literary history. Coxere's *Relation* bears a close affinity to the picaresque novels of travel and is more readable than most; Ellwood's skilful linking of selected incidents anticipates the fictitious autobiographies of the early eighteenth century; Fox imposes his personality on an artless sequence of reminiscences and welds them into a coherent world.

NOTES

1 Caton, sig. A2.
2 Howard, p. 24.
3 Banks, p. 9.
4 Burnyeat, p. 25.
5 Cf. Crisp, *Memorable Account*, pp. 21–2.
6 Crouch, pp. 9ff.
7 Whiting, sig. a2.
8 *Ibid.*, sig. a3.
9 Thomas Story, p. i.
10 *Ibid.*, p. 7.
11 George Whitehead, sig. A2v.
12 W. C. Braithwaite, *The Second Period of Quakerism*, 1919, p. 177.
13 Coxere, p. x.
14 *Ibid.*, p. 19.
15 Fox, p. xxv.
16 *Ibid.*, p. 1.
17 *Ibid.*, p. xliii (from William Penn's Preface).
18 *Ibid.*, p. xliv.
19 *Lycidas*, 119.
20 Ellwood, pp. 24–5.
21 *Ibid.*, p. xxxi (from The Preface, by Joseph Wyeth).

Chapter 12

A Language of Spiritual Experience

Something needs to be said of two issues which every writer was involved in through the very act of undertaking a spiritual auto-biography. One was the nature of the individual identity presented through narrative and commentary – how this was formulated and understood first by the writer and then by his readers. This image of the 'Puritan self' will be discussed in the next and final chapter. The other was the problem of finding an adequate language in which to express religious experience and its effects.

Communication problems

We have seen how the major Puritan contributors to the genre displayed individual features of language and style which helped them to achieve the effects they wanted: Goodwin, for example, by the use of a preacher's similitudes; Bunyan by his personi-fication of Scriptural texts, his imagery of landscape, and by what has been described as his tendency 'to assault his audience with the weapons of spiritual melodrama'.[1] Norwood, Baxter, Fox, and Ellwood likewise each achieved a recognizable style through characteristic means, some of which I have tried to identify. They had a tradition to work in, which they expressed in a personal accent.

Now many of the people we have been concerned with were neither preachers nor teachers and mostly lacked the skills of these better known men, but so thoroughly and so persistently had Puritan preachers anatomized the soul and the content of the Christian life that any of their followers had the means both to relate behaviour to the inner process of regeneration and to describe what was happening. Their language came from the Bible, from devotional literature, from the preachers, and from common usage among fellow believers. So prevalent was the tradition that many people may not have been aware either of the extent of the problem or of the resources they inherited.

One example will illustrate the way in which the language required lay ready to hand. This was a use of the passive voice which seems to have been adopted without question because it conveniently expressed something that everyone was aware of. When a Baptist said, 'Trouble came thick into my mind', when texts were 'brought in' or comforts 'darted in' to the heart, when a Quaker said that he was 'acted in sin', and when Jane Turner said of herself, 'there was not only a doing good but a love to it',[2] we are made aware of that sense of contact with something other which is the essence of religious experience, and the device itself helps to suggest the user's perception of himself as a lonely soul at the mercy of mighty spiritual forces.

Complaints that words could not be found to express what had happened were based not on the fear that the reader would quite fail to understand, but that he would simply not feel it in his heart with all the force that he should. 'I confess I find my self insufficient to declare these things to the utmost',[3] wrote Will Caton, acknowledging what was essentially a limitation in literary competence. This was needed particularly when writing of spiritual or psychological matters, though if any episode in a man's life was worth mentioning at all, it would certainly help to have it realized in the most graphic manner possible. When Robert Blair, as a student at Glasgow University, came upon an edition of Petronius it did not take him long to decide what to do with it: 'I went to the fire, and with my tongs I lifted out the best burning coal, and laid in this book in the place of it, laying on the burning coal above it.'[4] Why did Blair not just say, 'I burnt this book'? The reason, presumably, was that he wanted his readers to respond to the deliberation and thoroughness with which he acted, attitudes which he would have regarded as essential in any attempt to deal with evil. Hence his references to the tongs, to the choice of the 'best burning' piece of coal, and to the way the book was effectively engulfed in the fire. There is no remarkably literary skill shown here, but Blair's ability to evoke the particular details of his action contributed to his ultimate purpose which was, of course, a didactic one.

Many writers (though not all) coped well with incidents of this order, and occasionally showed a flair for anecdote, but to achieve precision and particularity in less tangible areas of experience was more difficult. One solution was to turn to the frame of reference provided by the familiar language of the Bible. Even Bunyan, attempting to be 'plain and simple and lay down the things as it was',[5] constantly took his bearings from Scriptural terms. And Isaac Penington, the Quaker, must have spoken for many when he said that the imaginative language of Scripture was most effective, 'because ye are more able to receive things from Scripture-expressions, then from the nature of the thing it self, spoken as it is felt in the heart'.[6] It was, after all, the language in which God had chosen to reveal Himself.

Biblical prototypes

This, then, was the source to which confessional writers instinctively turned when they wanted to communicate their own knowledge of God. Paul's description of spiritual conflict was diffused into more general terms, and they too found themselves sorely buffeted by Satan or met him disguised as an angel of light. The comparatively narrow range which was drawn on is emphasized by the continual recurrence of certain phrases. Not one but many of them had a heart like a cage of unclean birds, turned with the dog to their vomit, watered their bed with tears, or had been plucked like a brand from burning.

The narratives of the Old Testament were even more extensively adapted. Friends portrayed their inward warfare as a conflict between the seed of the Serpent and the seed of the woman, or as the struggle of Esau and Jacob in the womb. To all Puritans the calling of the Israelites out of Egypt was a prefiguring of the release of man from bondage to sin. Every detail of the exodus and wanderings was found to have a parallel in the lives of Christians. Anna Trapnel's conversion involved passing 'from Mount *Sinai*, into the Regions of Mount *Sion*', and she found her old sins 'dead and drowned in that red Sea', the blood of Christ.[7] The Quakers' extensive use of this imagery, already discussed, was hardly more insistent than anyone else's.[8] The whole range of

Israelite history presented a kind of map on which believers could plot their exact spiritual position.

Identification with Biblical scenes and characters are found at several levels, all of which can be illustrated from M.K.'s account in *Spirituall Experiences*. We notice in the first place a straightforward application of Scriptural language when M.K. adopts the prayers of a psalmist because they apply to her situation, or when she implicitly compares herself with Martha, 'cumbred about many things, but quite neglecting that one thing which is needfull'.[9] Secondly, the imagery may be at a more consciously interpretative level as when, describing a time of spiritual dejection, she says, 'my God hiding his face I was troubled, the Sunne, the Moone and the Starres, seemed in their courses to fight against me, my neighbours fell out with me, and mocked me'.[10] The relationship between physical and spiritual conditions is crudely but effectively made explicit in this juxtaposition of literal and figurative language. There is also a third level, at which an inward experience is given meaning and context as it is identified with a historical episode of Scripture, so that M.K. can define the impact of Dod's first sermon on her as a reliving of a Biblical event: 'my God did not onely make a scourge of small cords, and whipped out the buyers and sellers, but he did over-turn, and over-turne, and over-turne.'[11] Since an autobiographer could rely on his readers to recognize any Biblical allusion, he had at his disposal an immense range of materials from which to find an image, an episode, or a situation which could embody an otherwise elusive and perhaps incommunicable experience.

Because the Bible showed all types of men meeting God, anyone could find some parallel to his own experience in what had happened to patriarchs, kings, prophets, or humbler people. Arise Evans was anointed like David, called like Abraham, and eventually driven to justify himself like Paul. Coppe lived with the beasts like Daniel, Salmon wept with Mary at the sepulchre, others fed on husks like the prodigal son, worshipped Samaritanlike they knew not what, felt the despair of the exiled Cain, or were ready with Judas to destroy themselves. The mention of these names and events was enough to arouse in the reader all the sympathetic associations he had felt in pondering the sacred stories for himself. The writer could thereby be certain of the response he was evoking. Not until the antinomian prophets exploited the situation in order to bolster up their claims to be a second Ezekiel or Jeremiah would the pious seventeenth-century reader pause to question the validity of the language. It is evident that Biblical language was used in everyday speech as well as in writing. John Dod's biographer said, for instance, that 'When he saw a Christian to look sad, he would use that speech which *Johnadab* did to *Amnon, Art not thou a King's Son?'*[12]

Derived from the Bible in a more general way was the martial imagery in which M.K., like many others, constantly interpreted her situation, from the time when as a child she resolved to show her Captain 'how valiantly I would fight under his banner, and what a faithfull souldier I would be'.[13] Passing references to running away from the colours, laying down her arms, or yielding to the enemy are evidence of how popular preaching on the Christian's spiritual warfare had helped to condition the believer's perception of his difficulties and temptations. His struggle became meaningful when it could be seen in a cosmic setting, and even an unimaginative writer could venture beyond the particular images of Scripture to create new ones from within the same field which were appropriate to his own experience. M.K. spoke of the Captain whom she had deserted sending a herald to recall her to battle, and on another occasion making her run the gauntlet, 'and every souldier had a lash at me'.[14] The images of warfare were not organically related in her account, they were simply used to heighten the sense of conflict, and sometimes God Himself was thought of as the opponent: 'I thought will the Lord reason with sinners? will he vouchsafe a parley?'[15]

Vogue words

As well as the common pool of imagery, incident, and character which the Bible gave them, orthodox Puritans and Quakers had each their own jargon, which gave emphasis to the kind of experience they tried to communicate. A typical Baptist might testify that having been brought up under the means, he sooner or later found that solid and weighty preaching showed him his miserable state by nature; he then became burdened and pressed down by his sin, and lived in legal bands and slavish fears. He was exposed to waves or floods of temptations, and only delivered when Christ was presented to him so that he could cast himself upon Him. In thus rolling his soul on his Redeemer his heart was melted into a gospel sorrow, and he found faith in laying hold on the promises.

It was phraseology like this that Robert South attacked when he complained of those who amused their consciences

> with a Set of fantastical new-coin'd Phrases, such as *Laying hold on Christ, getting into Christ,* and *rolling themselves upon Christ,* and the like; by which if they mean any Thing else but obeying the Precepts of Christ, and a rational Hope of Salvation thereupon, (which, it is certain, that generally they do not mean) it is all but a *Jargon* of empty, senseless Metaphors.[16]

The Covenanters were another group that had their own phrases, recently castigated by Professor Sutherland as 'all the canting and snuffling piety of the Kirk expressed in an uncouth dialect'.[17] As far as the English sectaries were concerned, South was perhaps unjust in stigmatizing their motives; at all events their language met the immediate needs of the writer and his circle. The danger was that with its constant use men would become more and more facile in expressing the hidden operations of the heart and so it would rapidly become impossible to detect what genuine feelings or attitudes they had, if any.

One Anglican view was that as fashions changed the ministers found it necessary to be continually coining new phrases in order to keep their reputation; eventually they so obscured the simple message of the gospel that many of their followers turned to the Quakers:

> And thus it came to pass, that every one, striving not so much to speak what would profit, as what would please, dressed up Religion in affected Language of his own making; and new Expressions, if not new Notions, were heaped one upon another every year; till none knew what Christianity was. For at last there arose a Company of fine Youths, who judged even their Masters to be in a low and dull Form of Religion, *sticking in the beggerly Elements,* and *the dead letter,* and *the Old-Testament spirit,* as their manner of speaking was. These imagine not only we [Anglicans], but you [Dissenters], know *Jesus* only in the *Flesh,* and stand in the *outward Court*

and are not yet come within the *Veil* to discern the *Spirit*
and the *Mystery*, which they alone bring to light.[18]

Another Anglican critic, however, emphasized the continuing
popularity of such expressions because people wanted security and
a sense of belonging to their sect, and so, 'they love to have every
thing in the phrases to which they have been accustomed, and
according to the phancies they have entertain'd'.[19]

Quaker symbolism

The language of the Quakers themselves was even more striking
and they carried the use of set terms to a greater length. Some
were peculiar to the early Friends, but many were sanctioned by
Scriptural example, though used in accordance with the Quaker
interpretation of the Bible. Any increase in religious feeling was
referred to as 'breathings or stirrings after God', or as 'a motion
of the Seed within'; that which opposed it was 'the power of the
serpent' or a 'flaming sword barring the way to the Tree of Life';
in the inner tension thus set up, a man might be 'tossed from
mountain to hill' in search of peace. A relapse into worldliness
was almost invariably referred to in the terms of Revelation xi:
'I was led into vanities and so was one with them who made
merry over the witness of God.' Trust in 'the fig leaves of morality'
was rejected, as was the doctrine of imputed righteousness, since
this was 'a covering for sin'.

The cumulative effect of this language and much like it was to
express a religious experience radically different from that of
orthodox Puritans. It has been shown that the Friends' purpose
in recording their confessions was decidedly the more evangelistic;
there was often some effort to explain anti-social behaviour, but
the primary objective was to make an unequivocal testimony to the
new way of life, which would rouse the slumbering seed of God in
the reader and excite him to action. So whereas the Baptist or
Independent could rely on the reader bringing his own associations
to much of the language he used, the Quaker had to force his
impact by more violent expressions and an individual use of
Biblical imagery. The story of his conversion had therefore to be
told in such a way that the power and energy of the inner Light
would be apparent to the sceptical reader. And it was of times of
crisis that the most startling language was used. Some writers,

such as Howgill, were content to use a fairly subdued tone throughout the first part of their personal history, and then to emphasize the tremendous significance of the actual conversion by letting loose a flood of apocalyptic imagery to describe the birth of the power of God in them and the purging of their inner nature. Some of this can be seen in the passage quoted on p. 163 above. The fact that this was the kind of language used by Ranters could have done little to reassure the many people who already saw little difference between the two groups; nevertheless it was an important part of the technique of the early Friends because it communicated a sense of vitality that would otherwise have been lacking – that we certainly do not find, for instance, in the autobiography of Richard Coppin, whose conversion was very much like that of the Friends and who also was convinced that he had lived through a private Day of Judgment. All but a very few of the early Friends interpret the final crisis of conversion as the fall of spiritual Babylon in the heart, with scenes of cosmic destruction, the raising of the witnesses, the judgment of the Harlot and the plague of the Beast, mingled with fragments from the Psalms. As Isaac Penington said, 'truly, if ever ye espy the Dragon, the beast, Antichrist, the whore, the false Prophet, ye must look at home, and read within.'[20]

But this symbolism did more than attempt to portray a religious crisis convincingly. Its very violence and extravagance emphasized the Friends' assertion that immediate freedom from sin was possible because the power of God was a power that changed man's nature and utterly destroyed the inner root of evil. The orthodox Puritan's lifelong struggle to achieve sanctification had to be compressed into the brief time when the convert submitted his rebellious will to judgment; hence the cleansing of his corrupt nature was correspondingly more dramatic. Moreover the identification of Biblical Babylon with a man's inner self was consistent with the practice of finding the true importance of all revelation in subjective experience. The outward events of the Bible, the 'outward' redemption of man by the historical Christ, were only figures of the true redemption which had to take place within. It was not enough for a man to believe that Christ had died for his sins; if he stopped there he was still 'all in the veil and outward'. In fact, all Christians have taught that rebirth brings about a change in man's nature as well as in his status, but the

P   215

Friends were here protesting against what they considered to be the excessive deference paid to intellectual belief and forms of worship.

One of the best illustrations of the way Friends used Biblical imagery is found in *The Discovery of the Great Enmity of the Serpent*, by William Dewsbury. He succeeded at the cost of some obscurity in identifying his spiritual development with the whole sweep of the Scriptures, and the passage in which he did this is worth quoting in full because it shows the completeness with which an exclusively 'spiritual' interpretation of the Bible had been assimilated. After several years spent searching for God, during which a flaming sword repeatedly barred the way to the Tree of Life, Dewsbury discovered that the kingdom of Christ was within; then his mind was 'turned within to waite upon the Lord':

> . . . and this I witnesse, the administration of *Moses* in which *Caine* is banished, *Esau* reprobated, *Pharoah* plagued, the first borne of *Egypt* slain, and my will brought into subjection for the Lord to doe with me what his will was, if he condemned he might, and if he saved me it were his free love; and in this condemned estate I lay crying in the depth of misery without any hopes of deliverance by any thing I could doe to pacifie the wrath of God, till the administration of the Prophets, that witnessed to my soule there were free redemption laid up for me in the Lord Jesus, and by the power of the word of their testimony there was a secret hope raised up in me to waite for his coming, there I waited till the administration of *John*; and I witnesse that of all that is borne of a woman there is none greater than *John*; for he is a burning and a shining light, who discovered more of the mystery of iniquity in me in his administration, and the sence of my condition were more manifest, the cry of my condemned soule was great and could not be satisfied, breathed and thirsted after Christ to save me freely through his blood or I perished for ever, and in this condemned estate I lay waiting for the coming of Christ Jesus, who in the appoynted time of the Father appeared to my soule, as the lightnings from the East to the West, and my dead soule heard his voyce, and by his voyce was made to live, who created me to a lively hope and sealed me up in the everlasting

Covenant of life with his blood; then I witnessed the wages of sin and death, and the gift of God, eternall life through Jesus Christ my Lord; and I witnessed according to testimony of Scripture, death reigns over all from *Adam* to *Moses*, and *Moses* untill the Prophets, and the Prophets untill *John*, and *from this day the kingdome of Heaven suffers violence, and the violent take it by force*; there is no rest to the soule till Christ be manifest, and this the Scripture witnesseth; and I witnesse these Scriptures fulfilled in me, in the year according to the account 1645.

The witnesses that stood before the God of the earth, and had power to plague the earth; having finished their testimony, the beast ascends out of the bottomless pit and makes war against them and kill[s] them, and their dead bodies lay in the streets of the great Citty Spirituall *Sodome* and *Egypt*, where our Lord was crucified; and this Scripture was fulfilled in me in the year according to account, 1648.

Then Kindreds tongues and the Nations of the earth made merry over the witnesses; and I see the abomination that maketh desolate, which is spoken of by *Daniel* the Prophet, standing in the holy place where it ought not; and then was I led by the Spirit into the wildernesse and tempted of the Devill, that the Scripture might be fulfilled, *Luke* 4.1.

In that day and hour of temptation, which was in the time as the lines following giveth testimony: I witnessed these Scriptures fulfilled in me of *Pauls* condition, wherein he complained as I then did, who found a law in my members warring against the Law of my minde, that when I would doe good evill was present with me; the sence of which cause me to cry, oh wretched man that I am! who shall deliver me from the body of this death? And as I was crying to the Lord to free me from the burthen I groaned under; the word of the Lord came unto me saying, My grace is sufficient for thee, I will deliver thee; and by the power of his word I was armed with patience to waite in his counsell groaning under the body of sin in the day and hour of temptation, untill it pleased the Lord to manifest his power to free me, which was in the year according to the account, 1651.

The spirit of life from God entred into the Witnesses and they stood upon their feet, then great fear fell upon all that saw them; and the Temple of God was opened in Heaven, and I saw in his Temple the Ark of the Testament, and there were lightnings, voyces, thunder, earthquakes, and great hail: then mystery *Babylon* the great, . . . she was discovered in me . . .[21]

Confirmation that this was the usual Quaker interpretation of things came from Howgill, who told his readers that if they waited patiently in the light they would see prophecies opened in them, and many of the examples he gives are those experienced by Dewsbury. The titles of many testimonies imply a similar perspective: *Jacob found in a Desert Land; The Discovery of the Great Enmity of the Serpent against the Seed of the Woman; Mercy Covering the Judgement Seat.* The crowded scenes and exuberant imagery of the Apocalypse made it easily the most popular source, however.

The exact way in which the Quakers learned the use of this language is obscure, but their interpretation of the Bible seems to have been based ultimately on the teachings of German mystical writers of the sixteenth century, notably Sebastien Franck, Caspar Schwenckfeld, and Jacob Boehme.[22] They in turn probably derived many ideas from the undercurrents of medieval thought which found expression in such organizations as the Brethren of the Free Spirit. Franck preached the necessity for a religion which was entirely inward, claiming that the letter of Scripture brought knowledge but not power, and its true purpose was to direct the reader to the inward Light, God Himself. In *The Tree of Knowledge of Good and Evil* Franck said that the Garden of Eden was within, that the sin of man was therefore self-chosen and not inherited, and that the religious history of the Bible was a type of the experience of every man. Boehme taught that the man who tried to cover his evil self with 'the purple mantle of Christ's death' was still only a follower of Cain: each must follow the journey of Christ for himself by living a life like His. Franck's teachings were popularized in this country by the sermons of John Everard, who was the author of an unpublished translation of *The Tree of Knowledge*. Boehme's works began to be published here in 1647, and some of the early Friends are known to have read them. A number of English writers of this time show the influence of the continental mystics: John Saltmarsh saw all history as the struggle between the two seeds, and Everard wrote, 'there is no part of holy writ but is fulfilled always, in all times in every part thereof, either in every member of the church or in the enemies of the church at one time or other. Always the same things are in fulfilling, in doing, throughout the ages.'[23] Gerrard Winstanley, the Digger, told his readers that the seed of Abraham lay despised in them, that Christ was crucified within as long as they were under the dark clouds of inward bondage; and like Everard he found in Scriptural history a type of spiritual autobiography, with Christ and Satan, heaven and hell, actually present within the soul. The heavenly city, he said, 'is the heart of every one in whom the truth dwells'.[24]

Quaker historians have not been able to establish the existence of any direct contact between men like Everard and Winstanley and the early Friends, but there seems to be no doubt that their teachings and modes of expression were widely known and followed among the groups of 'seekers' from whom Fox drew his largest following at first. Joseph Salmon and Richard Coppin also show the influence of the same doctrines. The seekers, like similar groups in Holland, believed that for the most part the outward rites and organization of the Church were a perversion of the true gospel, and they were awaiting a new revelation which should direct them to the kingdom of God within; they described themselves as 'doves without their mates', a phrase that had been used by Caspar Schwenckfeld. Thus Fox found the ground already prepared for him, and when his followers came to describe their own experience of accepting the Light as a result of his teaching, they used the language they had inherited from the followers of Franck, Boehme, and the others.

Inevitably, such a specialized language came in for abuse at the hands of opponents. South recognized the connection between the Friends' way of speaking and that of the followers of Boehme, when he found an opponent's book written 'in the *Seraphick* way and style of *Jacob Behmen* or *George Fox*, it being nothing from first to last but a meer Jargon of Unaccountable, Incoherent, Obscure, *dark* stuff, and nothing so fit as a Dark Room to speak it in'.[25]

We have seen that the chief grievance of Simon Patrick against some dissenting preachers was that they rendered Christian teaching meaningless with the use of empty phrases. John Faldo, an Independent minister, found that the peculiar danger of Friends' language was that they enticed ordinary men to listen to them by dressing out their teaching in the terminology of the orthodox. He therefore undertook to make sense of the 'many Usurped and Unintelligible Words and Phrases' used by them in their writings, and said in a preface to a glossary of these terms:

> There is not any thing in the Quakers Method of deluding, which doth more tend to the insnaring of unwary Souls, than their asserting their false, Antichristian, and Anti-Scriptural Tenets, under Scripture-Words and Phrases, and in those very Terms wherein are expressed the Truths of God.[26]

His key contains about 200 words and phrases, some of which are defined with a touch of sarcastic humour:

> DENYING CHRIST COME IN THE FLESH. Denying Christ come in the Flesh of *Joseph, John, Sarah,* or any other who are Quakers.
> POLLUTIONS OF THE WORLD. . . . whatever customs they dislike . . .
> PRIDE OF MAN. A not submitting to their light . . .
> REFRESHINGS IN SPIRIT. Something they are pleased with they know not why, and come by they know not how . . .

Many others confirm the 'inward' and subjective interpretation of the Bible apparent in the testimonies:

> BONDAGE. Not only our selves in bondage to sin, but the light within, the seed of God, or Christ, being in bondage under the disobedience of men.
> CRUCIFYING OF CHRIST. Not that crucifying on the Cross of wood, but a crucifying within us, by disobedience to the light in our Consciences.
> THE JUDGEMENT, DAY OF JUDGMENT. Sin being judged in the conscience by the light within in this life.
> SLAYING THE WITNESS. Disobeying the light within; but especially a resolved rejecting it as our only Rule, Teacher, and Saviour.[27]

Although Faldo's definitions were coloured by his hostility to the Friends, it is clear that their language did perplex many people when they heard it for the first time. George Rofe, in his testimony, said that when he first heard the Quakers preach in the market place at Halstead, Essex, they 'spoke there some few words which I did not then understand'.[28] Thomas Zachary said, 'I went to the *Bull* and *Mouth*, but my expectation (being to hear some high matter) was disappointed, and I felt the man that spake, as a rushing winde; yet it went by, and I see little in it.'[29] And the use of language was an important criterion by which people's spiritual state could be assessed. Jane Turner, when she wrote of her brief flirtation with the Quakers, was thus judged by Edward Burrough in a criticism of *Choice Experiences*:

> . . . her selfe declareth in the 109. *pag.* of her *Booke*, of being brought out of *Babylon* into *Syon*, but all along through her *Booke*, her language is one and the same, before her comming out of *Babylon*, and in *Syon* (as she saith) . . . for I know her voyce, its the language of her City where she now dwells, which is in confusion in *Babylon*.[30]

The use of plain language in conversation, like the refusal of 'hat honour', was regarded as a cross to be taken up by the convert in his new life, and was also the product of Friends' literal separation from the world. The names of days and months were discarded in accordance with the injunction of Exodus xxiii.13, and titles of honour were dropped, so that St Paul's Churchyard, for instance, was referred to as 'Paul's Yard'. Qualification in the use of words loosely used by others becomes almost a formula in the following sentence of Francis Howgill: 'I . . . often went five or six miles, to hear some more excellent meanes (as they called it) . . . I posted up and downe after the most excellent Sermons, so called, and so became acquainted with all the eminent Christians so called in the region, where I lived.'[31] Perhaps this sprang in part from a desire to show up the beliefs and practices of the orthodox as empty formalism, but it came also from Friends' literal-mindedness and stubborn intellectual honesty, the scrupulosity that forbad them to sing the psalms of David unless they too were in David's condition. Richard Baker, writing in 1670, epitomized the sharply defined, black and white terms in which they viewed both names and conduct, when he spoke of Quakers as

> . . . the People of the Lord, who are at this time distinguish'd by the name Quakers, as the People of the Lord were in Ages past called Christians. Which name is now given to

Drunkards and *Swearers*, and all manner of *prophane Persons*, by the Sons of *Belial* one to another.[32]

Intimations of immortality

Finally, there is an area of experience that presented peculiar difficulties to the autobiographer, and this concerned the way he was to write of the blessings of the Christian life.

Because of the importance the Puritans attached to individual responsibility, most of their personal records deal with stresses and doubts, with several kinds of conflict and the weary battle with sin. But central to the believer's response was the joy of the new life and the hope of heaven which inspired it. 'Never take [your heart] to be right till it be delighting itself in God', wrote Baxter, and 'Delight in God is the health of your souls . . . holy delight adjoined to love is the principal part of our religion.'[33] That this is not usually conveyed to the reader at such length or with so much force as trials and temptations are is a measure of the difficulty of finding a language for it that is both fresh and meaningful.

The way the Old Testament speaks of a heavenly inheritance in terms of temporal blessings had been eloquently demonstrated by Calvin, and so the imagery of the prophets and psalmists is widely used by Puritans to portray the comfort of communion with God.[34] Most of the testimonies in Walker's and Rogers's collections end with an expression of assurance like 'I can sit down under his shaddow with great delight', or 'I have a fountain to go to'.[35] Anna Trapnel enjoyed 'wine upon the lees, wines well refined', 'milk and hony', and 'feasts full of marrow'.[36] The Englishman could not have known in his own life the Oriental's peculiar delight in milk and honey, and feasts full of marrow, nor could he know the quality of blessing that the desert-dweller found in shadow and fountains; but these things were felt to be adequate symbols for the refreshment and peace obtained through trust in God. He therefore derived from Hebrew literature an image of a spiritual arcadia where every need found fulfilment.

Now while a 'public' Biblical language of this kind could be tolerably effective in conditioning the reader's response to some aspects of spiritual experience, its limitations are such that the unique personal vision which the reader *must* be made aware of cannot be fully expressed by it just as it stands. The reader merely revives his own associations and does not get any further. So if Biblical language is used, it must be set in a context which can carry the reader beyond, either into territory that he has not yet explored or at least to somewhere that offers a new perspective on familiar landmarks.

The only writers to do this at all effectively among the Puritans are those major figures whose general literary competence has already been most apparent. We find it in Norwood's exposition of the *summum bonum*;[37] there are hints of it in Goodwin's glimpses of the community of saints and his lonely encounters with a mighty redemptive power;[38] and it meets us everywhere in a Bunyan 'all on a flame to be converted to Jesus Christ'.[39] Baxter, surprisingly, has no passage in his autobiography which explicitly presents the hope that was in him, though his utterance is everywhere loaded with the 'unexpressible weight of things Eternal'.[40] Perhaps this comes nearest to the surface in the account of his pastoral work at Kidderminster, where his passion for the kingdom of God is enshrined in a portrait of a model church community deriving its strength from worship and teaching, social relationships, and church unity.

Baxter is, however, quite detached and realistic in his references to parishioners and ministerial colleagues. Other Puritan writers, though, draw on their experience of church fellowship to convey some of the warmth and transforming power that conversion brings, but which eludes them when they try to write directly of the presence of God. They write, therefore, of their changed perception of the phenomenal world and of the brethren in particular. 'They shone,' says Bunyan, 'they walked like a people that carried the broad Seal of Heaven about them.'[41] It is here, if anywhere, that we find an individual vision most frequently expressed. Anna Trapnel, in a passage I have already quoted, speaks of an experience like Bunyan's,[42] and from an eighteenth-century Quaker we get a typical example of how the memory of a powerful corporate experience can quicken a cliché-ridden narrative into life for a few lines. Though still relying heavily on familiar New Testament language, he has produced 'something . . . of his own preparing':

And every one had something to offer to God of his own

preparing, whether a Sigh, a Groan, a Hymn, a Psalm, or a spiritual Song; and so soon as they stood up to speak, one after another, they seem'd to me rather Angels than Men, come down from Heaven to preach the Gospel again to Mankind; for there was such a Power accompanied their Words, especially *J. Gratton*'s, that as Face answers Face in a Glass, so every Word was confirm'd in the Hearts of the Hearers by the Spirit of God, . . . [43]

NOTES

1 Daniel B. Shea, Jr., *Spiritual Autobiography in Early America*, p. 96.
2 Turner, p. 39.
3 Caton, p. 7.
4 Blair, p. 16.
5 Bunyan, pp. 3f.
6 Penington, *Babylon the Great Described*, p. 6.
7 Trapnel, *Legacy*, pp. 14, 17.
8 Cf. p. 167 above.
9 *Spirituall Experiences*, p. 164.
10 *Ibid.*, pp. 180f.
11 *Ibid.*, p. 178.
12 Clarke, *Lives of Thirty-Two English Divines*, 1677, p. 174.
13 *Spirituall Experiences*, p. 163.
14 *Ibid.*, p. 181.
15 *Ibid.*, p. 182.
16 *Sermons*, 6th ed., 1727, III. 165.
17 J. R. Sutherland, *English Literature in the Late Seventeenth Century*, 1969, p. 302. Professor Sutherland, however, relies heavily on South and other hostile sources such as Samuel Butler for his assessment of Puritan religion. But cf. the childhood experience of William King: 'My father was accustomed at night, before he commenced the reading, the family being assembled, to offer a prayer, but since his prayers were conceived in words and phrases in a manner peculiar to those times, and to the sect, I understood them very little, and I did not pay much attention to what was done, nor could they be easily understood without a dictionary to explain them.' Sir Charles Simeon King, *A Great Archbishop of Dublin, William King, D.D.*, 1906, p. 10. (Passage translated from the Latin.)
18 Simon Patrick, *A Friendly Debate between a Conformist and a Nonconformist*, 3rd ed., 1669, p. 38.
19 Joseph Glanvill, *An Essay concerning Preaching*, 2nd ed., 1703. For

other attacks on the jargon of the sectaries, see C. Smyth, *The Art of Preaching*, 1940, pp. 138ff.

20 Penington, *Babylon the Great Described*, p. 9.
21 Dewsbury, pp. 17–19.
22 Cf. Rufus M. Jones, *Studies in Mystical Religion*, and *Spiritual Reformers in the Sixteenth and Seventeenth Centuries*, London, 1914.
23 *The Dead and Killing Letter*, quoted by George H. Sabine in the introduction to his edition of *The Works of Gerrard Winstanley*, New York, 1941, p. 30.
24 *The New Law of Righteousness Budding Forth*, in *Works*, 1941, p. 180.
25 *Tritheism Charged*, 1695, p. 80 (published anonymously). I owe these references to South to Mrs Winifred Nowottny.
26 *Quakerism No Christianity*, 1673, Part III, pp. 61–2.
27 *Ibid.*, III. 62–90, s.v.
28 Rofe, p. 17.
29 Zachary, p. 6.
30 *Something in Answer to a Book called Choice Experiences*, 1654, p. 3.
31 Howgill, p. 6.
32 R. Baker, p. 9.
33 *Works*, IX. 283, II. 420.
34 Cf. *Institutes*, Bk. II, ch. xi, sections 1–3.
35 *Spirituall Experiences*, pp. 15, 16.
36 Trapnel, *Legacy*, p. 13.
37 Cf. pp. 72–6 above.
38 Cf. pp. 85–7 above.
39 *Grace Abounding*, para. 73.
40 Baxter, I. 3.
41 *Grace Abounding*, para. 74.
42 Cf. pp. 92–3 above.
43 Bromfield, p. 80.

Chapter 13

The Puritan Self

All the experiences here examined have been those recorded by the subjects themselves, so if our knowledge of what was involved has been one-sided it has at least been 'inside' knowledge. The very concept of experience implies this, since an experience cannot be found in an event on its own, but only in the interaction of the event and the person. So if an autobiographer is honest – that is, if he does not deliberately mislead his readers – we have a guarantee of authenticity: he writes only of what he believes to have happened and of what he believes its significance to have been. As Professor Roy Pascal has pointed out, even an inaccurate or treacherous memory is not a serious problem in autobiography because its purpose is not to reconstruct the past but to interpret it and thereby find a meaning in the individual life; he goes on to quote Stendhal: 'I do not at all claim to write a history, but quite simply to note down my memories in order to guess what sort of man I have been.'[1]

The Puritan would not have put it quite like that, but he was certainly concerned about whether the kind of man he was meant that he were a child of God. If so, he would also hope to find out the extent of his growth in grace, the precise pattern of spiritual maturity that could be traced in different areas of his life and character. In publishing his record he would repudiate the idea that it should be read because he was an exceptionally interesting person, a unique personality; no one in the seventeenth century could have done this without having to admit to the most monstrous egotism. Even the vulgar prophets claimed a hearing because they had an urgent message for the world or because they found themselves being used as instruments of a mighty power: it was not

226

ostensibly a matter of their personality, except when they had to reply to attacks which discredited their message and work. But, of course, whether the writer's concern was pastoral or evangelical or prophetic he found himself involved in presenting a 'self' to the reader, if only because he was the main subject of the story.

Dr Paul Delany, in his study of British autobiography in this period, has commented on 'the age's widespread concern with pinning down a personal identity which had become more elusive than it had ever been before'.[2] A potent cause was probably the increasing pressure upon men to make choices. This was most apparent in respect of political and religious controversies, but many other areas of life were beginning to offer a new range of possibilities. Changing views about science and man's relationship to nature; social mobility; exploration and travel; and the wider circulation of news, ideas, and information: all challenged existing habits of thought and traditional loyalties. Roles which men had hitherto accepted without question were no longer perceived as inevitable, and the fact that decisions had to be taken, or were at least now seen to be possible, led inescapably to self-assessment and increasing self-awareness. Thus the growing complexity of human society and culture brought increased awareness of the complexity of human nature; hence the elusiveness of any personal identity which seemed to be emerging from all this activity and thought.

The self and God

One characteristic of the Puritan approach to these problems was the way in which a personal identity was formulated primarily through its relationship with God. And the initial impetus for this was almost invariably provided by a sense of sin. John Rogers, in telling how he was awakened at the age of ten by the preaching of Fenner, commented, '(for what I was before I know not, a meer – I know not what)'.[3] Only when it began to know its alienation from God did the soul begin to know itself. And it was through the long experience of change from alienation to reconciliation that a true self-image could be built up step by step. That is why the Puritan self was most adequately expressed in the form of narrative rather than in self-portraiture or meditation. 'His spiritual self-exploration is always temporal: How have I progressed (or regressed) from day to day? rather than, What am I like as a human being?'[4] So writes Miss Joan Webber, who also observes that what the Puritans called self-knowledge was an 'anxiety to determine whether one's every experience fits the proper pattern (or, more accurately speaking, [a] zealous effort to make all experiences fit)'.[5] This is an extremely perceptive definition; it emphasizes the Puritan's concern with the *process* of his experience as well as his constant need to measure himself against an ultimate standard. It also suggests a limitation which is all too apparent in many of the testimonies we have been concerned with: the tendency to select for the record those episodes which could be seen to belong to a recognizable sequence. This is particularly true of the short testimonies submitted for church membership admissions and of the early Quaker confessions. Most of these writings relate the pattern of events to the pattern of dispensations favoured by the groups concerned – law and gospel, for instance, or the characteristics associated with the major Biblical prophets in chronological order. If the writer has insight he gives us no evidence for it, the complexity of his interaction with events is unrealized, and we are not made to feel the power of alternative possibilities. In such works we must assume that anything uniquely personal has been left unnoticed, or unexpressed, or subsumed into a standard form of words. In this respect sincerity is not enough. Elizabeth Webb began her story by declaring, 'I have no learned method in which to deliver my religious experience, either by word or writing, but plainly and simply as the Spirit of Truth directs.'[6] Yet she was one of the most prolific users of Quaker jargon.

However, the 'zealous effort to make all experiences fit' did not have to lead to lifeless conformity, although the possibility of anything else might appear unlikely. In spite of the incredible variety of God's world, man did not in the Puritan view have an unlimited range of possibilities open to him in the search for the good life. He had, in fact, just two models: Adam and Christ, the former being the natural and necessary prototype of everyone who did not choose the latter. The one brought an inheritance of depravity and death, the other made man the heir of unsearchable riches. To be made conformable to the image of Christ was not a restrictive experience, it was the only way to be set free from the chains of self love. All seventeenth-century Christians believed that man was made to know God and enjoy Him for ever. But *how* was He to be known? The Puritan answer was that God was to be known in the ministry of word and sacrament, in public worship, in church fellowship, in private devotions, and in the life of disciplined obedience starting with repentance and faith. These means of grace were defined in the Scriptures, as were all the stages of salvation. So the pattern sprang from the demand for an objective basis for knowledge. Fundamentally, as we have already seen, it was not complicated. The essentials could be summed up in Goodwin's reflections on what he actually understood at the time of his own conversion: 'I knew no more of that Work of Conversion, than these two general Heads, That a Man was troubled in Conscience for his Sins, and afterwards was comforted by the Favour of God manifested to him.'[7] It was when the implications were worked out and interpreted in detail – as they had to be if the whole scheme were to be popularly understood – that the pattern might become rigid and confining. Much depended on the quality of the subject's perception of what he was striving to conform to, and this in turn would largely determine his ability to convey the personal impact of the experience. Men like Norwood, Bunyan, and Baxter all strove to bring their lives into harmony with ideals which we recognize as being basically the same, but our discussion of them has been enough to suggest that they became more rather than less diversified in the process.

Judgments about their powers of self-analysis are difficult to establish or refute. Professor Pascal finds Baxter 'diffuse and pedestrian, without psychological insight', and *Grace Abounding* 'limited in its range' because of Bunyan's sectarian piety.[8] But in default of supporting evidence one can only assume that it is the critic himself who is limited – by his own interests and a stereotyped image of Puritanism. 'What would one not give', he goes on revealingly, 'to know more about how he fared as a soldier in the Civil War!'[9] Bunyan's own account of this would certainly be worth having, but it might not have made *Grace Abounding* a better book.

The Puritan concept of himself as God's instrument also contributed to the form of his self-realization. And here the three main traditions show very different emphases. For the orthodox Puritans man's highest faculty, the feature in which he most distinctively bore the image of God, was his reason; it was thus of the first importance to serve Him with understanding. Then, given the will to serve, the believer would know how to bring his other faculties into subjection to the regenerate reason and all would work harmoniously together. The response of the affections was, as we have seen, held to be equally critical, but this emphasis was shared by the Quakers and vulgar prophets, whereas the importance of the rational faculty in self-assessment was not. Bunyan's stress on the damage inflicted by his ignorance and on how he gained the knowledge to overcome Satan; Goodwin's concern to explain the meaning of his premature satisfactions; Baxter's testimonies to what he learnt from books, and his exhaustive portrayal of his intellectual growth: all are examples of this.

The Quakers constantly deprecated the use of the 'understanding', and even discredited human learning. William Bayly said that it was 'the Serpent' who 'led out my mind wholly to delight in the Art of Arithmetick, and the study and practise of navegation'.[10] The Christian could not be fully committed until he had overcome his 'reasoning part', which was identified by all the more radical Puritans with what was worldly and unregenerate. Francis Bampfield, the Sabbatarian Baptist, burned all his notes and papers when he was converted, even though they contained 'a little somewhat that was true and good', because he thought it essential to 'begin (as it were) Religion, and all anew, and take all from Christ'.[11] There was little continuity between the old self and the new. The Puritan dualism of matter and spirit, and the effort to distinguish sharply between a state of apostasy and a state of grace, here found their most insistent expression. The change had to be as complete as possible, and it had to be a felt change. The Quaker Josiah Langdale thought his confirmation useless because 'upon a neer Search into my Self, I found I was not changed, or in the least altered'. What did bring about regeneration for him was when 'earnest Desires were begot in me, that I might settle more and more down to the Foundation'.[12] It was in these terms of a search into the depths of his being that the Quaker found God; he did not conceive of Him as a Being 'out there', but always in terms of an indwelling Spirit. Hence, as we have seen in chapter ten, his expectations of himself and of his pattern of life differed in many ways from those of the orthodox. The Friends seldom mention

God, as such, in their narratives, and for communication with Him they placed more reliance on human sensibility and intuition than on objectively identified means of grace, though the doctrine of the inner Light brought a measure of rational control that was altogether lacking in most of the vulgar prophets.

The self and other men

Like men everywhere, the Puritans evolved their own identity in terms of their relationship with others; for them this meant especially those of the same faith and order. We have had several occasions to notice the immense reassurance they gained from finding that their experiences could be related to those of others. And it was their intention that preaching and testimonies should help to generate a particular kind of experience; so it is sometimes difficult to distinguish between cause and effect, since doctrine and experience constantly interacted to confirm and redefine each other. It is significant that self-examination could be seen as the discovery with one's own faculties of a pre-existing objective condition, and so could be spoken of in the same terms as an autopsy: 'As a Chyrurgion, when he makes a dissection in the body, discovers the *intestina*, the inward parts, the heart, liver, arteries: so a Christian anatomizeth himself; he searcheth what is flesh, and what is spirit; what is sin, and what grace.'[13] The inner landscape had already been mapped by experts. A man knew what he ought to find, because everyone was alike.

For Calvinists the most influential group norms were doctrinal ones. They are sometimes accused of making an 'unholier than thou' claim for their unregenerate days. 'The doctrine of childhood depravity', writes Dr Delany, '. . . led Calvinist autobiographers to compete with each other in confessions of precocious wickedness.'[14] And critics often go on to say that the 'wickedness' involved is usually something quite innocuous. But the Puritan understanding of sin was that it essentially related to a corrupt nature, of which wicked actions were merely an inevitable outcome. Since all men were equally sinful (because all were totally alienated from God) every act without exception was self-centred, and there could be no question of one man claiming to be more depraved than another. Some men's behaviour might be more unrestrained or socially harmful, but this would be because they lacked such supports as a godly home, which were a channel of common grace, and most Puritan writers placed at least as much emphasis on the outward helps they had had as on their sinful behaviour. There is no evidence that they competed with one another. The common self-accusation of being the chief of sinners must be carefully interpreted. There seems to have been almost no 'lateral' dimension in this concept, it was not arrived at by a man comparing himself with others. Rather, it sprang from the full impact of discovering his total estrangement from God, from the failure to find in his own life and character even the most fragile basis for reconciliation. He was as far from God as anyone could possibly be; hence the only adequate language for the situation was in terms of being the 'chief of sinners'. So it was not in this context that a Puritan defined his individuality by relating himself to his fellows, though the identification of particular practices as symptoms of depravity was, of course, made possible by the existence of particular group values.

The Quakers testified to a common experience in that what had happened to them all was explained as the work of the Spirit of God within, but their doctrine was far less complicated than the Calvinists' and group influence was expressed most prominently in the code of conduct which the Spirit moved them to conform to. The striking unanimity of Friends' witness against war, tithes, oaths, and any form of ceremonious behaviour both established every member's identity with the group and was the most noticeable expression of it. It also represented a measurement of the self against the demands of the world. Like all Puritans, the Friends found in their supernatural allegiance the standards by which to judge the world, and in doing so they found it wanting. The outcome was a chronically hostile stance, which on the whole the world heartily reciprocated. The Quaker self was certainly moulded by Friends' unanimity about the implications of convincement with regard to behaviour towards one another and unbelievers.

We should expect the vulgar prophets, each with an exclusive personal revelation, to show more individuality than either Calvinists or Quakers. And because of the vigour with which they asserted their uniqueness they do indeed avoid the lifeless conformity which is the hallmark of many of the other narratives. Evans, Claxton, Muggleton, and the rest emerge as sharply defined individuals, glorying in their self-revelation and non-conformity, but their obsessions ultimately become monotonous, and we are forced to conclude that their unbridled subjectivism was a less effective agency of self-awareness than the Puritan tradition of disciplined reflection as practised by a Bunyan or a Goodwin, or by one of the more sensitive Scottish divines such as Halyburton. I cannot decide whether this is a literary judgment or not. The prophets certainly produced work of more consistent literary interest than the other Puritan groups as a whole, but they did so accidentally and not because they fulfilled their objectives in writing; we respond to their graphic evocation of situations and feelings, we are made to see things as they saw them, but we are not persuaded in the way they hoped to persuade us, because their self-portrayal often involved too much of self-betrayal. With the orthodox Puritans and the Quakers, on the other hand, we get in general much less literary vitality; but when the writing does rise above the level of expository competence their intended message gets through to us in a way that is at least consistent with their aims. 'The difficulty of literature', wrote Robert Louis Stevenson, 'is not to write, but to write what you mean; not to affect your reader, but to affect him precisely as you wish.'[15] It seems to me that the orthodox Puritans and Quakers meet this criterion occasionally, but the prophets hardly at all, primarily because of the nature of the self which emerges from their story. But this, as I have already implied, may be less of a literary judgment than a moral one. It brings us to the question of an author's relationship with his readers through the quality of his self-portrayal.

The self and the reader

All these works had a 'palpable design' upon the reader. They were written to persuade, to cause reading to issue forth in action. Inevitably the various writers saw their readers differently and this affected the stance they adopted. Indeed, it is seldom that the writer-reader relationship was limited to a single role, for a writer might present as many selves as there were motivating factors behind his effort to communicate.

The pastoral role was the one most widely acknowledged, the writer presenting the fruits of his experience so as to help his fellow-believers in day-to-day Christian living. For the lay folk this was an extension into the world of print of the obligation which all Puritans accepted to admonish and exhort one another and build one another up in the faith. The skill and confidence needed to do this had been developed through years of family worship, repeating sermons, wrestling with Biblical interpretation, and participating in church life generally. Consequently they saw themselves as competent to exercise the 'ministry of the Word'; and published autobiographies were a highly appropriate medium. 'Christians know not what they loose, by burying their experiences: they disable themselves for strengthening the weake hands, and confirming the feeble knees of others: and it is a great disadvantage to themselves.'[16] This observation by Samuel Petto illustrates yet another way in which self-knowledge was regarded as related to the 'zealous effort to make all experiences fit'; for the process which he commended presupposed a common pattern of experience as well as common aims and standards. The writer's role as a commentator was as prominent as that of subject, a factor particularly important to laymen, who would lack the outlet of sermon or treatise for any urge they had to give pastoral advice.

Among the Quakers this pastoral function was most clearly seen in the posthumously published journals, which were intended to edify those already convinced. The role, however, does not seem to have been consciously undertaken by the writer concerned, who usually had had no thought of publication: it was rather one bestowed on him by his editors when they prefaced the journal with testimonies to his character. These were often very numerous – as many as twenty-two in the case of William Edmundson – and they had the effect of presenting the narrative as an exemplum.

The Quaker who wrote of his experiences for immediate publication was more likely to have seen himself as a preacher or prophet, a distinction that became blurred when a message was proclaimed in the heightened emotional language appropriate to a unique inspiration. A prophetic attitude might even be blended with a pastoral one, as when William Dundas, writing for Friends who were not facing up to the demands of their faith, described his urge to 'be set up as a *Beacon* to those who are travelling *Sion*-ward'.[17] But content and tone tended to be the same whether the author addressed himself specifically to such widely different audiences as 'seekers after the truth', or 'Loving Neighbours and

Acquaintances', or 'all the Inhabitants of the Earth'.[18] He was the bearer of a message which exactly confirmed the experience of others, but which had nevertheless come as a personal revelation. Fox certainly saw himself as a prophet, while the Ranters and other wild men were even more explicit. Muggleton wrote about the need to leave a record behind him, 'as other Profits have done before me, as *Moses* and others'.[19] His autobiography was to become holy writ which the faithful would read and believe after he was gone.

Whether pastor, preacher, or prophet, the autobiographer was also aware of himself as a man speaking to men. Having chosen personal experience as the basis for his counsel or message, he knew that its acceptability depended heavily on the reader's assessment of his character. Epistles of recommendation were an important means of reassurance about this, and they reinforced the author's own concern to justify his ways to men. This concern is not always obtrusive but it is present in all but the most summary narratives. The very act of writing about oneself presupposes it, and fortunately, the enterprise itself is to a great extent its own recommendation. For because he implicitly appeals for our understanding, and enables us to stand where he stands and see life as he sees it, the autobiographer enjoys a strong initial plausibility and needs to be unusually insensitive to lose the reader's good will completely. The Puritan appeal for understanding might be primarily a personal one, or as a spokesman for a particular group, or with the emphasis on behalf of 'the truth'. Anna Trapnel evidently found some difficulty in sorting out some of the interconnections here, but she at least managed to make it clear that her heart was in the right place:

> I do not go about to vindicate my self, but Truth; which indeed stands in no need of mine or any ones vindication; but I would shew love and respect to it, in opposition to those who with spades and shovels dig up mire and rubbish to throw upon it.[20]

When going about to defend themselves most writers recognized the conflicting claims of self-justification and the glory of God. They anxiously discounted vanity as a motive and professed to have been drawn into print only with great reluctance. Bampfield, for instance, said he 'had intended to have lodged this Historical

Declaration within him, and when he had died away into Glory, to have made report of it to Heavenly Fellow-Citizens', but earlier publication was made necessary by persistent attempts to 'blast his Call'.[21] Difficult though it was to reconcile divine and human interests, the seventeenth-century Puritan probably found it easier to present himself acceptably to his readers than any secular auto-biographer who ventured upon self-revelation. It was still taken for granted that a human life could most naturally find meaning through its relationship with God, and the honour of God was admittedly bound up with the good name of His servants. The charge of vainglory would more readily stick to the writer who implied that his life and character were of intrinsic interest because of his career, travels, or other adventures, and distinct from the particular ways he fulfilled his function as God's instru-ment or exemplified God's workmanship. A modern reader's reaction is likely to be different. The mere claim to be God's instrument is apt to be regarded as arrogant, and theories of unconscious motivation complicate our reading of a man's self-portrayal. Perhaps, faced with our evidence of his repressions and rationalizations, a Puritan autobiographer would simply declare himself confirmed in his conviction that the heart of man was deceitful above all things and desperately wicked. Had not years of self-examination uncovered layer upon layer of self-deception? But he might not have been able to detach himself from his record sufficiently to make such a comment. For because it could only be justified on instrumental grounds the work, despite the presence of symbolic overtones, had in essence to be literally true, and this meant that the point of view from which it was written could not be discredited without the whole thing losing its validity. A spiritual autobiography, in the Puritan view, was not like a work of art, which could survive through qualities other than its accurate presentation of particular truths.

Self-definition

Whilst spiritual autobiographies were published in order to influ-ence their readers, they were often developed in the first instance for the benefit of the writer. To use Professor Starr's convenient terminology, they served both a didactic purpose and an auto-didactic one. We have seen that this was the reason the Puritans kept confessional diaries, and it was from them that the auto-biographies took their origin. Richard Rogers, as well as noting down experiences and evaluating them, preached to himself in his diary through reminders of his aims and duties: in attending to himself as subject he became also recorder, commentator, and counsellor. This suggests the possibility of a quite complex approach to the self, though the perspective of the diarist was of course limited to that of the time of writing. Now the auto-biographer had in addition involved his present self in the task of looking at his past self; he tried to re-create his experiences so as to convey both the impact they had on him at the time and their meaning in the light of subsequent experience and knowledge. And when he referred to what he understood at the time and why he took certain decisions in the past he also became a commentator on his past roles of commentator and counsellor. This happens in any autobiography, but because the didactic element was so im-portant in the works I have been discussing, they presented the self with especial clarity in these multifarious roles. Baxter in his self-review and Bunyan in his frequent interjections are only two of the most obvious examples of what I hope has been apparent throughout my study. The assured tone with which most of the writers moved from one perspective to another suggests that they were to some degree aware of the different attitudes involved, though necessarily lacking acquaintance with the actual categories I have named.

Conclusion

The Puritan self-image, then, emerged out of specific factors in the Puritan way of life – self-examination, doctrines of sin and grace, group pressures, mutual exhortation – which determined the form in which certain widely felt challenges of the age were identified, notably the need to clarify one's own position in relation to a ramification of fundamental controversies. For a hundred years or more discussion of these matters in pulpit, press, and private assemblies increasingly fostered popular concern at a personal level, and in so doing developed the concepts and language with which to articulate a growing sense of identity. The amount of reading and writing that went on, to say nothing of the talking, must alone have ensured rapid development. Calvinist doctrine, in requiring the believer to ensure constant growth in under-standing, emotional commitment, and the practice of good works, made demands which led to self-definition in terms of a whole range of relationships – to God, the Father, Son, and indwelling Spirit; to fellow believers, deviant groups, persecutors, and po-tential converts; to family, friends, and society at large; to one's own past, present, and ideal self as discerned in the act of writing about them. Because evidence consisted of particular phenomena and events made meaningful in a sequential pattern, a conscious-ness of time and history pervaded the subject's awareness. A man was what he was through the process of being remade. Narrative was therefore the most appropriate form in which to embody the emerging sense of the self, since this would help to ensure that no relevant factors were ignored.

The perspective and attitudes engendered by this tradition were shared by all Puritans. The Quakers and some of the indivi-dualist prophets went furthest in the subjectivity of their response, and while this can in some respects be regarded as a natural extension of orthodox Puritan sensibilities, it potentially impover-ished the range of media available for self-evaluation. The whole Puritan tradition itself was, of course, only one manifestation of a growing self-consciousness at this time, but the aspects of the self which it focused upon, and the language and techniques of the resulting spiritual autobiographies, were to be a potent force in Anglo-Saxon culture through the way they helped to determine the scope of men's attention in both life and literature.

NOTES

1 Roy Pascal, *Design and Truth in Autobiography*, London, 1968, p. 18.
2 Paul Delany, *British Autobiography in the Seventeenth Century*, p. 115.
3 Rogers, p. 419.
4 Joan Webber, *The Eloquent 'I'*, p. 8.
5 *Ibid.*, p. 137.
6 Webb, p. 164.
7 Goodwin, p. vii.
8 Pascal, *op. cit.*, pp. 33–4.
9 *Ibid.*, p. 34.
10 Bayly, p. 5.
11 Bampfield, p. 3.

12 Langdale, pp. 3, 19.
13 Thomas Watson, *Heaven taken by Storm*, 1669, p. 56.
14 Delany, *op. cit.*, p. 89.
15 *Virginibus Puerisque* IV. The Truth of Intercourse.
16 Samuel Petto, *The Voice of the Spirit*, 1654, p. 182.
17 Dundas, p. 4.
18 Cf. John Mulliner, John Higgins, title pages.
19 Muggleton, p. 4.
20 Trapnel, *Report and Plea*, sig. A2.
21 Bampfield, p. 37.

Bibliography

A. Puritan Spiritual Autobiographies written before 1725

The place of publication is London unless otherwise indicated. The edition listed here is normally the one quoted in the text.

ALLEN, HANNAH: *Satan his methods and malice baffled. A narrative of God's gracious dealings with that choice Christian Mrs. Hannah Allen, (Afterwards married to Mr. Hatt,) reciting the great advantages the Devil made of her deep melancholy, and the triumphant victories, rich and sovereign graces, God gave her over all his stratagems and devices* . . . 1683.

AMES, WILLIAM: *A declaration of the witnes of God, manifested in the inward parts.* Written by William Ames. The second edition. . . . 1681. (1st ed., 1656) Quaker.

ANDREWS, ELIZABETH: 'An account of the birth, education and sufferings for the truth's sake of that faithful Friend Elizabeth Andrews' in *Journal of the Friends' Historical Society,* Vol. 26, 1929, pp. 3–8. Quaker.

ANONYMOUS: 'The confession and profession of ane convert.' MS. in National Library of Scotland (Wodrow MSS. 4to XXIX. 9).

ANONYMOUS: 'Excerpts from a MSS. of a young gentleman's containing observations of the Lord's dealing with his soul from the 16 Novr 1696 being the 20th year of his age, but were not noted down till the beginning of May 1697.' MS. (eighteenth-century transcript) in Edinburgh University Library.

ANONYMOUS (WOMAN): 'A short account of the Lords way of providence towards me in my pilgrimage journey.' Dated 1724. MS. in National Library of Scotland (No. 1037).

ANONYMOUS (WOMAN COUSIN OF OLIVER CROMWELL): [MS. transcript of autobiography and diary] British Museum. Add. MS. 5858, pp. 411–427.

BACHE, HUMPHREY: *A few words in true love to the old long sitting Parliament, who are yet left alive,* . . . 1659. Quaker.

BAKER, RICHARD: *A testimony to the power of God, being greater than the power of Satan: contrary to all those, who hold no perfection here, no freedom from sin on this side of the grave. Which doleful doctrine is here testified against.* . . . 1699. Quaker.

BAMPFIELD, FRANCIS: *A name, an after-one; or* "Ονομα Καινὸν, *a name, a new one, in the latter-day-glory: or an historical declaration of the life of Shem Acher, especially as to some more eminent passages of his day, relating to his more thorow lawfull call to the office and work of the ministry, for about twenty years last past. Wherein Paul is propounded for an example, and the case, so far as it doth run parallel, is set down before it; tho the preheminence is given unto Paul,* . . . 1681.

BANGS, BENJAMIN: *Memoirs of the life and convincement of that worthy Friend Benjamin Bangs, late of Stockport in Cheshire, deceased; mostly taken from his own mouth, by Joseph Hobson.* . . . 1757. Quaker.

BANKS, JOHN: *A journal of the life, labours, travels, and sufferings (in and for the gospel), of that ancient servant, and faithful minister of Jesus Christ,* . . . 1712. Quaker.

BARCLAY, ROBERT: *Universal love considered* . . . 1677. ('The Introduction') Quaker.

BARCROFT, JOHN: *A brief narrative of the life, convincement, conversion, and labours of love in the gospel-ministry of that worthy servant of Jesus Christ,* . . . Dublin, 1730. Quaker.

BARRETT, JOSEPH: 'God's early dealings with Mr. Barret' in *A funeral sermon upon the death of Mr. Joseph Barrett, son of the Reverend Mr. John Barret Minister of the gospel in Nottingham. Preached Aug. 30th. by J. W. Junior,* . . . *To which is added, an account of his holy life, his evidences, experiences, holy resolves, divine meditations, and his constant course of self-examination. Being part of an exact diary written by his own hand.* . . . 1699.

BASTWICK, JOHN: *The confession of the faithfull witnesse of Christ, Mr. John Bastwick doctor of physick. Wherein he doth declare his education, and the grounds of his conversion, and constancie, in the true profession of faith.* . . . 1641.

BAXTER, RICHARD: *Reliquiae Baxterianae: or Mr. Richard Baxter's narrative of the most memorable passages of his life and times. Faithfully publish'd from his own original manuscript, by Matthew Sylvester.* . . . 1696.

BAYLES, THOMAS: *A relation of a mans return and his travaills out of a long and sore captivitie,* . . . *Written by one of Zyons travellers,* . . . 1677. Quaker.

BAYLY, WILLIAM: *A short relation or testimony of the working of the light of Christ in me, from my childhood, by one who is now a witness of the spirit of truth* . . . 1659. Quaker.

BEARD, THOMAS: 'A short account of the memorable passages of my life' in *The holy seed: or a funeral discourse occasion'd by the death of Mr. Thomas Beard. Sept. 15. 1710: soon after he had compleated the 17th year of his age. By Jos. Porter. With a review of his own life; written by himself while he was in perfect health* . . . 1711. (pp. 20–40.)

BEEVAN, JOHN: *A loving salutation to all people who have any desires after the living God; but especially to the Free-Will-Anabaptists. From one that desires the eternal good of all souls.* . . . 1660. Quaker.

BENNET, WILLIAM: *The work and mercy of God conducing to his praise; or a demonstration of the visitation of God's love to my soul in the dayes of my youth;* . . . *By a friend to all people* . . . *and a sufferer for the truth in Edmonds-Bury Common Goal in the year 1669* . . . *Re-printed with some additions in the year, 1677.* Quaker.

BEVAN, EVAN: [Letter to a friend containing an account of his convincement] In William Sewel: *The history of the rise, increase, and progress of the Christian people called Quakers.* . . . 1722 (pp. 705–7). Quaker.

BLAIR, ROBERT: *The life of Mr. Robert Blair, Minister of St. Andrews, containing his autobiography, from 1593 to 1636, with supplement to his life, and continuation of the history of the times to 1680, by his son-in-law, Mr. William Row, Minister of Ceres.* F/lited for the Wodrow Society from the original manuscript. By Thomas M'Crie, D.D. Edinburgh: . . . 1848.

BLANDFORD, SUSANNAH: *A small account given forth by one that hath been a traveller for these 40 years in the good old way.* . . . 1698. Quaker.

BLAUGDONE, BARBARA: *An account of the travels, sufferings & persecutions of Ba Blaugdone. Given forth as a testimony to the Lord's power and for the encouragement of Friends.* . . . 1691. Quaker.

BORLAND, FRANCIS: 'Memorialls of my pilgrimage, & the providences of the Lord toward me in all my changes to this day.' MS. in University of Edinburgh Library, Laing 262.

BOSTON, THOMAS: *A general account of my life by Thomas Boston, A.M. Minister at Simprin, 1699–1707 and at Ettrick, 1707–1732* printed for the first time from the original manuscript with introduction, notes, and bibliography by the Rev. George D. Low, M.A., Edinburgh . . . 1908.

BRAND, JOHN: 'Memoirs'. MS. in National Library of Scotland. (No. 1668).

BRIGGS, THOMAS: *An account of some of the travels and sufferings of that faithful servant of the Lord, Thomas Briggs.* . . . 1685. Quaker.

BRITTEN, WILLIAM: *Silent meeting a wonder to the world; yet practised by the apostles, and owned by the people of God scornfully called quakers. . . .* 1675. (1st ed., 1660). Quaker.

BROMFIELD, WILLIAM: 'The author's conversion' in *The faith of the true Christian, and the primitive Quakers faith* . . . 1725 (pp. 73–162). Quaker.

BRUSH, EDWARD: *The invisible power of God known in weakness, with a Christian testimony of the experience and sufferings of Edward Brush, aged ninety one years. . . .* 1695 (pp. 21–2). Quaker.

BRYSSON, GEORGE: 'Memoirs of George Brysson, merchant in Edinburgh. Written by himself' in *Memoirs of Mr. William Veitch, and George Brysson, written by themselves: . . . to which are added, biographical sketches and notes, by Thomas M'Crie D.D. . . .* Edinburgh and London 1825 (pp. 265–352).

BUNYAN, JOHN: *Grace abounding to the chief of sinners.* Edited by Roger Sharrock. Oxford, 1962. (1st ed., 1666.)

BURNYEAT, JOHN: 'An account of John Burnyeat's convincement: together with a journal of his travels' in *The truth exalted in the writings of . . . John Burnyeat. . . .* 1691 (pp. 1–72). Quaker.

BURROUGH, EDWARD: 'A true declaration, and a discovery to all the world of my manner of life; what I have been, and what now I am at present' in *A warning from the Lord to the inhabitants of Underbarrow, . . . with the manner of my passage through the dark world. . . .* 1654 (pp. 31–5). Quaker.

BURTON, HENRY: *A narration of the life of Mr. Henry Burton. Wherein is set forth the various and remarkable passages thereof, his sufferings, supports, comforts, and deliverances. Now published for the benefit of all those that either doe or may suffer for the cause of Christ. According to a copy written with his owne hand. . . .* 1643.

CAMERON, HUGH (attrib.): 'Some remarks on Providence and the Lords dealings with me in my tender years, and progressively carried on since' . . . MS. in National Library of Scotland. (34.6.30).

CARLETON, THOMAS: *The captives complaint, or the prisoners plea against the burthensom and contentious title of tythes. With a true relation of the prisoners spiritual progress, and travel towards the new and heavenly Jerusalem. . . .* 1668. Quaker.

CARPENTER, RICHARD: *Experience, historie, and divinitie. Divided into five books. Written by Richard Carpenter. Vicar of Poling, a small and obscure village by the sea-side, neere to Arundel in Sussex. . . .* 1642.

CATON, WILLIAM: *A journal of that faithful servant and minister of the gospel of Jesus Christ Will. Caton. Written by his own hand. . . .* 1689. Quaker.

CHUBB, THOMAS: *The posthumous works of Mr. Thomas Chubb: . . . To the whole is prefixed, some account of the author: written by himself.* . . . 1748.

CLARIDGE, RICHARD: *Mercy covering the judgement-seat, and life and light triumphing over death and darkness: in the Lord's tender visitation, and wonderful deliverance of one that sat in darkness,* . . . *Witnessed unto in certain epistles and papers of living experience.* . . . 1700. Quaker.

CLARKE, SAMUEL: 'A brief narrative of my life, and of the most remarkable acts of God's Providence in guiding and governing of the same' in *The lives of sundry eminent persons in this later age.* . . . *By Samuel Clark, sometimes pastor of Bennet Fink, London.* . . . *To which is added his own life,* . . . 1683 (pp. 3–11).

CLARKSON, LAURENCE: *Look about you, for the Devil that you fear is in you: or, the right Devil unfolded:* . . . *With many other divine secrets* . . . 1659. ('The Introduction'.)

CLARKSON, LAURENCE: *The lost sheep found: or, the prodigal returned to his Fathers house, after many a sad and weary journey through many religious countreys,* . . . *Written by Laur. Claxton the onely true converted messenger of Christ Jesus,* . . . 1660.

COAD, JOHN: *A memorandum of the wonderful providences of God to a poor unworthy creature, during the time of the Duke of Monmouth's rebellion and to the revolution in 1688. By John Coad, one of the sufferers.* . . . 1849.

COALE, JOSIAH: *A song of the judgments and mercies of the Lord:* . . . *Being a brief demonstration of the secret work of the Almighty in me his servant. given forth at the movings of the Spirit of the Lord,* . . . 1663. Quaker.

COPPE, ABIEZER: *Copp's return to the wayes of truth: in a zealous and sincere protestation against severall errors;* . . . *And the wings of the fiery flying roll clipt, &c. by Abiezer Coppe, the [supposed] author of the fiery flying roll. Herein is something hinted concerning the author, in reference to the sinfulness and strictness of his life. With a little t'uch of what he hath been, and now is; sparkling here and there throughout these lines, and in the preface.* . . . 1651.

COPPE, ABIEZER: *Divine fire-works. Or, some sparkles from the spirit of burning in this dead letter. Hinting what the Almighty Emanuel is doing in these wipping times. And in this his day which burns as an oven. In ABH I AM.* 1656–7. (Anonymous broadsheet.)

COPPE, ABIEZER: *A fiery flying roll: a word from the Lord to all the great ones of the Earth,* . . . *And all by his most excellent majesty, dwelling in, and shining through Auxilium Patris, alias, Coppe* . . . 1649.

COPPE, ABIEZER: *A second fiery flying roule: to all the inhabitants of the earth; specially to the rich ones.* . . . *Together with a narration of various strange, yet true stories: And severall secret mysteries, and mysterious secrets, which never were afore written or printed.* . . . *Per Auxilium Patris* . . . 1649.

COPPIN, RICHARD: *Truths testimony; and a testimony of truths appearing, in power, life, light & glory;* . . . *With the authors call and conversion to the truth, his practice in it, his publishing of it, and his several tryals for the same* . . . 1655.

COWPER, WILLIAM: *The life and death of the Reverend Father, and faithfull seruant of God, Mr. William Cowper, Bishop of Galloway* . . . *Wherevnto is added a resolvtion penned by himselfe, some few dayes before his death* . . . 1619.

COXERE, EDWARD: *Adventures by sea of Edward Coxere.* Edited by E. H. W. Meyerstein. Oxford, 1945. Quaker.

CRISP, SAMUEL: *Two letters writ by Samuel Crisp, about the year 1702, to some of his acquaintance, upon his change from a chaplain, of the Church of England, to joyne with the people called Quakers.* . . . 1722. Quaker.

CRISP, STEPHEN: *A memorable account of the Christian experiences, gospel labours, travels and sufferings of that ancient servant of Christ* . . . 1694. Quaker.

CRISP, STEPHEN: *A short history of a long travel, from Babylon to Bethel. Written in the 9th month, 1691.* . . . 1711. Quaker.

CROKER, JOHN: 'Brief memoir of the life of John Croker, who was born at Plymouth, in 1673. Written by himself. Now first published' in *A Select Series,* edited by A. R. Barclay, Vol. 6. . . . 1839 (pp. 281– 330). Quaker.

CROOK, JOHN: [Autobiographical letter] In; Isaac Penington: *To all such as complain that they want power.* . . . 1662 (pp. 23–6). Quaker.

CROOK, JOHN: *A short history of the life of John Crook, containing some of his spiritual travels and breathings after God, in his young and tender years: also an account of various temptations wherewith he was exercised, and the means by which he came to the knowledge of the truth. The manuscript hereof, written by his own hand, was found since his other works were published in print.* . . . 1706. Quaker.

CROUCH, WILLIAM: *Posthuma Christiana; or a collection of some papers of William Crouch. Being a brief historical account, under his own hand, of his convincement of, and early sufferings for the truth.* . . . 1712. Quaker.

CURWEN, ALICE: *A relation of the labour, travail and suffering of that faithful servant of the Lord Alice Curwen* . . . 1680. Quaker.

DANKS, JOHN: *The captives returne or the testimonys of John Danks, of Colchester, and Elizabeth Danks, his wife. To the mercy and goodness of God, in calling them back to his everlasting truth, after their o[u]t-runnings and seperation from the same.* . . . 1680. Quaker.

DAVIES, RICHARD: *An account of the convincement, exercises, services and travels of that ancient servant of the Lord, Richard Davies. With some relation of ancient Friends, and the spreading of truth in North Wales, &c.* . . . 1710. Quaker.

DEWSBURY, WILLIAM: 'The first birth' in *The discovery of the great enmity of the serpent against the seed of the woman,* . . . *A true testimony of him the world knows by name, William Dewsbury, and in scorn calls Quaker;* . . . *Also his call to the ministry of the everlasting gospel by the still voyce of the spirit of God* . . . *From the common goal in Northampton the 25 day of the 4 month 1655.* . . . 1655 (pp. 12–22). Quaker.

DICKINSON, JAMES: *A journal of the life, travels, and labour of love in the work of the ministry, of that worthy elder, and faithful servant of Jesus Christ,* . . . 1745. Quaker.

DIMSDALE, WILLIAM: *The Quaker converted: or the experimental knowledge of Jesus Christ crucified, in opposition to the principles of the Quakers, declared; in the narrative of the conversion of one in Hartfordshire, who was for some years of their faith.* . . . 1690. (An earlier edition was published some time before 1673.)

DISNEY, GERVASE: *Some remarkable passages in the holy life and death of Gervase Disney, Esq; To which are added several letters and poems* . . . 1692.

DOE, CHARLES: *A collection of experience of the work of grace: (never before printed) or the Spirit of God working upon the souls of several persons; whereby is demonstrated their conversion to Christ, or signs of being in the peculiar love of God to salvation.* . . . Collected by Charles Doe. . . . n.d. [Epistle dated 1700].

DUNCAN, HENRY: 'The most memorable passages of the life of M. H.D. containing many instances of divine goodness of holy wisdom and powerful providence towards a sinner the most unworthy and undeserving of the least of Gods mercies. Begun to be extracted of my diary this 19th of May 1708.' MS. in National Library of Scotland. (Wodrow MSS. 4to LXXXII. (3).)

DUNDAS, WILLIAM: *A few words of truth from the spirit of truth to all who are convinced of the truth, and stand in opposition to the cross. By one who remained in that estate above seven years, before he was brought to the true obedience of truth: and was whipped to it by the merciful rod of the Lord; for no less could do it.* . . . 1673. Quaker.

EDMUNDSON, WILLIAM: *A journal of the life, travels, sufferings, and labours of love in the work of the ministry,* . . . Dublin, 1715. Quaker.

EDWARDS, CHARLES: *An afflicted man's testimony concerning his troubles.* . . . 1691.

S   247

ELLWOOD, THOMAS: *The history of the life of Thomas Ellwood or an account of his birth, education, etc., with divers observations on his life and manners when a youth: and how he came to be convinced of the truth; with his many sufferings and services for the same; also several other remarkable passages and occurrences written by his own hand edited by C. G. Crump.* . . . 1900 (1st ed., 1714).

ELLYTHORP, SEBASTIAN: *A testimony wherein is shewed certain weighty reasons why the national ministers, their way and practice is conscientiously disowned,* . . . *also, a testimony, from a certain experience, to the people called Presbyterians,* . . 1692. Quaker.

EVANS, ARISE [or RHYS]: *An eccho to the voice from heaven. Or a narration of the life, and manner of the special calling, and visions of Arise Evans: By him published, in discharge of his duty to God, and for the satisfaction of all those that doubt.* . . . 1652.

EVANS, KATHARINE and CHEVERS, SARAH: *This is a short relation of some of the cruel sufferings (for the truths sake) of Katharine Evans and Sarah Chevers, in the Inquisition in the Isle of Malta,* . . . 1662. Quakers.

FARNWORTH, RICHARD: *The heart opened by Christ; or, the condition of a troubled soul that could find no true rest, peace, comfort, nor satisfaction in any thing below the divine power and glory of God,* . . . 1654. Quaker.

FORSTER, THOMAS: *A guide to the blind pointed to. Or, a true testimony to the Light within.* . . . 1659. Quaker.

FOSTER, GEORGE: *The sounding of the last trumpet: or, severall visions,* . . . *Lately shewed unto George Foster, who was commanded to print them.* . . . 1650.

FOWLER, ROBERT: *A Quakers sea-journal.* . . . 1659. Quaker.

FOX, GEORGE: *The journal of George Fox,* a revised edition by John L. Nickalls with an epilogue by Henry J. Cadbury and an introduction by Geoffrey F. Nuttall. Cambridge, 1952. (1st ed., 1694). Quaker.

FRANKLIN, MARY: 'The experiences of Mary Franklin' in *Congregational Historical Society Transactions,* Vol. 2, October 1906, pp. 387–401.

FRASER, JAMES: *Memoirs of the life of the very Reverend Mr. James Fraser of Brea, Minister of the Gospel at Culross. Written by himself* . . . *Now publish'd at the desire of some friends.* Edinburgh . . . 1738.

GATES, NICHOLAS: *A tender invitation to all, to embrace the secret visitation of the Lord to their souls.* . . . 1708. Quaker.

GILPIN, JOHN: *The Quakers shaken: or, a fire-brand snatch'd out of the fire. Being a brief relation of Gods wonderfull mercy extended to John Gilpin of Kendale in Westmoreland. Who (as will appear by the sequel) was not onely deluded by the Quakers, but also possessed by the Devill.* . . . Newcastle, 1653.

GOODAL, MRS: 'Memoir of Mrs Goodal, written by herself' in *Select*

Biographies. Edited by the Rev. W. K. Tweedie. Vol. 2. Edinburgh, Wodrow Society, 1847, pp. 481–93.

GOODWIN, THOMAS: 'The life of Dr. Thomas Goodwin; compos'd out of his own papers and memoirs' in *The works of Thomas Goodwin D.D. sometime President of Magdalen College in Oxford. The fifth volume . . . To which is prefix'd an account of the author's life from his own memoirs. . . .* 1704 (pp. v–xvii).

GOTHERSON, DOROTHEA: *To all that are unregenerated: a call to repentance from dead works. . . .* 1661 (pp. 88–95). Quaker.

GRATTON, JOHN: *A journal of the life of that ancient servant of Christ, . . .* 1720. Quaker.

GREEN, THEOPHILUS: *A narrative of some passages of the life of Theophilus Green from his youth: both before and after he received the truth, as professed by the people of God, in scorn called Quakers. . . .* 1702. Quaker.

GREEN, THOMAS: *A declaration to the world, of my travel and journey out of Ægypt into Canaan through the wilderness, & through the Red-Sea, from under Pharoah, . . .* 1659. Quaker.

GREEN, WILLIAM: *The sound of a voyce uttered forth from the mountaine of the lord of host, . . . By one that is passed from death to life, . . .* 1663. Quaker.

GWIN, THOMAS: 'The journal of Thomas Gwin, of Falmouth, a minister of the Society of Friends. Transcribed from a copy of his own MSS. made by various ffriends of East Cornwall.' 1837. Falmouth 1905. MS. in Friends House Library (MS. Vol. 77). Quaker.

GWIN, THOMAS: *The will and testament of Thomas Gwin of Falmouth; being some religious and serious considerations, . . .* 1720 (pp. 8–9). Quaker.

HALYBURTON, THOMAS: *Memoirs of the life of the Reverend Mr. Thomas Halyburton, Professor of Divinity in the University of St Andrews; digested into four parts, whereof the first three were written with his own hand some years before his death, and the fourth is collected from his diary by another hand; . . . The second edition corrected and amended. . . .* Edinburgh, 1715.

HAYES, ALICE: *A legacy, or widow's mite; left by Alice Hayes, to her children and others. . . .* 1723. Quaker.

HEYWOOD, OLIVER: 'Autobiography' in *The Rev. Oliver Heywood, B.A. 1630–1702; his autobiography, anecdote and event books . . .* edited by J. Horsfall Turner. . . . Brighouse . . . 1882 (Vol. 1, pp. 133–202).

HIGGINS, JOHN: *To all the inhabitants of the earth . . .* 1658. Quaker.

HILLS, HENRY: *The life of H. Hills With the relation at large of what passed betwixt him and the taylors wife in Blackfriars, according to the original. As likewise particular remarks of his behaviour ever since. Which proves (tho times change) him to be the same H.H. still. . . .* 1688.

HOLME, BENJAMIN: *A collection of the epistles and works of Benjamin Holme. To which is prefix'd, an account of his life and travels . . .* 1753. Quaker.

HOMWOOD, NICHOLAS: *A word of counsel: or, a warning to all young convinced Friends, or others whom it may concern, that are called forth to bear a testimony for the Lord in the case of tythes. . . .* 1688 (pp. 2–3). Quaker.

HOOTON, SAMUEL: 'Something concerning my travell, and of the dealings of the lord with mee, since the lord brought mee from my dwelling.' MS. in Friends House Library (Port. 3.80). Quaker.

HOPKINS, THOMAS: *A tender visitation and warning to those that profess the way of truth but are not in possession of it. . . . Giving some account of the tender dealings of God with the author, . . .* 1707. Quaker.

HOWARD, LUKE: *The seat of the scorner thrown down: . . . Whereunto is annexed my call from the Baptists, to walk in the true light. . . .* 1673. Quaker.

HOWARD, LUKE: 'A short journal of Luke Howard, . . . being left for his children and the whole world' in *Love and truth in plainness manifested: . . .* 1704 (pp. 1–34). Quaker.

HOWGILL, FRANCIS: *The inheritance of Jacob discovered. After his return out of Ægypt: and the leading of the Lord to the land of promise declared, and some information of the way thither. . . .* 1656. Quaker.

HUBBERTHORN, RICHARD: 'A true testimony of obedience to the heavenly call' in *A collection of the several books and writings of . . . Richard Hubberthorn . . .* 1663 (pp. 1–6). Quaker.

HUBBERTHORN, RICHARD: *The immediate call to the ministery of the gospel, witnessed by the Spirit. With a true declaration of the persecution and suffering of Richard Hubberthorn, James Parnell, Ann Blayling, by Will. Pickering, who is Mayor of Cambridge. . . .* 1654. Quaker.

JACKSON, JAMES: *The strong man armed cast out, and his goods spoiled: Or, the poor man sitting at Jesus's feet clothed, and in his right mind. Being a true convert's testimony . . . Formerly given forth in writing unto my relations and acquaintance, the professors, called Independents, in Nottingham-shire; . . .* 1674. Quaker.

JAFFRAY, ALEXANDER: *The diary of Alexander Jaffray, . . . to which are added particulars of his subsequent life . . .* By John Barclay . . . 1833 (pp. 1–64 are retrospective).

JEFFRYS, JOHN: *A serious address to the people of the Church of England, . . . To which are prefixed, some passages of his life, written by himself.* Dublin, 1739. Quaker.

Bibliography

JESSEY, HENRY: *The life and death of Mr. Henry Jessey, late preacher of the gospel of Christ in London;* . . . 1671 (pp. 25–31).

KEIMER, SAMUEL: *A brand pluck'd from the burning: exemplify'd in the unparallel'd case of Samuel Keimer, offer'd to the perusal of the serious part of mankind, and especially to those who were ever acquainted with, or ever heard of the man.* . . . 1718. Anti-Quaker.

KELSALL, JOHN: 'A journal or historical acct. of the chief passages, concerns and excercises of my life since my childhood; with some preceeding relations thereto.' MS. in Friends House Library. (MS. Vol. S. 194). Quaker.

KIFFIN, WILLIAM: *Remarkable passages in the life of William Kiffin: written by himself and edited from the original manuscript, with notes and additions, by William Orme.* . . . 1823.

KILBY, RICHARD: *The burthen of a loaden conscience: or the miserie of sinne: set forth by the confession of a miserable sinner.* . . . Cambridge, 1608.

KILBY, RICHARD: *Hallelu-iah: praise yee the Lord, for the unburthening of a loaden conscience: by his grace in Jesus Christ vouchsafed unto the worst sinner of all the whole world.* . . . Cambridge, 1618.

KNOLLYS, HANSERD: *The life and death of that old disciple of Jesus Christ, and eminent minister of the gospel, Mr. Hanserd Knollys, who dyed in the ninety third year of his age. Written with his own hand to the year 1672, and continued in general, in an epistle by Mr. William Kiffin.* . . . 1692.

LACY, JOHN: *The prophetical warnings of John Lacy, Esq; pronounced under the operation of the Spirit; and faithfully taken in writing, when they were spoken.* . . . 1707 ('The Preface').

LACY, JOHN: *A relation of the dealings of God to his unworthy servant John Lacy, since the time of his believing and professing himself inspir'd* . . . 1708.

LAMPE, HENRY: *Curriculum vitae, or the birth, education, travels, and life of Henry Lamp, M.D., written by himself for the information of his own children* . . . *With an introduction, supplement, and notes, by Joseph J. Green.* . . . 1895. Quaker.

LANGDALE, JOSIAH: 'Some accot. of the birth education religious exercises and visitations of God, to . . . Josiah Langdale . . .' MS. in Friends House Library (MS. Box 10(10)). Quaker.

LAYTHES, THOMAS: *something concerning my convincement of God's truth, the way, work and manner thereof.* . . . 1686. Quaker.

LEA, FRANCIS: *Judgment brought forth unto victory, and mercy kissing judgment; being the work and mercy of God, (upon my soul) which conduceth to his praise* . . . 1671. Quaker.

LILBURNE, JOHN: *The resurrection of John Lilburne, now a prisoner in*

Dover-Castle, declared and manifested in these following lines penned by himself, . . . 1656. Quaker.

LILLIE, SAMUEL: [Untitled MS. account of himself.] MS. in National Library of Scotland.

LIVINGSTONE, JOHN: 'A brief historical relation of the life of Mr. John Livingstone, minister of the gospel. Containing several observations of the divine goodness manifested to him in the several occurrences thereof. Written by himself, during his banishment in Holland, for the cause of Christ.' In: *Select Biographies,* edited by W. K. Tweedie. Edinburgh: Wodrow Society, 1845 (Vol. 1, pp. 127–97).

LIVINGSTONE, PATRICK: 'The heavenly seed and its light plainly proved to be in all mankind, . . . also some things of my own travel and experience, . . .' in *Selections from the Writings of Patrick Livingstone,* edited by L. A. Barclay. . . . 1847. (pp. 21–39) Quaker.

LOMBE, HENRY: *An exhortation given forth at the requirings of the Lord,* . . . 1694. Quaker.

LURTING, THOMAS: *The fighting sailor turn'd peaceable Christian; manifested in the convincement and conversion of Thomas Lurting, . . . First written for private satisfaction, and now published for general service.* . . . 1710. Quaker.

MARSHALL, CHARLES: 'A short and brief narrative of my pilgrimage in this world' in *Sions Traveller Comforted, and the Disobedient Warned.* . . . 1704 (sigg. d-g3v). Quaker.

MARTINDALE, ADAM: *The life of Adam Martindale, written by himself, and now first printed from the original manuscript in the British Museum.* Edited by Rev. Richard Parkinson, B.D., Chetham Society Remains, Vol. 4, 1845.

MATERN, JOHN: *The testimony of that dear and faithful man, John Matern,* . . . 1680. Quaker.

MAYNFORTH, ROBERT: *An exhortation to all people. Together with a warning to the drunkards of England, who were my companions in the kingdom of darkness,* . . . 1691. Quaker.

MELLIDGE, ANTHONY: *A true relation of the former faithful and long service, with the present most unjust imprisonment of Anthony Mellidge, sometime called a Captain; now in scorn called a Quaker.* . . . 1656. Quaker.

MOWSLEY, THOMAS: 'An accompt of God's dealings with this young man, before and at his conversion' in *Death unstung. A sermon preached at the funeral of Thomas Mowsley, an apothecary, who died July 1669. With a brief narrative of his life and death:* . . . By James Janeway, . . . 1671 (pp. 79–119).

MUGGLETON, LODOWICK: *The acts of the witnesses of the Spirit. In five parts. By Lodowick Muggleton: one of the two witnesses, and true prophets of the only high, immortal, glorious God, Christ Jesus. Left by him to be publish'd after's death.* . . . 1699.

MULLINER, JOHN: *A testimony against periwigs and periwig-making, and playing on instruments of musick among Christians, or any other in the days of the gospel.* . . . *By one, who for good conscience sake hath denyed and forsaken them,* . . . 1677. Quaker.

MURRAY, JAMES: 'Mr James Murrays diary. Or a succinct account of quhat was remarkable wh relation to him for ye glory of god & his own shame & downcasting.' MS. in National Library of Scotland (No. 3045).

NAYLER, JAMES: *To the life of God in all* . . . 1659. Quaker.

NAYLER, JAMES: *What the possession of the living faith is, the fruits thereof, and wherein it hath been found to differ from the dead faith of the world,* . . . 1659. Quaker.

NEWCOME, HENRY: *The autobiography of Henry Newcome, M.A.,* edited by Richard Parkinson, D.D., F.S.A. Chetham Society Remains, Vols. 26 and 27, 1852.

NIMMO, JAMES: *Narrative of Mr. James Nimmo written for his own satisfaction to keep in some remembrance the Lord's way dealing and kindness towards him 1654–1709.* Edited from the original manuscript with introduction and notes by W. G. Scott-Moncrieff . . . Edinburgh: Scottish Historical Society, 1889.

NORWOOD, RICHARD: *The journal of Richard Norwood surveyor of Bermuda with introductions by Wesley Frank Craven . . . and Walter B. Hayward* . . . Published for the Bermuda Historical Monuments Trust by Scholars' Facsimiles and Reprints, New York, 1945.

OSBORN, ELIAS: *A brief narrative of the life, labours and sufferings, of Elias Osborn.* . . . 1723. Quaker.

PARNELL, JAMES: *The fruits of a fast,* . . . 1655. Quaker.

PEARSON, ISAAC: *The implacable cruelty, of the people call'd Quakers, in the County of Cumberland, against Isaac Pearson, one of that persuasion.* . . . 1713.

PENINGTON, ISAAC: 'The account of his spiritual travel.' From 'A testimony concerning I. Penington by Tho. Ellwood' in *Works,* 1681, Vol. 1, sigg. c2v-c4. Quaker.

PENINGTON, ISAAC: *Babylon the great described.* . . . 1659. (The Preface). Quaker.

PENINGTON, ISAAC: 'A brief account of my souls travel towards the Holy Land' in *Works,* 1681, Vol. 2, pp. 48–50. Originally published in 'Observations on some passages of L. Muggleton', 1668. Quaker.

PENINGTON, MARY: *Experiences in the life of Mary Penington (written by herself).* Edited with introduction and notes by Norman Penney.

Philadelphia and London, n.d. [1911]. Reprinted from an edition of 1821. Quaker.

PENN, WILLIAM: *An account of W. Penn's travails in Holland and Germany. Anno MDCLXXVII. For the service of the gospel of Christ, by way of journal.* . . . 1694. Quaker.

PERROT, JOHN: *A narrative of some of the sufferings of J.P. in the city of Rome.* . . . 1661. Quaker.

PERRY, EDWARD: *Something of the dealings of the Lord with and towards one, who hath been asking the way to Zion, with his face thitherward;* . . . n.d. [Written 10.9.1689, and published 'long after the author's decease'.] Quaker.

PETTO, SAMUEL: 'Choice Experiences' in *Roses from Sharon. Or sweet experiences gathered up by some precious hearts, whilst they followed on to know the Lord. Published for publick soul-advantage.* . . . 1654.

PIKE, JOSEPH: 'Some account of the life of Joseph Pike, written by himself about the sixty-fifth year of his age, and continued to the seventy-first' in William Evans and Thomas Evans (ed.): *The Friends' Library*, Vol. 2, Philadelphia, 1838, pp. 351–97. Quaker.

PLEDGER, ELIAS: [Autobiography and diary] MS. in Dr Williams's Library, London (MS. 28.4, Shelf 545).

POWELL, VAVASOR: 'Mr Powel's account of his conversion and ministry' in *The life and death of Mr. Vavasor Powell, that faithful minister and confessor of Jesus Christ.* . . . 1671 (pp. 1–19).

PRINGLE, WALTER: 'The memoirs of Walter Pringle of Greenknow; or some few of the free mercies of God to him, and his will to his children, left to them under his own hand' in *Select Biographies*, edited by W. K. Tweedie. Edinburgh: Wodrow Society, 1845 (Vol. 1, pp. 411–94).

'PRIVATE GENTLEMAN': *An account of some remarkable passages in the life of a private gentleman; with reflections thereon. In three parts. Relating to trouble of mind, some violent temptations, and a recovery; in order to awaken the presumptuous, and encourage the despondent. Left under his own hand, to be communicated to the publick after his decease.* . . . 1708.

RAWLINSON, THOMAS: *Light sown for the righteous, and gladness for the upright in heart.* . . . *that all honest people may see what I was in profession, and also what I now am by the grace of God.* . . . 1657. Quaker.

REEVE, JOHN: *A transcendent spiritual treatise upon several heavenly doctrines* . . . *John Reeve and Lodowick Muggleton, the two last witnesses and true prophets of the man Jesus,* . . . *If any of the elect desire to speak with us concerning any thing written in this treatise, they may hear of us in Great Trinity Lane, at a chandlers shop, against one Mr. Millis, a brown baker, near the lower end of Bow-lane.* . . . n.d. [1651] (p. 5).

REID, ALEXANDER: *Life of Alexander Reid, a Scottish Covenanter. Written by himself, and edited by Archibald Prentice, his great grandson.* Manchester . . . 1822.

RICH, MARY, FOURTH COUNTESS OF WARWICK: 'Some specialities in the life of M. Warwicke', edited with introduction and notes as *Autobiography of Mary Countess of Warwick,* London: Percy Society . . . 1828.

RIGGE, AMBROSE: 'A true relation of Ambrose Riggs, by way of journal' in *Constancy in the truth commended:* . . . 1710 (pp. 1–28). Quaker.

ROFE, GEORGE: *The righteousness of God to man,* . . . *with, a true declaration how I lived before I knew the truth, and how I came to know the truth, and overcame deceit.* . . . 1656. (pp. 14–18) Quaker.

ROGERS, JOHN: 'Examples of experience' in *Ohel or Beth-shemesh. A tabernacle for the sun: or irenicum evangelicum. An idea of church-discipline, in the theorick and practick parts;* . . . *By John Rogers* . . . *Declared for the most part in Christ-Church, Dublin in Ireland.* . . . 1653 (pp. 354–450).

ROSS, KATHERINE: Untitled MS. ('some remarkable passages of my life', p. 1). MS. in National Library of Scotland (Wodrow MSS. 34.5.19(5)).

SADDINGTON, JOHN: *A prospective-glass for saints and sinners whereby may appear and be seen, 1. The authors life expressed in the first epistle* . . . *and several other things necessary to salvation.* . . . 1673.

SALMON, JOSEPH: *Heights in depths and depths in heights. Or truth no less secretly then sweetly sparkling out its glory from under a cloud of obloquie. Wherein is discovered the various motions of an experienced soul, in and through the manifold dispensations of God. And how the author hath been acted in, and redeemed from the unknown paths of darkness;* . . . 1651.

SAMBLE, RICHARD: *A testimony unto the truth, and a warning unto the world in general,* . . . 1676 (pp. 38–44). Quaker.

SANSOM, OLIVER: *An account of the many remarkable passages of the life of Oliver Sansom; shewing, his convincement of the truth, and the exercises, tryals and sufferings which came upon him for his obedience thereunto:* . . . 1710. Quaker.

SELLWOOD, JOHN: *An invitation of love to all people: but especially to the inhabitants of the parish of Stepny* . . . 1678. Quaker.

SHAW, JOHN: 'The life of Master John Shaw' in *Yorkshire diaries and autobiographies in the 17th and 18th centuries.* Durham: Surtees Society, Vol. 65, 1877 (pp. 119–62).

SIMPSON, MARY: *Faith and experience or, a short narration of the holy*

255

life and death of Mary Simpson, late of Gregories parish in the city of Norwich: who dyed, anno 1647. in or about the thirtieth yeare of her age, after 3 yeares sicknesse and upwards. Containing a confession of her faith and relation of her experience, taken from her owne mouth. To which is added, sermon preached at her funerall, . . . by John Collings, M.A. . . . 1649.

SMITH, DANIEL: Untitled tract beginning, 'The 20th day of the 6th moneth, 1673 . . .' Quaker.

SMITH, HUMPHREY: *Man driven out of the earth and darkness, by the light, life, and mighty hand of God.* . . . 1658. Quaker.

SMITH, HUMPHREY: *To all parents of children upon the face of the whole earth.* . . . The second edition. . . . 1667. (First published 1660). Quaker.

SMITH, NICHOLAS: *Wonderfull prophecyes revealed to Nicholas Smith shoe-maker, living at Tillington neer Petworth in Sussex,* . . . *Manifested unto me Nicholas Smith on Matthias Day last, by a Spirit from God; and am now come up to London to doe the work I am commanded, and lie at the signe of the Flying-Horse in Thames-street, where I will by the grace of God be ready to attest the truth hereof with my life.* . . . 1652.

SOMMERLAND, RICHARD: *A general testimony to and for the everlasting truth of God, partly for my relations and neighbours, that have known me from my childhood in Wishaw & Sutton. Wherein there is a short relation of my manner of convincement.* . . . 1678. Quaker.

STEEL, LAURENCE: *Jacob the plain man wrestling with God until the break of day,* . . . (*Whereby all may see, how I was* . . . *brought off from professing and preaching that for gospel which made not free from sin in this life.* . . .) 1677. Quaker.

STEPHENSON, MARMADUKE: 'Marmaduke Stephensons paper, of his call to the work and service of the Lord, . . .' in Daniel Gould: *A brief narration of the sufferings of the people called Quakers; who were put to death at Boston in New-England.* . . . 1700 (pp. 21–3). Quaker.

STEVENSON, JOHN: 'A rare soul-strengthening and comforting cordial for old and young Christians: being an exact account of the author's experience . . . By John Stevenson, land-labourer in the parish of Daily in Carrick, who died in the year 1728' in *Select Biographies,* edited by W. K. Tweedie. Edinburgh: Wodrow Society, 1847 (pp. 411–77).

STIRREDGE, ELIZABETH: *Strength in weakness manifest: in the life, various trials, and Christian testimony of that faithful servant and handmaid of the Lord,* . . . 1711. Quaker.

STORY, CHRISTOPHER: *A brief account of the life, convincement, sufferings, labours and travels, of that elder and minister of Christ Jesus, . . .* 1726. Quaker.

STORY, THOMAS: *A journal of the life of Thomas Story: containing an account of his remarkable convincement of, and embracing the principles of truth, as held by the people called Quakers; and also of his travels and labours . . .* Newcastle upon Tyne, 1747. Quaker.

STRUTT, JAMES: *A declaration to the whole world, to try themselves by Gods witness in them, . . .* 1658. Quaker.

SYMONDS, THOMAS: *The voice of the just uttered: his passing out of Egypt through the Red Sea: through the wilderness to the Promised Land where rest and peace is injoyed. . . .* 1657. Quaker.

TAYLOR, CHRISTOPHER and FRANCES: *A testimony to the Lord's power and blessed appearance in and amongst children: Here are also added . . . several pretious testimonies. . . .* 1679. Quakers.

TAYLOR, JOHN: *An account of some of the labours, exercises, travels and perils, by sea and land of John Taylor of York: and also, his deliverances; by way of journal. . . .* 1710. Quaker.

TAYLOR, TIMOTHY (attrib.): *The hidden life of a Christian, exemplified in the diary, meditations, and letters of a young minister.* Published from authentic manuscripts. By Thomas Gibbons, D.D. . . . The third edition. Edinburgh, 1770 (pp. 15–21 are retrospective).

THOMPSON, THOMAS: *An encouragement early to seek the Lord: and be faithful to him: in an account of the life and services of that ancient servant of God, . . .* 1708. Quaker.

TOLDERVY, JOHN: *The foot out of the snare. . . . Being a brief declaration of his entrance into that sect called (by the name of) Quakers. . . . Also, what desperate delusions he was led into . . . With the manner of his separation from them. . . .* 1656.

TOMPKINS, ANTHONY: *A faithful warning to all backsliders, who hold the truth in unrighteousness, . . .* 1668. Quaker.

TRAPNEL, ANNA: *Anna Trapnel's report and plea. Or, a narrative of her journey from London into Cornwal, the occasion of it, the Lord's encouragements to it, and signal presence with her in it. . . .* 1654.

TRAPNEL, ANNA: *The cry of a stone: or a relation of something spoken in Whitehall, by Anna Trapnel, being in the visions of God. . . .* 1653.

TRAPNEL, ANNA: *A legacy for saints; being several experiences of the dealings of God with Anna Trapnel, in, and after her conversion, (written some years since with her own hand) and now coming to the sight of some friends, they have judged them worthy of publike view; . . .* 1654.

TRENCH, EDMUND: *Some remarkable passages in the holy life and death of the late Reverend Mr Edmund Trench; most of them drawn out of his own diary . . .* 1693.

Bibliography

TROSSE, GEORGE: *The life of the Reverend Mr. Geo. Trosse, late minister of the gospel in the City of Exon, who died January 11th, 1712–13. In the eighty second year of his age, written by himself, and publish'd according to his order. To which is added, the sermon preach'd at his funeral. By J. H.* . . . Exon. . . . 1714.

TRYON, THOMAS: *Some memoirs of the life of Mr Tho. Tryon, late of London, merchant: written by himself* . . . 1705.

TURNER, JANE: *Choice experiences of the kind dealings of God before, in, and after conversion; laid down in six general heads. Together with some brief observations upon the same. Whereunto is added a description of true experience. By J. Turner wife to Cap. John Turner* . . . 1653.

VEITCH, MRS WILLIAM: 'An account of the Lord's gracious dealing with me and of his remarkable hearing and answering my supplications.' MS. in National Library of Scotland (No. 34.6.22).

VOKINS, JOAN: *God's mighty power magnified: as manifested and revealed in his faithful handmaid* . . . 1691. Quaker.

WALKER, HENRY (editor) (attrib.): *Spirituall experiences of sundry beleevers. Held forth by them at severall solemne meetings, and conferences to that end. With the recommendation of the sound, spiritual, and savoury worth of them, to the sober and spirituall reader, by Vavasor Powel, minister of the gospel. The second impression, enlarged with the experiences of forty two beleevers, wherein is wonderfully declared Gods severall workings in the various conditions of his chosen ones.* . . . 1653.

WENTWORTH, ANNE: *A vindication of Anne Wentworth, tending to the better preparing of all people for her larger testimony, which is making ready for publick view.* . . . 1677. Quaker.

WEST, ROBERT: *The voice of him that is escaped from Babylon. Reasons given forth to all sober minded people, why I departed from the ministery of those called ministers of parishes; and why I departed from the ministery of those called Anabaptists; and why I have, and what I have contended for, some years past.* . . . 1658. Quaker.

WHITEHEAD, GEORGE: *Jacob found in a desert land: Or a recovery of the lost out of the loss . . . wherein is discovered the work of the Lord in the creature, and how I travelled through the night of thick darkness . . . into the true light and truth.* . . . 1656. Quaker.

WHITEHEAD, GEORGE: *The Christian progres of that ancient servant and minister of Jesus Christ, George Whitehead. Historically relating his experience, ministry, sufferings, trials and service, . . . In four parts. With a supplement to the same.* . . . 1725. Quaker.

WHITEHEAD, JOHN: *The enmitie between the two seeds: wherein is discovered the subtiltie and envie of the serpents seed: who rules in the man of sin, that is born after the flesh, and persecutes him that is born after the spirit; which spiritual birth is here witnessed* . . . 1655. Quaker.

Bibliography

WHITING, JOHN: *Persecution expos'd, in some memoirs relating to the sufferings of John Whiting,* . . . 1715. Quaker.

WILDE, SAMUEL: *The last legacy of Samel Wilde, weaver, being an humble and penitent recantation of him, an old wretched sinner, who besides his sinful course of living in licentiousness, jollity, mirth and drunkenness, &c. used among his companions to deride and scoff at the people called Quakers,* . . . 1703. Quaker.

WILKINSON, ELIZABETH: 'The life and death of that eminent saint of God, Mris Elizabeth Wilkinson, late wife to Dr. Henry Wilkinson Principall of Magdalen Hall in Oxford' in *A sermon preacht at Great Milton in the county of Oxford: Decemb: 9. 1694. at the funerall of that eminent servant of Jesus Christ Mris Elizabeth Wilkinson . . . by Edmund Staunton D.D.* . . . Oxford, 1659.

WILLIS, R.: *Mount Tabor. Or private exercises of a penitent sinner. . . . Written in a time of voluntary restraint from secular affaires. By R. W. Esquire. Published in the yeare of his age 75. . . .* 1639.

WILSFORD, JOHN: *A general testimony to the everlasting truth of God; . . . wherein there is some short relation of the manner of my convincement . . . By J.W. a sufferer in Leicester-County-Goal. . . .* 1677. Quaker.

WILSON, THOMAS: *A brief journal of the life, travels and labours of love, in the work of the ministry,* . . . Dublin, 1728. Quaker.

WINDER, HENRY: *The spirit of Quakerism, and the danger of their divine revelation laid open: in a faithfull narrative of their malicious prosecution of Henry Winder, and his wife, as murtherers, at the publick assize at Carlisle,* . . . 1696.

ZACHARY, THOMAS: 'An account of my own condition' in *A word to all those who have bin convinced of the truth,* . . . *but hold a league and friendship with this world.* . . . n.d. [*c.* 1659] (pp. 4–8). Quaker.

B. Modern Studies

All the following contain information or discussion on Puritan spiritual autobiographies.

BARBOUR, HUGH: *The Quakers in Puritan England.* New Haven and London: Yale University Press, 1964.

BOTTRALL, MARGARET: *Every Man a Phoenix; Studies in Seventeenth-Century Autobiography.* London: John Murray, 1958.

DELANY, PAUL: *British Autobiography in the Seventeenth Century.* London: Routledge & Kegan Paul, 1969.

FIRTH, SIR CHARLES: 'Some Seventeenth Century Diaries and Memoirs' in *Scottish Historical Review,* Vol. 10 (1913), pp. 329–46.

HALLER, WILLIAM: *The Rise of Puritanism: or the Way to the New*

Jerusalem as set forth in Pulpit and Press from Thomas Cartwright to John Lilburne and John Milton, 1570–1643. New York: Columbia University Press, 1938.

LERNER, L. D.: Introduction to *Milton, A Selection*. Harmondsworth: Penguin Books, 1953.

MORRIS, JOHN N.: *Versions of the Self: Studies in English Autobiography from John Bunyan to John Stuart Mill*. New York–London: Basic Books, 1966.

NUTTALL, GEOFFREY F.: *The Holy Spirit in Puritan Faith and Experience*. Oxford: Basil Blackwell, 1946.

SHARROCK, ROGER: *John Bunyan*. London: Hutchinson, 1954.

SHARROCK, ROGER: 'Spiritual autobiography in "The Pilgrim's Progress" ' in *Review of English Studies*, Vol. 24 (April 1948), pp. 102–19.

SHEA, DANIEL B., Jr.: *Spiritual Autobiography in Early America*. Princeton University Press, 1968.

STARR, G. A.: *Defoe and Spiritual Autobiography*. Princeton University Press, 1965.

SUTHERLAND, JAMES: *English Literature of the Late Seventeenth Century (Oxford History of English Literature, Vol. V)*. Oxford: Clarendon Press, 1969.

TALON, HENRI: *John Bunyan: the Man and his Works*. English translation by Barbara Wall. London: Rockliff, 1951.

TAYLOR, JOHN H.: 'Some seventeenth century testimonies' in *Congregational Historical Society Transactions*, Vol. 16 (December 1949), pp. 64–77.

TINDALL, WILLIAM YORK: *John Bunyan Mechanick Preacher*. New York: Columbia University Press, 1934.

WEBBER, JOAN: *The Eloquent 'I': Style and Self in Seventeenth-century Prose*. Madison, Milwaukee, London: University of Wisconsin Press, 1968.

WRIGHT, LUELLA MARGARET: *The Literary Life of the Early Friends 1650–1725*. New York: Columbia University Press, 1932.

Index

Biblical characters and places are indexed under 'Bible'.

T　　　263

Index

265

Index

267